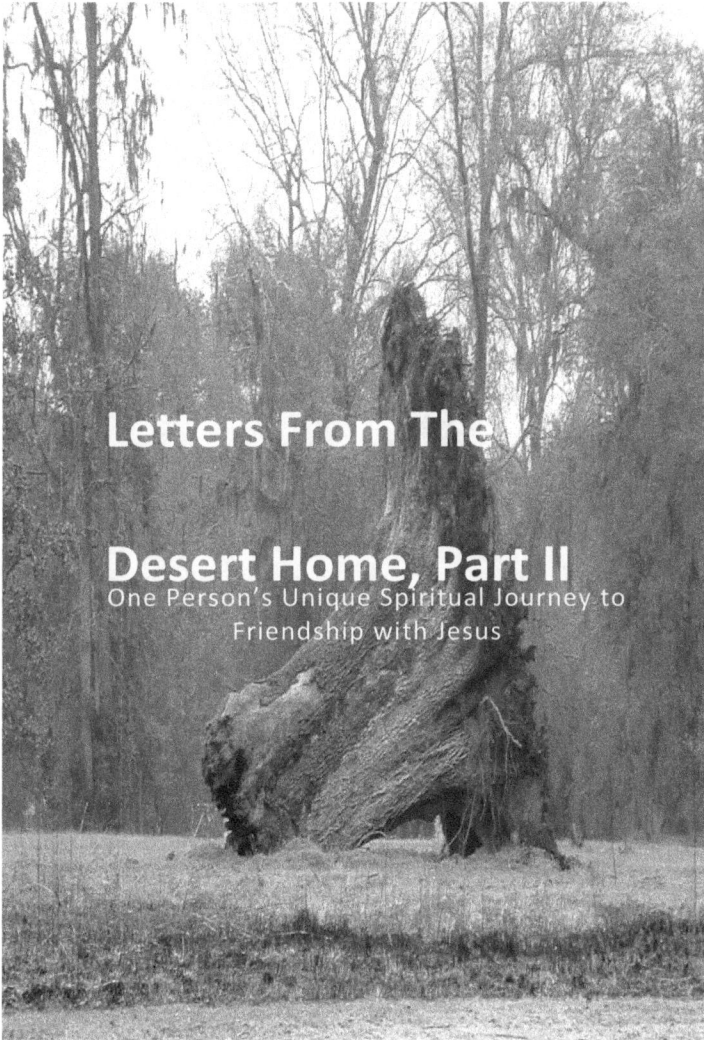

Letters From The

Desert Home, Part II
One Person's Unique Spiritual Journey to
Friendship with Jesus

By Rodney K. Odom

Personal Letters from the Desert Home, Part II

One Person's Unique Spiritual Journey
to Friendship with Jesus

The Author

Rodney K Odom [Brother Anthony-Maria]
photograph by other, 2014

Rodney prepared for monastic life from 2004 to 2009. He entered a Trappist monastery in 2009 and was formally a monk from 2010 to mid-2015 when he returned to Philadelphia, PA. His early educational focus was scientific and technical. He is also the author of an unpublished work of poems: "Writings from the Desert. A Compilation of Poems on the Way to First Vows as A Trappist Monk."

While self-publishing this book, he is a practicing Roman Catholic and looking toward living a life as a hermit.

Personal Letters from the Desert Home, Part II

One Person's Unique Spiritual Journey
to Friendship with Jesus

Published Methuzala.com
Philadelphia, PA

Personal Letters from the Desert Home, Part II
One Person's Unique Spiritual Journey to Friendship with Jesus

Cover Photograph is by Rodney K. Odom. Used by permission.

contact email: admin@methuzala.com

Biblical References in this book are taken from The World English Bible™. The World English Bible™ (WEB) is a Public Domain (no copyright) Modern English translation of the Holy Bible. That means that you may freely copy it in any form, including electronic and print formats. The World English Bible™ is based on the American Standard Version of the Holy Bible first published in 1901, the Biblia Hebraica Stutgartensa Old Testament, and the Greek Majority Text New Testament. The companion Deuterocanon/Apocrypha is derived from the Revised Version Apocrypha and the Brenton translation of the Septuagint into English.

New Testament References in this book are taken from the World English (New Testament). "You may freely quote up to 500 verses of this New Testament without permission." Taken from THE JESUS BOOK - The Bible in Worldwide English.

ISBN: 979-8-9890917-2-0

I am grateful for the mystery of life. And the help of Mary as my mother. I am grateful for a holy purpose that gives direction to my being and existence. I thank God for making his presence known to me and others. And I am grateful for this chance to come to terms with my ways and realize the Mercy of God as my help.

Table of Contents

Acknowledgements

Thank you, Mary, the lovely, kind, merciful Blessed Virgin, for all your help. My parents and sister Barbara for struggling to maintain their sanity and doing all they could to support me as I did "my thing." My sister and her husband, James, for truly supporting and carrying my parent's efforts. I thank Mrs. Barbara A. Sylla for her editing recommendations to help me write according to the rules. I did the best I could.

To the Late Fr. Jude Duffy, O.F.M. Cap **(Order of Friars Minor Capuchin)**, Deacon Curtis Todd, Ms. Dale Brown and all the human effort persisting behind them making my transition into the Roman Catholic church and monastic life possible despite my many difficulties.

I am grateful to all the brothers of Methuselah Abbey and their entire support system of volunteers. They make the continuation of the abbey possible.

To those who allow me to use their image to enhance the collection of writings, letters, and essays, I also thank you!

The Font: Chapbook used in various places throughout the book is based on typefaces found in publications during the mid-seventeenth century. Chapbook is licensed under the SIL Open Font License (OFL.) It is free for personal and commercial use. Thanks to Foerag from Edinburgh, Scotland for making it available through https://www.1001fonts.com.

Preface

Some names of people and places are changed to protect the privacy of those involved. The overall journey or story detailed in this book is factual.

I wrote the book for those who have a tolerance for the intimacy of human frailty; to convey a very personal experience without interference. While it may teach a lesson or two about life, it is not a basis for anyone's personal belief system. I tried my best not to focus on the public relations involved with everyday human communication. It is a perspective to make life more palatable. Sometimes it distorts the facts beyond proper understanding. Thus, you may find some language harsh and some situations intimate or uncomfortable.

If, in my encounter with God, in seeing the truth that God wants me to see, I lash out and attempt to circumvent the reality shown me, I would not gain what I have. Let that be the same for the one who comprehends my intentions in writing this book as they read. We need the full array of reality to grow and change regardless of the pain involved. It would be immature for me to pick and choose what sounds proper to my ear and ignore the needs of my heart.

Complete communication is often difficult, if not impossible. I do not know your version of "our language." A particular word to me often has a slightly different meaning to you. Thus, I miscommunicate. For instance, I grew up thinking spicy food meant it contained an abundance of spices. And I found to my surprise, that spicy food to most people means hot to taste or burning to the tongue. I misunderstood for a long time!

Communication becomes even more complicated if you are not a professional writer and must deal with aesthetics with little firm definition, as with many spiritual subjects.

In places in the book, if it turns out not to be factual, I apologize. I do not think I intended to be purposefully wrong.

Introduction

According to www.Merriam-Webster.com, an online dictionary, one of the definitions of the word 'desert' is a "desolate or forbidding area." And to the uninformed observer, it may seem as though there is not much to see in a desert. It may seem dried up and devoid of life. Interestingly, this is true of any circumstance that imitates desert-like conditions. A visitor to the monastery once asked me, "What do you do? I mean, don't you get bored doing the same thing every day – never leaving the monastery?" He saw as an outside observer a group of people in a monastery, with nothing interesting to do and nowhere to go or "nothing to do but pray."

All this discussion of deserts leads to the title of this book. To interpret the title of my little book and the meaning of its contents properly, you need to look at the word desert in a symbolic sense. This "Letters from the Desert" collection is not from a physical desert. Instead, the letters were from me, a desolate and forbidding person. I am "desolate" because I have withdrawn from my ordinary life activity and seek a life of physical and mental separation. I am "forbidding" because I refuse to accept the world around me as offered. Instead, I only allow what I seek and nothing else. So if in my understanding, I perceive something as a threat to what I seek, I filter it out and/or outright reject it for the sake of focusing my energy on what it is I truly seek. What I seek is God. So the letters reflect my unusual state of being. I later discovered that it is a state of being for someone on a unique spiritual journey. It is a journey seeking to create a more sheltered life based on my understanding of the circumstances I encounter as I go along. I make my path as I proceed and simultaneously put it before me. I walk in faith as I wrestle and fight with the objectionable part of myself and the world around me.

Go in by the small gate. The gate is big and the road is wide that goes to death. Many people go that way. The gate is small and the road is not wide that goes to life. Not many people find it. **Matthew 7:13-14.** (14)

This writing started as a mere collection of letters documenting the activity associated with seeking the heaven within. They demonstrate my understanding of the world around me. But as I gathered the letters together, I decided to tell more of a story. I decided to add some of my creative writing. Also, I figured it would be more readable if each chapter, designated by year, had a chapter introduction. I thought it would add a transition to the material. Over time, I decided that adding some engaging lessons that I learned along the way was essential. So I inserted short writings on various topics called "Welcome to Monastic Life" that offer some of what was important to me as I lived the monastic journey. Thus, the collection is a volume of letters and other forms of communications from me, the desert, to the people who choose to read it. This writing is clearly not a book for everyone.

Though not a theological collection, it is predominantly a Roman Catholic- Christian spiritual journey. Or a journey that transitions me from a guy who was at best described as agnostic into life as a Roman Catholic Christian. Due to the emphasis on science in our culture, we are increasingly creating a world that finds offense with who practice traditional faith. There seems to be hostility toward traditional religious values. Religious people seem scarier now. Faith in "God" is perceived more and more extreme. It seems our worship of science is replacing the worship of God.

I recently noticed several social situations. For instance, while walking and praying my Rosary, some of the people present felt and looked at me nervously. I saw the same thing while traveling on an airplane and reading scripture. I am baffled by the look of fear on people's faces. Moreover, while I am surrounded by people doing the exact opposite, I seek something other than physical accomplishment. I find myself following something not seen with my naked eye. And in my mind, I am doing so intelligently, wisely, and, yes, guided by God, not by fear.

When the people whom God has chosen call to him day and night, he will save them from their enemies. He may let them wait a time. But I tell you, he will save them from their enemies soon. But when the Son of Man comes, will he find any people who believe in him? **Luke 18:7-8.** (14)

Faith in Christ is critical on this journey.

200X

How I Exist

Life being what it is;
A timeless event of evolving interactions,
Imbued by layers, sources disclosed to me,
Disclosed through complex human machinery.

Though I do not know where or what I am,
Though I know I am forever,
I think of no better way to encounter this process
Except as evolution.

Change as I may,
Be Eternal,
Comprehend what I am,
I am of this nature.

My substance is real,
My awareness is intelligent,
And love is the glue that keeps this form.
For this and all else I am truly grateful.

Chapter Introduction

The years 2000 through 2009 were a remarkable personal struggle and growth phase. It was a time of incredible pain, fear, and insufficient explanation. It was a time of making decisive decisions about my most important values. I discovered too much of my life was "lies." Far too much of it involved segments that were either unknown, not true, or based on unrealistic fantasy. I once prayed to God that I might live "the truth," and it seemed that he answered my prayers. Unfortunately, the horror of that truth made me run. I was desperate. I saw that I needed drastic change. It was also clear that I did not belong to the world around me—these critical conditions created for me a mission. I was on a mission to some ethereal place and on the run from a horrible state. Both were occurring simultaneously. I had every reason in the world to abandon life as I once knew it because I now knew different. I now knew better. And I had a powerful drive within me to seek what I thought was better. I seem to know that following this drive would change my horrible state.

As a result of this new knowledge or wisdom, I acted differently. One might say I was strange or weird. And the people who cared for me most and who were comfortable with the world as they saw it wanted to "help me." As for me, their help meant going back to what was, and to me, that made no sense. Their support did not mean that what they valued was unnecessary; it was simply no longer enough for me. I needed to learn and change - to evolve in some way. And that meant seeking a new depth of being. All this radical change and activity led to a deeper understanding and a changed perception. I did not have any answers, nor did I need them. This way of being is equivalent to feeling your way through life with no detailed road maps except a Holy Book and faith in God.

Radical change is just that – extreme. One is changing quickly. But drastic change often draws people's fear. It makes them want to grab you and pull you back. The only way I could go after what I needed was to do what Peter (biblical disciple) did; he wanted to walk on water as he saw Christ doing. My task was to escape an imprisoning mental state that produced an unacceptable human. And when I began to sink into the dangerous water, as did Peter, I had to learn to call out for help. And this I learned to do. In that scary process, I realized that I had wings of mercy that could help me walk on water and not drown in it. I experienced the God I followed, the angels he directed, and those around me inspired to help. Read the following and imagine how it applied to my immediate situation:

> *Jesus said to another man who followed him, `Come with me.' But the man said, `Lord, let me go first and bury my father.' Jesus said to him, `Let those who are dead bury their own dead people. As for you, go and tell people about God's kingdom.' Another man said to Jesus, `Sir, I will go with you. But let me go first to my home and tell them I am going.' Jesus said to him, `Any person who starts doing something and then keeps looking back is not fit for the kingdom of God.'* **Luke 9: 57-61** (2)

Between 2003 and 2007, I moved three times. I moved from Philadelphia, Pennsylvania, to Delaware with my sister Barbara. And after a few months, I left her home in Delaware and moved to Greenville, North Carolina. I lived in Greenville for about eighteen months before moving to Charlotte, North Carolina, where I lived for three years. And from there, I went on to what I thought was the last leg of my journey, a move to Monk City, South Carolina, near Charles City.

It was a journey filled with intimate encounters with my weaknesses and corruption. My perception broadened to allow for many mystical possibilities. At the same time, I discovered a more profound truth about the world around me. While I am a product of a loving experience, I am also a twisted, tangled, corrupt one. And because of my habit of authentic profanity, I must struggle to accept new truthful ways. During this journey, I discovered my life was a co-developed fantasy catering to my internal or selfish satisfaction. While I had "decency," I was certainly not living the truth of what God intended for me.

It was a time of Grace initiating a more profound sense of what is true. And that deeper truth was my incentive for the journey ahead. I thank God for the wings of mercy keeping me afloat as I traveled the journey. It turns out God is the only one who can rightfully promise to heal. If the Son sets you free, you are indeed free.

Jesus said, `I tell you the truth. No person can see God's kingdom if he is not born again.' **John 3:3.** (14)

Anyone who loves his father or his mother more than he loves me, is not good enough for me. Anyone who loves his son or his daughter more than he loves me, is not good enough for me. Anyone who is not willing to carry his cross and suffer with me, is not good enough for me. Anyone who tries to keep his life, will lose it. Anyone who gives up his life for my sake, will find it. **Matthew 10:37-39.** (14)

Comments on email: *While removing myself from society, I was fortunate in the financial sense. After selling my house, I had enough money left over to pay off all my student loan debt, credit card debt, and other financial obligations I created for myself. I also repaid money I borrowed from my mother and father to seed a business idea: years earlier, I designed, coded, and marketed a software application I was selling on a website I maintained.*

Now I was "deleting it all." I am not sure what this whole radical experience means in the greater sense of life, but it was a profoundly emotional life encounter. I took years of stressful, strenuous hard work and investment and dissolved it all into nothing. I made these changes in my life with the idea of being like some relatively unknown person I read about and wish to imitate - Antony of the Desert. Most people I knew never even heard of Saint Antony, and the few that did took his life story as a fable passed down by the Church for inspirational purposes. He did not seem real to them. Below is a copy of an email I sent to the state government requesting information on how to dissolve a corporation. On my own, paying my business taxes was hard enough; now I had to figure out how to dissolve a corporation? All of this was very intimidating for me; somehow, I made it through. I have changed the names to protect the innocent! The email correspondence is displayed in the order in which it is sent. (There are multiple forms that need to be filed to dissolve a corporation in the commonwealth of Pennsylvania. The names of the forms seem very complicated and intimidating. In this email I was seeking clarification on which form to file first.)

Email Correspondence:

From: Customer Service [mailto:service@amazingsoftware.com]
Sent: Monday, June 05, 2006 4:17 PM
To: RA-CORPS@state.pa.us

Subject: order of form filing?

To whom it may concern:

Do I first file for a clearance with the Dept of Revenue to dissolve the corporation or first file Articles of Dissolution-Domestic with the State for dissolution of the corporation? Or does it not matter the order in which you file the forms?

Thanks

Rodney Odom
Unique Business Software, Inc.

Please see us for software, forms and software greeting cards!
http://www.amazingsoftware.com

Response:

> **From:** "Last name, First name" <last name@state.pa.us> wrote:
> **Subject:** RE: order of form filing?
> **Sent:** Fri, 9 Jun 2006 15:07:41 -0400
> **To:** <service@amazingsoftware.com>
>
> **CC: "ST, CMAIL"** <ra-st-cmail@state.pa.us>
>
> Dear Rodney, thank you for taking the time to visit our web site. In response to your recent inquiry: You will need to contact the Dept of Revenue to obtain the tax clearance application and follow the instructions on that application, then wait for the clearance certificates. One will be from the Revenue Dept. and the other is from the Dept of Labor & Industry, once you have both clearance certificates you then need to submit the dissolution & clearance certificates to us.
>
>
> First name Last name
> Business Processing
> 717-787-1057 option #X
> last name@state.pa.us
>
> _____

Comments on email: *If I truly wish to have a chocolate bar, I need to make some effort in that direction to accomplish the task of acquiring it. I gave all I had to the garbage collection people and hopped on a bus to Charlotte, North Carolina. I talked to a deacon at Saint Peters Catholic Church in Uptown-Charlotte, N.C. He directed my initial steps. And after settling in on a Catholic parish with an RCIA class that matched my schedule (Our Lady of Consolation on Statesville Road), I connected with Ms. Brown. I eventually reached out to the people at the monastery who were the object of my interest. The email below is documentation of my initial contact with the second monastery in my search: Our Lady of Methuselah Abbey. The email correspondence is displayed in the order in which it took place.*

-----Original Message-----
From: Rod Odom [mailto:rod_odom123@yahoo.com]
Sent: Wednesday, October 24, 2007 6:24 PM
To: Name

Subject: another question

Hello Father (Fr.) Thomas,

Not to pester you, but do you think I should try to come in the winter coming up for one week or try for 2 weeks in the spring? My job is basically busy during the summer outdoor months and also, I could plan financially for a longer time if I waited till the spring?

Also, Deacon Todd thought I should ask you about coming there after I become Catholic. He seems to think people considering monastic life actually live at the monastery? I am about to sign a lease for one-year on an apartment since I found out I have to wait 2 years to become Catholic and enter. Just thought I should ask...

Rodney
"May the Peace of Christ be with you always"

Do You Yahoo!?

His Response:

Name <thomas@Methuselahabbey.org> wrote:

Dear Rod,

Thank you for contacting me. Can you call me on Thursday morning at 10a.m.? I will be sure to be available at that time.

with prayers,

Father Thomas

My Response to His Response:

From: Rod Odom [mailto:rod_odom456@yahoo.com]
Sent: Wednesday, October 31, 2007 1:03 PM
To: Name

Subject: RE: another question
If you see this email in time, I will try calling today through Friday morning. I am off work Wednesday (today 10/31) and Thursday...

His Response to My Response 2:

From: thomas@Methuselahabbey.org
To: rod_odom456@yahoo.com
Sent: Wed, Oct 31, 2007 at 5:25 PM

Subject: re: another question

I look forward to speaking with you in the morning.

My Response to His Response 3:

From: Rod Odom [mailto:rod_odom456@yahoo.com]
Sent: Wednesday, October 31, 2007 3:09 PM
To: Name

Subject: RE: another question
Thanks Fr. Thomas,
I will call tomorrow at 10am. I will set my phone. I will very likely be out of the Mass for All Saints Day by then.

Rodney

Welcome to Monastic Life! - The Divided Self

The Divided Self

Each day for weeks, months, and even years, I was mentally processing the stress of leaving all that I think of as "life" in the past as I tried to enter a new, radically different way in the monastery. It is better to leave mental baggage or personal history outside the monastic gates. But that did not happen. And the psychological and physical effect of simultaneously living two different ways of life is like carrying an invisible load of logs everywhere you go, with everything you do, and with everyone you speak. I was living two lives at once. The task of ridding oneself of all possessions and physically moving some other place requires tremendous personal effort. Yet, it is still another massive effort to dedicate oneself to this radically different lifeway, even if accomplished gradually.

Meanwhile, my mind is still seeking and recycling the pleasure sources of my former ways. I formed the habit of sitting in front of my house on my porch at night and relaxing as I planned my next day. At night, behind our monastic cells (think monks' living quarters), I would look out over the river at the dim lighting of the homes on the other side. I imagined the people in those homes watching television and thinking about their work the next day. Just watching the lights in their homes and listening to their dogs barking made me feel like I was "home again." I suspect this naturally occurring fantasy was a distraction from the stress of this radical monastic change.

Without trying to create it, a mental emptiness opened within me as I strived each day. I distinguish emptiness from homesickness. While homesickness occupies a space in your mind, emptiness lacks any mental occupation. Some people describe that emptiness in terms of a feeling of dryness. And, at times, it can seem painful to the mind and body. I don't think any of these circumstances develop without God's help. I firmly believe God is actively at work reforming a person at this point. I see God creating the emptiness and not allowing anything else to occupy it. In this new life, I naturally tended toward introspection, evaluating my behavior and the behavior of the people around me. I struggled to avoid my poor habit of criticizing and judging others. And I was successful at times. If you see it in others, people say it is because you know about it firsthand within yourself. Before entering, one book I read, written by a priest, indicated that the mind would tend toward thoughts of sex and food when left with nowhere to focus and nothing else for occupation. I found this to be 100 percent accurate. Over time, I struggled with demanding sexual thoughts to trying to stay focused on the present. Then I had to struggle with persistent romantic ones.

In retrospect, I see giving away what I own as a process that requires years of planning and long-term decision-making. I made a personal decision to pay all debts, cut all social and economic ties to the society I was leaving and give up all further investment in career activities. I froze my credit files. I did this well in advance of entering the monastery. But for some who enter monastic life, they are giving up licensed careers, vital education, and critical opportunities. In some professions, stepping away for a mere year sets them back in a gaping professional way. I met a lawyer trying to decide whether to renew his license to practice law (he did.) The married or previously married forego communication with family and close friends (including their children). Having that loving interaction with immediate family members reduced to one or two visits per year is very stressful for anyone. And many do it all to go live with a bunch of strangers, eat an odd diet and be part of a very unusual and foreign daily schedule.

I did quite a bit before I entered. I gave up my car and depended on public transportation. And in a small city like Greenville, North Carolina, where I first moved when leaving the Philadelphia area, I discovered the public bus transportation came once an hour. The system was very informal. If I missed a bus, I ruined my entire day's plan. If the driver decided to skip my stop that day, I was just out of luck! For me, the consequences of such changes were a divided self, divided thinking, split values, and divided dreams and fantasies about how life is supposed to be—living two different value systems at once.

Interacting with a whole new family of strangers was stressful, as I never socialized much. I indeed visited the monastery multiple times before entering. And I lived the monastic life with the monks for periods before deciding to enter. And it is also true that certain critical people of the monastery have gotten to know me administratively. They know my background, education, social record, and more interesting habits. One of the questions a senior monk asked me was, "what kind of music do you like?" Because the monastery tended to listen to chant or classical music, he thought that might be an issue for me. It was not. They can know certain things about me beforehand, but I suspect it is difficult for them to know, for instance, what I will say or do when I open my mouth to speak while angry. This emotional event may not happen on a short visit or may take years to observe. I compare entering the monastery to dating and then eventually getting engaged.

I expose my more personal habits to the folks there on my initial visits. But there are personal habits they do not discern immediately. These habits require more prolonged periods of observation. Also, I discover just how much I enjoy the monastic life during more extended visits. I will learn if I can grow to appreciate it more. In this process, the divided self is leaning toward the monastic life or rejecting it for a life outside. Over time the monks learn that they want you to be there with them, or if you stay long enough, they may learn to dislike you. In that case, they know to put up with you anyway. They will either think you are a great guy or someone who makes them frown. They will have private complaints about you, the new person, and say nothing about them. Or they will communicate their observations to someone with authority or come to you publicly and speak to you with compliments or criticisms.

October 31, 2007

Dear Family,

How are you? I do hope everyone is okay. I truly do. I am writing to update you all on my progress here in Charlotte. Some people in Philadelphia know that my seeking monastic life has become like a crusade for me. Others think I am on an exciting trip for a thrill, Jackie, a friend from high school, asked me if I thought I was having a "mid-life crisis." I told her that if I am, it started when I was about 29 years old. Whatever your thoughts are, it's a life in progress, so it is supposed to be serious.

I have a permanent job now working for Frito-Lay in South Charlotte. The pay is much better than the temp jobs I worked, and I am in the process of moving closer to the new job since it currently takes me about five hours by bus to travel each day to work and back. I am used to public transportation, but the travel time does get to me.

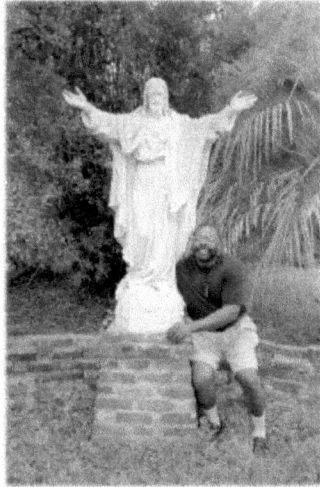

Methuselah Abbey, Sacred Heart of Jesus, 2007

Frito-Lay is great. But like I told my parents, when I visited them in Durham, North Carolina, during the Labor Day holiday, it has been a rough start. My first week here, I was in a nasty mental battle with my supervisor because I don't work Sundays. I told them five times before they hired me that I do not work on Sundays. No one seems to have heard that. The managers said they were only supposed to hire those who could work Sundays. It turns out they started a new shift, and I was hired to work specifically Saturdays. It seems, Veronica, my other boss, forgot to tell everyone. Before all this, my immediate supervisor sarcastically implied that I should be fired because it was unfair to the other people that I do not work on Sundays. Anne, his boss, didn't listen to him. So I am still here. I offered to quit because I would not have left my other job, knowing my schedule would have changed to working on Sunday.

I have become susceptible to people's emotions recently. And it is such that when people are pleased about me, I feel their joy when they speak to me and when they are angry, I feel that too. I state this as an observation and not as a fact. When I first started working on Saturday, my boss Veronica, was having inventory problems, and when she detected a mistake on my part while doing counts, she became upset. And even though she called herself sneaking up behind me to observe my technique, I could feel her anger scraping my "mind" like a knife. I didn't acknowledge her, but I knew she was there. Again, however, Anne, my other boss, was angry because we didn't load eight boxes of an order on a delivery truck. The driver complained the following day when he drove off with an empty truck and had to come back. She boiled over and made us all sign documents for our personnel files. Because I was new, she made me sign a document indicating I was being cautioned about that specific incident. She was angry when she came to talk to me, and the anger from her attitude as she walked off was like being hit in the head with a hammer. So I must approach each day in this place with caution. And there are days when I am filled with fear of going to work. I don't know when I will end up feeling like I have been hit by a moving truck.

I talked to Ms. Brown (she's the parishes' Pastoral Associate) when I first came to Our Lady of Consolation Catholic Church. And she said something to me that helps. She said, "When I run out of energy and become weak, I should pray for strength." And I can honestly say that has saved my life and mental state. It is truly a battle making it through the day when you are working around so many people with so many different backgrounds coming at you from so many different directions. So when I come home and fall on my bed, babbling like an idiot (sometimes in tears), and I fall to the

Photo: Ms. Dale Brown was the Pastoral Associate of Our Lady of Consolation Roman Catholic Church. She also directed the RCIA Classes. Author unknown.

foot of my little cross, I tell God that I have no more sanity. And if I am to go on, I truly need his help. I tell you, you have no idea what it is like

to have immediate renewal. It used to take me weeks to recover, if at all. And I would spend my days in silence, avoiding everyone I could to avoid disrupting my recovery. But God does it immediately.

Photo: Frito-Lay truck leaving the lot in S. Charlotte, NC

Maybe this is the reason God has made it clear that to receive mercy, you must give mercy. Because when people are angry and criticize or silently call you names, you tend to react with anger at their insults. But God requires mercy, which eventually leads to understanding and peace between you and other people. Since I have started at Frito-Lay, it has been a constant struggle to survive. To me, this is a sure sign that God is at work because if you stay focused on him, your sufferings make you stronger and purify your mind and heart. Read below:

Week 1 through 2: In a dispute over working on Sundays, I should be fired.

Week 2 through 4: I stink and need to shower before I come to work. People move away from me when I sit down. My manager counsels me that it's probably a chemical reaction and change deodorants or soap.

Week 4 through 8: I don't contribute enough. I use public transportation as an excuse to leave work before the work is complete (buses stop running at 1 a.m. in Charlotte). The other employees say they want more dedication from me.

Week 6 through 8: I am gay. Now all the guys avoid being seen talking to me. People start whispering about me.

Week 4 through current: I am having a sexual affair with Veronica, my boss. They say to each other that that's why I was hired. In Veronica's defense, she is cute. People can't help but dream up stuff under these working conditions. Truthfully, I didn't know Veronica until I started working here!

Now, after five months on the job, I have emerged more aware of my dependence on God. I see the victories in my struggles are his mercy in action. In this way, heaven teaches me how to survive the world I am in in its rawest form. And time tells the truth. Frito-Lay now thinks I am one of their better employees (even though I tend to mumble to myself). And there is no way whatsoever I could have survived this long without heavenly help. Thy rod and staff, they comfort me.

Photo: Employee unloading and scanning in new inventory to the warehouse.

But now, also, I think about Jesus. When he was in a crowd walking, and a lady touches his robe to heal from her disease, why did he turn and ask, who touched me? He already had people pressing against him from all sides. I don't think he is asking who physically touched him. Although this is speculation, I think he felt a distinct draining of something from his being. And, from all these struggles, I know that if I stick with God, he will teach me this invisible or spiritual warfare. Because it is just as I understand St. Paul to say,

We are not fighting against people of flesh and blood. But we are fighting against rulers and powers whom we cannot see. We are fighting against those who control the darkness of this world, and against bad spirits who have power in the air. So use everything that God has given you, that you can fight when the bad time comes. You will need to do everything you can do to stand! So then, stand and hold on tight to the truth like you put on a belt. Do what is right. Wear it as a cover for your body. You have the good news of peace. Wear that like shoes on your feet. You believe in God. Take that and cover all of yourself with it. With that you can stop all the poison arrows of the devil. **Ephesians 6:11-15.** (14)

I recently came back from a three-day visit to Methuselah Abbey (formally known as Our Lady of Methuselah Abbey). Methuselah is in Monk's City, South Carolina (about one hour from Charles City). Established in 1949, Methuselah is located along the Jordan River's western branch in Berkeley County. It was owned by the Lucens family, a prominent Revolutionary War family. Lucen is also a U.S. Constitution participant. The family traded slaves at one point and eventually became farmers growing rice. According to a 2007 conference at Methuselah on the Trans-Atlantic Slave Trade, some slaves came from a specific part of West Africa and were specialists in growing rice. The Lucens family is buried at Methuselah Abbey, and the family's descendants still visit Methuselah to this day. Another plantation owner, J. W. Johnson, sold the Methuselah Plantation to the Lawsons in 1936. [11]

Mr. Lawson is well known as a publisher of *Great* magazine. Methuselah Abbey is two thousand acres of the Methuselah plantation donated by the family foundation to be a Roman Catholic monastery. To my knowledge, neither Elizabeth, his second wife, nor Henry Lawson were Roman Catholic. It is a most beautiful place. There are flowers from around the world and birds there that exist nowhere else on earth.

During my stay, when I asked if I could come to Methuselah to stay, they broke my heart. If I were interested, I would have to wait two years. Not because they are overcrowded, because they only have 23 monks, but because two years is how long you must wait after expressing interest in a Trappist monastery. I should mention that one of the monks is in Columbia, South America. He serves with the convent of Trappistines nuns.

Photo: Fr. Jude Duffy was a Franciscan Capuchin, Friar and Priest who pastored Our Lady of Consolation during my time as a member. I updated him on my progress at Methuselah Abbey. Author unknown.

I'll have to be Roman Catholic for two years to enter Methuselah. The two-year period is a time of discovery and self-understanding. This waiting is to assure my interest is not trivial. But, once I discovered this, I went

Photo: Entrance. Our Lady of Consolation Roman Catholic Church on Statesville Road in Charlotte, N.C. (2008). Some buildings not pictured.

into deep mourning for about 20 minutes. I knew that I did not have the stamina to wait for two more years on top of what I have already been through to date. So I went back to my room, mentally reeling, my mind filled with doubts about my whole purpose. I even thought that all this that I am going through is some great illusion. I thought I must be mentally ill, and maybe I need to go to a hospital or something. I thought to myself, "here I am, way out here on some illusion of a twisted mental story!" I fell on my bed, and I began to speak to God openly. "Lord, there is no way I can go through this for another two years. And if this is what you will for me, then you have to deal with it!" As I thought these things, I began to lean on my past experiences. I remembered the many times God answered my prayers. As I lay there, I concluded that it couldn't be a dream. It must be authentic. I thought, No! If God needs me to wait two more years, and I don't do it, then something is wrong with me. I need to change – I need more patience! And miraculously, as I left my room to go to prayer, I was restored completely. Fr. Thomas reassured me that even he had to wait for two years. He said he saw the disappointment on my face after telling me about the waiting period. Everyone does have to wait, though according to my research, he only waited one year. Then I began to think. I got a warning weeks earlier when I read about the Trappist monastery in Kentucky. I read that they require two years also. But I didn't focus on that till after my encounter at Methuselah.

Now I realize that I must focus on what I am taught regardless of where I end up, monastery or not. I probably need a personal plan, but just as critical is the need to learn from my circumstances while making progress with God. From all my readings of the saints, I knew that I was being taught. I read that God can expose your weaknesses and strengthen you to overcome them simultaneously. One of my weaknesses was and still is patience. This learning process is excruciating but necessary. And I pray for strength to carry on, falling literally on my face but having enough direction now to ask God for help.

Photo: Train pulling into Uptown Station, Charlotte, North Carolina, 2007

Methuselah Abbey is a Trappist Monastery. Trappist monasteries are guided by the Rule of Saint Benedict. The Rule of Saint Benedict is precisely how it sounds; Saint Benedict developed a set of rules for governing a monastery. The lifestyle entails: intense silence and prayer, physical labor for a living, and deep reflection. The monks refrain from speaking. There is no vow of silence. They often use their hands to indicate what they are trying to communicate, like Sign Language. Trappists were made more famous by Thomas Merton, who wrote an autobiography, The Seven Story Mountain. Thomas Merton, who is now deceased (the Abbot calls him Fr. Louis), has a small but popular following because of his many spiritual writings. The Abbot was one of his students as a monk at Gethsemane Abbey in Kentucky. This occurred in the 1960s.

Now (in Charlotte), I am moving to an apartment and signing a one year lease starting in December 2007. The apartment complex is in south Charlotte and is called Sun Valley. (I will send you all my address information later after getting the exact apartment number.) It is significantly closer to work. And I will be able to ride the train which starts running in November (I hope). [I ended up riding

Photo: Me, Rodney, staring out of the window of the new Charlotte train as it pulls through a train station. Author unknown.

the bus because the new train system went in a different direction.]

I felt comfortable with the monastery because Fr. Thomas asked me a million questions when he first met me. And I learned from my reading that you must make every effort to be completely honest with this questioning. I did my best to be open and try not to hold back or hide anything. Not only is patience a prime monastic virtue, but so is honesty, and even though my story probably sounds utterly absurd to the average person, to Fr. Thomas, it was quite normal. There are underlying politics when you deal with any group of people; overall, the monks were very sincere, helpful, and praying for me to make the right decision. One monk, who was elderly and sickly, was in a wheelchair. He had a disease in which he was losing his skin pigmentation (he is African-American). We had a short conversation. And when I left, he asked my name. I knew he was going to pray for me. The open display of private effort is always a good sign. Sometimes I thank God for answering prayers beforehand because somehow I know it will obtain what I request.

Welcome to Monastic Life! - Formation!

Formation!

In a book on tape I listened to some time ago, the author suggested that all they see are pockets when a pick-pocket walks down the street. Anyone who has occupied a continuous period of time focused on a subject, art form, or hobby knows something similar. By living a monastic life, I am trying to focus my time, efforts, and energy toward God alone. It is supposed to be part of my work, exercise, and even walk to dinner!

> *Do not keep many things for yourself on earth. Insects and rust will spoil them. People will get in and steal them. But keep things for yourself in heaven. Insects and rust will not spoil them there. People will not get in and steal them. The place where you keep things is where your heart will be also.* **Matthew 6:19-21.** (14)

For the modern person, who is very much schooled in facts or using the scientific method as a basis for their reality, thinking about far-off, ethereal, heavenly things is a challenge. The rules are not fixed in the mind of a small child. So what we teach them, they more or less accept. This acceptance is not necessarily so for the older person or adult. The idea of "stores" for some heavenly future that may not be real because it cannot be measured or proven scientifically is asking too much! It would seem that knowledge and understanding of our physical universe eliminate the need for or effort for a heavenly one. All our planning goes into today, this week, or even this month. But few people plan for years from now, and even fewer can afford to think about passing away or after they are physically dead. And they will not unless the entire group is doing so!

I now see that thinking about heavenly things takes time and energy. As Jesus was said to have told one monk, "time is the currency for our friendship." Or restated, I reap what I sow from my relationship with God based on the time I put into it! And to me, understanding my relationship with God also means understanding self (me). What and how I think is the "substance" I use to connect with God. Christ can take my experience and revamp it to a clearer view of his will. To me, I must transcend what the world thinks of God (and thus what it passes to me) and seek a much more personal understanding. My understanding of God then comes not from me, but from the church that feeds me and from God himself.

God seems to work hand in hand with my tendency "come as you are" is proof of that. I did not end up in a monastery because I decided to make it happen; I ended there because my God wished to fulfill my heart's desire. My need to be closer to God manifested itself as a destination of "monastery." And out of Mercy, he created a path in my life to end up at a "monastery." If I seek, I find; if I ask, I receive. And if I knock, the door is opened for me. It is my Heavenly Father's wish for me to be with him and not to live in fear of death or hell.

And so, to me, practice makes perfect. When I pray every day and place God first, spend time learning about what I believe, engage with the Living God, I transform into a child of God who can know my God as more real than I am myself. And not a God who is a figment of my imagination or an illusion. I learn according to his direction and not my own. For me and probably any Christian, change is a human challenge to be like Christ by focusing on Christ. For me, the reward for this focus has been more than a hundred-fold. And yes, the path is paved with both struggles and rewards. With God, reality bends and transforms in ways you do not realize is even possible. And Christian life forms you regardless of your circumstance, background, or prior knowledge.

September 18, 2009

Hello Family,

Just a short note to say what's up! It has been a while since I last contacted anyone. I have talked to a few of you on the telephone. I spoke to T.J.(Timothy Junior)... and I talked to T.J.'s cousin - Laiene on Labor Day weekend. It is hard to believe that T.J. and Laiene are about to finish high school. T.J. said he doesn't do email [that is why he doesn't answer mine.] I bet if his girlfriend did email, he would do email. I read an article that said that email is outdated for younger folks nowadays; they text each other instead. Texting is just another form of email! I heard Lee (the third) is married. Happy Bliss, congratulations Lee (and wife!) I emailed a particular person's sister for some pictures and am ignored on the matter. But she is a parent, so I am giving her a break on her response. Who knows if I will ever meet the bride! I would have sent a cheese sandwich if I had his current address!

Anyway, let me thank everyone again for the little get-together at your house when the Abbot visited Philadelphia. He said he had an enjoyable time. And he seemed to appreciate the food Barbara put together and the hospitality of the family. Everybody here enjoyed the chocolate you sent me. No, I didn't give all of it away, but it would have been wrong not to share some of it. People here like an occasional treat, and that was an incredible one! I am ashamed to say it is all gone now! I ate most of it within three weeks. And that is probably stretching the time a bit. Not to worry, I am currently preparing for a one-month workout and fast. This refrain is where I fast from any exercise or workouts (smile). The only thing I am allowed to eat is pizza, steaks, and hoagies filled with meat!

Seriously, I am about to fast for 30 days in October to help me with my emotional attachment to food. It's a "spiritual-mental" thing. It will be challenging, but with God's help and the Virgin's guidance, I will make it through. By the way, the Abbot used to go to the same movie theater we went to when he was younger. He attended about 25 years earlier than we did. It was still called the Erlen Theater back then. His best friend lived at 19th Street and Cheltenham Avenue. He said they used to play ball in that field behind that strip mall on the Cheltenham Township side where the bowling alley used to be. He said he lived about three miles outside the city limits in the Jenkintown area.

We recently had a movie night here at the monastery. The brothers gather in the conference room and watch popular commercial films on DVD. We usually have pizza on movie night. The restaurant where we get the pizza makes a near-perfect pie. It is far better pizza than the chain pizza stores. Perhaps that is not saying much, but you don't complain when you usually have three different cheese slices as your variety of sandwich choices.

Since I last wrote, I have learned how to drive a tractor. It is a very long story. You see, we had a forest fire. Well, maybe you should call it a tall weed fire. In any case, no one around at that moment knew how to drive the tractor with the bushwhacker. So we could not stop the spread of the fire. We didn't have any access to water out in the middle of the big field; that is to say, our hoses will not stretch an entire cotton field. Consequent to that situation, I said to myself: "Self! Never again

Photo: This is a picture of the large field filled with beautiful green cotton plants. At the time of the fire, it was not so green, grass was taller and fire spread easily.

are you going to be stuck with only a broom to put out a fire that large!" And within two weeks, I was driving the tractor -not bad for a city boy!

Br. Joseph eventually arrived and hopped on another tractor and mowed a path around the fire, and then we had time to walk around the edges of the fire and beat out the flames. It was exciting and new but scary since the fire would have eventually reached the trees before long. Br. Joseph has been a monk for sixty-five years. And he pretty much knows the monastery in intimate detail. He still has screws and bolts from 30 years ago because "they might come in handy someday." He and Ted (the manager) pretty much fix everything at the monastery. Alas, it was he who started the fire! While trying to burn some old branches, he decided it was safe to go to dinner and leave it alone. Some embers flew too far! When we came back from lunch, half the field was ablaze. The fire arrested. The remains burned themselves out. Someone did stand watch for a while to make sure no fire restarted.

You may be interested to know I am becoming a snake "expert." Since the summer is a popular time for snakes looking for the cooler shade, I learned they crawl to any space to do so. They will even crawl into a split in a window screen. I used to carry a large stick to kill any snake I saw near me. Now, I simply watch them. With a bit of knowledge from Google, I learned that I don't need to kill them unless they are poisonous and threatening. That may not seem like much but, it is somewhat different for someone like me to become so comfortable with snakes that I grab a broom and chase them off. One time I told Br. James that Satan was behind the mushroom cooking room wall, was about four feet long, with gray and black stripes. He just looked at me and started laughing. Most of the time, they don't want any trouble from us, so they run. But there is a snake called a black racer. It is swift, and it moves in such a way as to seem as though you are in its path as it weaves back and forth trying to get around. I asked Br. Joseph why was this snake in such a hurry. He said that the snake is probably trying to get back to where he came from(smile)!

My two foster turtles are doing fine. They pretty much eat, sleep and crawl under the mud I put in the box to help them stay cool. They like the water, but they can be messy in water. Fr. Bartholomew should be back from Asia soon to take them back. They are his, not mine! Though, strangely, we have yet to hear from him since July. As I walk, I am always on the lookout for worms for fishing and feeding the turtles. One turtle is called Hansel, and the other is called Gretel. Fr. Bartholomew named them and then dumped them on me [Where did he get turtles? Sometimes when it rains, the turtles wash out of the rivers and creeks onto the road.]

We are doing a fine job advancing the mushroom business. I am doing my share of work in that part of the abbey. I am helping to solve a lot of technical problems and helping to design new equipment. It is not very high tech, but my little inventions help with all the heavy work. More than anything, I help with communication. We monks are not effective in communicating, so I started writing memos to everyone about mushroom issues. Within a few months, everybody was helping to solve all our problems. Now my memos are a standing joke! But I think I serve to integrate the bigger picture of related issues and help communicate technical ideas.

We've had quite a few classes over the last six months. And theology is a big part of our monastic learning. Our learning is not organized like a seminary, but monks learn quite a bit over time, both in personal reading and through formal teaching.

Fr. Gerry(teaching) on the right, me in blue Observer shirt in the middle. Author unknown.

We had Fr. Trappist of Monk Abbey come and teach us about the "culture of God" during our one-week retreat in early September. He spoke on the Baptism of Jesus. I had no idea that the Baptism of Jesus meant so much. Before that class, I thought, why? Why on earth did Jesus need to get baptized? And since Jews didn't have baptism as part of their practices, why? Why do we call this particular Jewish prophet John the Baptist? None of this made any sense to me! Fr. Trappist says we learn the psychology of Jesus and his culture through the Gospels. And we understand the "culture of God" through Jesus. Jesus went into the Jordan River, and when he rose from the water, the heavens burst open. And the Spirit of God descended on Jesus like a dove. And it stayed with Jesus. And it was from that point on that Jesus' entire language and thinking began to openly and actively demonstrate His God-nature with acts "only God" could perform. Who else can walk on water without a whole bunch of special equipment and bring dead, decaying corpses back to life? It gets kind of complicated after that. But, all in all, it seems like excellent information and interesting theology and it answers many questions I had about that part of Jesus' life.

I was surprised to learn that not too long ago the Roman Catholic Church didn't recommend that the laity(non-ordained) read the bible. And when you start to see the theology that is developed from it, you begin to understand why it was not recommended. The bible can be easily misinterpreted. (It would be like each person has their own version of scripture.) I think the problem with stopping the laity is that they miss out on "nourishment" that living scripture provides in a spiritual way. Anyone can read the bible and walk away enlightened from it in some way since it is "food from God." Anyway, the Church does now recommend all read holy scripture.

This monastery didn't always have so many non-monastics visiting in the past. Still, after the Second Vatican Council, they decided it was best to open the entire church up to everyone (In other words, all church members should participate in the monastic spirituality.) It is now everyone's job to represent Christ and to evangelize. So most monasteries are now required to be more open to public view and laity visits.

I have more jobs now. I am an Altar Server (I did that for a short while at Our Lady of Consolation in Charlotte.) I am the bell binger. The bell ringer sounds the buzzer five minutes before each event, including the prayers. So I have to keep a constant eye on the daily schedule. And boy-oh-boy if I miss a schedule change! Everybody looks at me with outrage. It isn't very comfortable

Photo (l to r) A monastic guest, me (Rodney) and another monk prepping large mushroom columns. Author unknown.

when I walk in the room after everyone else because I did not realize the time and miss the bell.

I am a mushroom column "stuffer." Those mushroom columns can weigh about 70 pounds at times. I sing on the schola. (A schola is a small religious choir.) When I know the songs, singing goes well for me. People go out of their way to tell me they LOVE my voice. During lunch, they whisper compliments in my ear. Some people stare at me with their mouths open when I sing. However, I am not used to reactions like this since I don't sing, don't read music, and am experiencing compliments like this for the first time ever. A priest visiting from Peru said, "Thank God for your voice!" (I often wonder what they hear that I don't.) When I don't know the song, forget about everything! Anyway, soon I expect to be cooking and reading in the dining hall at meals. Someone always reads a book during lunch using a microphone. Reading happens every day except Friday and Sunday. It is usually non-fiction. The books are fascinating. I learn much.

Okay, what is monastic life like for me? Is it heavenly? No! Most days, it is tolerable. On a bad day, it is merely a more intense version of the previous day when it is not okay. The intensity of the experience does not disappear entirely on the best days. It is a lot like living with a constant ailment. Some days you forget you have it for a little while. Fr. Thomas seems to think I am experiencing what people call "A Dark Night." It is a concept made famous by Saint John of the Cross. Here are some lessons for all the people just waiting to break down the door and be monks and nuns:

Rumors: Goodness! Rumors are the currency of the monastery. I ask myself: How do you stay cordial with someone who spies on you to see if you are stealing chocolate or cake between meals? Or worse yet, when someone had a dream that you were eating at midnight. And you get questioned about it as if you did eat at midnight! It is only by the Grace of God I am still here! Who could survive this craziness without God's help?

Follow Through: We meet, and we plan. We meet, and we plan. We meet again, and we plan. We collect information, and we meet again. And then? Maybe we need another meeting? We take forever to do things, and when we do act, the follow through is rare. In other words, implementation of plans is rare, and only by the Grace of God do I survive this way of life! I admit my way of thinking is biased. I come from the outside, and my tendency has always been toward action. My biggest challenge in recent years has been patience. Having said all that, I think I suffer less from fear of failure than most people, having failed at implementing so many bizarre, inspired plans in my own life. And so, I tend toward action without so much fear, whereas the monks are much more conservative. They look for much more certainty, and they seem harsh in their recall of people's failures.

Fishbowl Effect: We are affected by visitors. We sing louder. We worry about what they might think. We must worry about offending women with our "all male organization." The nuns who visit are used to this separation, but mainstream people are not. If I look at a woman for too long, it might cause issues. It is only by the Grace of God I have survived thus far! I don't think most people who come to a monastery realize the hormonal effect of sexual separation. Nor do they realize how much satisfaction they get from being near the "other gender." The change in the body and on the mind is tremendous. The effect of separation seems less obvious after long periods. But it never goes away completely.

Under Staffed: We have a sprawling, multi-industrial and community-type organization, and most of the monks are 70, 80, and 90 years old. Need I say more? Only by the Grace of God have I survived this new life! The monks don't think of it as any big deal to have empty buildings sitting about neglected, but I have seen what happens when something is not properly maintained. I know the complexity of what we have here. We don't have the people to properly care for all this according to what is usually required. That is why buildings are failing, equipment is neglected, and the new business does not receive the needed attention. The psychology of the monks is one of "let it go" and "don't worry"). Religious call these conditions "poverty."

Thoughts and Thinking: I have a thought or question today; he answers it in his conversation with someone else tomorrow. I have an idea today; he claims he had it yesterday. Somehow, someway our thoughts get mixed and messy, and far too often, it isn't easy to track an idea to its origin. You thought you told him yesterday, but you didn't. But he knew somehow and didn't remember who told him or when. **Only by the Grace of God am I still here!**

Openness In Monastic Life: We should tend toward transparency. We should struggle for less and less to hide. We believe that God sees all and that Jesus emerges in the one with nothing to hide. Yet, there persists (in my opinion) a certain tendency toward privacy. We have an "us" versus "them" mentality toward outsiders. We tend to look at our flaws as an embarrassment to be covered up and not placed in public view. We pray, work, eat and sleep! We do have very little to hide. And so, we are not perfect people? I say this to indicate the level of stress created trying to "act" as if there is some real reason to protect and defend what doesn't seem to exist in the first place. Can I speak freely about anything here without some form of "shushing going on". For me, the most challenging issue is understanding when to speak and when not to speak. Knowing what is the secret and what is not the secret. Every time you open your mouth at the wrong time, you get a nasty look, and you begin to gain a reputation for speaking out of line.

Only by the Grace of God am I still here. My experiences here, the love of Jesus, and Mary's help keep me where I don't ordinarily want to be. I cannot see any other explanation. It would be so much easier for me to get a quiet little job somewhere and live as a hermit, go to church, go home, eat and sleep. The place is filled with people that all say something similar or did at one point in their history. "I am clearly not here under my own power! All I did was say YES to being here." I have learned that casually talking to people outside the monastery about Jesus and Mary is something of a challenge. You want to write to people about it, but they have no interest or deep belief in such things. So I should consider myself lucky for these experiences!

Well, now it is time to say goodbye, Hasta luego, and Peace be with you. And over the coming months, I will be following up with three true stories that might blow you away. Trust me, you will be amazed at what has been going on over the last 10 years, starting with a year or two before I first left Philadelphia. All the weird things and strange issues are still current in my mind. It all comes together like a big giant puzzle. And the answers didn't come until I entered the monastery and was here for a good year.

Love,

Br. Rodney

2010

I was traveling this morning

It was a bright, sunny day. And it was a pleasant day. Like something out of a perfect dream, but then I woke up. Still groggy from sleeping, I thought that the day was coming to an end, that maybe it was about 7:30 p.m. or so. But it was not; it was 1:30 a.m.. Yes, it is still very early in the morning. It is slightly earlier than before my day normally gets started! And where was I just now, before I realized I was dreaming, and became so confused about what time of day it is this moment? I was on a trip with my Guardian. And the day I experienced was tomorrow; that is to say, it was the next day coming into being. Still, it had come; and it had gone. When I woke up, tomorrow was just about over.

While I slept, I never left my bed. But as I slept, I searched and observed the next day or maybe several days. I find nothing of interest. I see no reason for fear or worry. It is a day filled with extraordinary, warm weather, a bright, sunny sky, and endless satisfaction. I live out the entire day, or so it seems, in a matter of minutes. And I am tired when tomorrow was over.

Suddenly my alarm clock sounded! And after I awoke and realized where I was, I wondered with incredible astonishment how it was that I thought the day was nearly over, but the clock insisted it was merely just getting started. It is now actually about 2:15 a.m.. And I lay in my bed to think on the matter. In fact, I thought about this unusual matter of "temporal disorder in my reality" all day long. It never left my mind even for a moment. And when that same tomorrow came again, I expected little and enjoyed what I did expect, a bright sunny day with few hassles and endless blue sky.

When tomorrow was "really" over, I remember thinking to myself, O how I love Jesus, for he has truly set me free.

> *The holy writings say, `No eye has seen the things God has made ready for those who love him. No ear has heard about them. No person's heart has ever thought of them. `* **1 Corinthians: 2.** (14)

And I am not even dead yet! Free to even travel the days ahead and see and observe. Then return to my current time and experience tomorrow again today.

Chapter Introduction

After nearly three years (2006 to 2009), I left Charlotte, North Carolina, headed for Charles City, South Carolina. Charlotte is also where I became Roman Catholic on Easter of 2008. I already packed the personal items I was keeping. I shipped them via United Parcel Service freight or the United States Postal Service to the Abbey for safekeeping. Everything else I either sold, gave away, or tossed in the trash.

I left my job of two years at a South Charlotte Frito-Lay warehouse. I started there as a temporary worker folding and sorting reusable boxes and finished as a parking lot sweeper. In addition to walking

Photo: I bought the first cake, and another made by a coworker is almost gone (Million Dollar Pound Cake) - in the middle.

around a massive warehouse with a train of carts picking and loading orders for various stores and supermarkets, my other job was making sure the vast truck parking lot was swept spotless. It was a happy goodbye. When my bicycle was stolen from in front of a store I was in while in Uptown, Charlotte, some of the employees found out and took up a collection. They bought me a new one! When they told me about it, I thought they were joking! We had a little going away party when I left, and one coworker made me a "Million Dollar Pound Cake." I manage to get a piece of it for myself.

I caught Amtrak (train) to Charles City, South Carolina, if I remember accurately. Br. Mark met me and drove us to Methuselah. I do remember that the Abbot was out of town. During the first nine months at Methuselah, I was classified as an Observer. I was not officially a part of the community. And as such, I wore a blue, hooded, pull-over shirt. It was tailor-made for me by Methuselah volunteer, Mrs. Ruddy. Postulants are part of the community and wear a white, hooded, pull-over shirt instead of the robe that other members wear. The daily schedule was the same every day but Sunday. Over time I settled into the routine of waking up at 3 a.m.. for Vigils, a period of meditation, Lauds as morning prayer, breakfast, and daily Mass. After Mass, there is Terce. We then gather with Br. Mark or Ted. (The monastery facility manager.) They assigned daily work.

The brothers had recently stopped keeping chickens to sell their eggs as a business, a business they were in for decades. And they started growing various kinds of mushrooms for sale. They were growing gold, grown, pink, and white oyster mushrooms. They recently gave up on raising a specific type of mushrooms on logs. We eventually ended up producing just the white oysters. The others were either not selling or were not growing reliably. They tried different growing methods in various containers to see which worked best. We started with small 10-pound flower pots with holes cut in them for mushrooms to grow out. We then moved on to giant, 75 pound, hanging plastic columns hung in truck trailers maintained for humidity and temperature. We punctured those plastic columns too. The mushrooms grow through the column holes. We used this method for a few years until we finally designed and built actual mushroom growing houses. We reduced the column sizes by about two-thirds. They were much easier to lift at about 20 pounds and fit perfectly on shelves. We eventually started growing shiitake mushrooms also.

The Trappist monk's daily day at Methuselah Abbey is community prayer seven times a day and personal prayer as often as one can to include meditation in the morning. Our day most often ends at about 7:30 p.m. After daily morning work, we have Midday prayer, lunch (called dinner), daily afternoon work, Vespers (evening prayer). The night ends with Compline and on Sunday Benediction. Sunday is a day of rest, and there is very little work. The period following Compline and ending the following morning is called Grand Silence. There is no talking and no work during this period

Photo: White oyster mushrooms columns growing inside environmentally controlled truck trailers.

without permission from the Abbot. Many people think Trappist monks take a vow of silence. If it ever was true, it is no longer. Speaking is allowed but strongly discouraged. But unnecessary talking, casual chitchat, and horsing around are unacceptable. The older monks often use sign language they developed long ago for communication. It is not uncommon to have a room full of monks sitting around in a room in total silence. Learning silence is usually a matter of time and proper behavior reinforcement.

January 31, 2010

Dear Family,

How are you and the family? Doing well, I hope. This letter is just to let people know why I am in the monastery (*few ask, but many still wonder why*)? I suppose one cannot help but wonder about a life choice of this nature. I have sent this letter mostly to my family and friends. If you have read any of my other letters, this letter shouldn't surprise you a bit. And if not, well, take your time...if you find it interesting read more. If not, toss it. Some people think I choose to enter monastic life because I committed some legally horrible crime (as in guilt). They think that I entered to "atone for my legal sins," so to speak. That is simply not true. For people who believe in my version of God and know my history, they know me better than that. While I sin as everybody else has sinned, what sent me to a life of atonement was a very clear picture of my life as I lived it- a sort of graphic inner picture of my soul. It was pitch black, diseased, and scary. It was so powerful and graphic that it brought me to my knees. It scared me deeply. I could barely look at it. And clearly, I accepted and believed that picture that I saw with my own inner eyes, and through my reading monastic life or subjects like it was my response. [I discovered something through all this. God can have a conversation with you without your being consciously aware that it is in fact God. God's power is such that he knows you better than you know yourself. And while I have some freedom to choose evil over good, I don't have the power to not answer God. If I am a child of God, I must respond. If I am shown myself as I actually am, my response says a lot about my needs in life. My response to this incident indicated my need to repair my spiritual "corruption."] Some of my knowledge of myself was clearly physical and some I would say was spiritual. And intuitively, I knew what I needed to do. I had to "stop my life in its track" and change its course dramatically. Generally, this is who I am and how I act in life. So between the year 2003 or so and 2009, I was "stopping my life in its track" and changing its course. I entered this monastery Our Lady of Methuselah Abbey. And may God help me with all this change going on here!

To a friend: I just heard from my dear and long-time friend Peter (via email, no less) that the two of you are no longer together. I don't know how long you are apart now (or that you are remarried to someone else), but had I known that prior to now, I certainly would not have been addressing your mail the way I am. My oldest sister divorced a few years back and she is still in contact with her ex-husband's parents. They are relatively active in the lives of their grandchildren.

Mary, though Peter and I don't talk as we used to, you were and still are both very important people to me. I have admired you from the start of our friendship and still adore you very much. I truly hope all is well with you. Though you probably have no reason too, please when you have time (whatever that means to a parent nowadays) keep in touch. If you have an extra picture of the family, please send it or email it to me.

I pray for my family and friends everyday...especially my friend Peter (smile).

Much love to you all and **may the Peace of Christ be with you,**

Br. Rodney

My new address:
Rodney K Odom
Methuselah Abbey
1234 Methuselah Abbey Rd
Monk City, SC 29333

Welcome to Monastic Life! - Meditation

Meditation

Since the early 2000s, I have been learning about and practicing meditation. My exposure to meditation was from a Buddhist perspective. While understanding meditation and implementing it in my lifestyle, I also read or listened to audiobooks on Buddhism. I did not know, nor did it ever occur to me, that Christians meditate. Once I arrived and entered the monastery, I realized that meditation was essential to a Trappist monk's spirituality.

But Christian meditation is used as a form of prayer, listening, and responding to God. In contrast, Buddhists use it as a path to self-enlightenment. In other words, Christians and Buddhists use the same word but with two distinctly different purposes in mind. We had talks and guest speakers at the monastery on how and why to meditate. But in the end, meditation requires that you get started. It requires that you do it frequently and reliably. And for Christians, the fruit is not just from meditation; it is also from the action of Grace.

We had a designated time for meditation, usually after the prayer of Vigils and before breakfast. And it was usually a period of half an hour. However, it seemed to me we needed more time than 30 minutes. I meditated in my room or the Chapel. In the Chapel, I felt I was in the direct presence of Christ. But it should not have mattered where I meditated. And over time, I realized that I would have left the monastery much earlier without meditation and its fruits.

Photo: My sister Kimberly, meditating in the church chapel during her 2013 visit to Methuselah.

My mind is always racing on from one subject to the next, solving problems that it sometimes created on its own. I found things to worry about and produced anxiety levels to match. My mind was not separate from me; however, I most certainly learned to participate as an observer of my behavior. And because I read some psychology-related material, I developed a language for describing myself and my activities.

For me, meditation turned out to be not only a tremendous path for self-discovery, but it also led to a method of release from an overly active mental state. I found I was no longer enslaved to the endless mental demands created in my mind. In other words, sometimes, my mind was busy just for the sake of being busy. I was in the habit of looking for "something to do," and my body would, without question, follow its commands.

I reached levels of inner peace that I never knew possible. It was probably an earthly peace, but one brought about through heavenly help. My whole lifestyle was now changing. Mental urgency was waning, and thus worry was less, false goals were disappearing, and so was the vain mental activity created by it. Much of this activity is vanity. It literally just filled the space of time inefficiently. I suspect that I focus more on truth when I concern myself less vanity.

Happy Easter!

By Br. Rodney K Odom, Postulant
Our Lady of Methuselah Abbey

Why is God so Beautiful?

When I woke this morning and left my cell for the church, I noticed God over the Jordan River. And I said to myself, Lord, why are You up there being so beautiful. Like a perfect circle of a giant moon too close to the earth, but yet so far away?

God appeared to be checking on the fish. And I thought to myself, today, all the fish in all the rivers, lakes, seas, and oceans are blessed forever because of the Lord's presence here!

Then God provoked more questions in my mind. And I asked, Lord, why is it you are so beautiful this morning? Why did you make the quiet, dark, early morning so mysteriously wonderful? Why do you cause me to ask so many questions about your creation? What is all this scenery for anyway, plants and water, trees, and fish...insects of every kind! Creatures, rustling about in the bushes. Strange odors!

And why do I always ask why? What's going on with me? Why can't I enjoy what you gave me? Do you think my questions make any sense? Will I ever stop asking questions? Do you think I am just a simple-minded slave to some strange pattern of thinking? Is there no end to the mess I create in my mind from all this?

I think it is all God's fault for being so beautiful this morning...Isn't it?

May 23, 2010

Dear Mary and Joseph,

It is official! I am a monk. I entered the Postulancy on May 18, 2010. I wear white now! The strange thing is I went through so much screening, and nothing special happens. The Abbot announced it at Vespers, and that was it. I did get quite a few hugs from friends of the monastery. People are happy for the monastery and me. To them, I was a good "choice." But of course, look who's doing the choosing!

We had Mass the next day, and during the intercessory prayer, there was only one prayer. Br. James (a monk in simple vows) offered thanks for me becoming a community member. He prayed for grace to sustain my efforts to the last day. There was no other prayer. It was silent. It was not planned. I see it as the Holy Spirit acting especially for Methuselah Abbey and me. You could hear a pin drop. No more prayers of any kind were offered. Two days later, Fr. Bartholomew (46 years old) from East Asia requested entrance to the monastery. We are hopeful, but he still must apply. He leaves in June and has much work to finish before he goes back to Asia.

I am grateful. The Abbot is grateful. I thanked Jesus, Mary, my Guardian Angel, and the Saints. I thanked God for all the support and prayed for strength to continue to do His will regardless of the circumstances ahead.

Love,

Br. Rodney Odom

June 1, 2010,

Dear family,

Just a little note to say hello! I hope all is well. The school year is coming to an end. So I trust no one is scared about passing on to the next grade? Or at least not unnecessarily worried! As you ought to know by now, my new name is Br. Rodney Odom. I am a Postulant now. I feel a special reverence for what I wear and why I wear it. But other than that, nothing has changed.

Since my last letter, I have killed my first snake. It was either him (or her) or me, right? And I had the shovel, so I won. However, it was all in ignorance. I found out it was non-poisonous and mostly ate mice or small squirrels. I had no reason to murder this harmless creature. To my surprise, I did learn how mean squirrels can be. You have not seen the meanness of a squirrel until you see them go up against a snake. Those cute little jowls turn tight and vicious! I think the squirrel I observed was protecting her young. Though you could not see the young, the squirrel knew what the snake had planned, and she went to work, trying her best to scare it away. Like us, squirrel too have a limited attention span. The snake freezes its motion for a little while, and the squirrel becomes baffled. The squirrel eventually goes about her business as if there is no threat. Suddenly, the dinner bell rings, for the snake, that is, and off she goes up the tree to eat the young squirrels.

I recently found out I will probably end up on the choir and cook supper for the brothers every fourth Sunday or so. I attended my first Monk Funeral. Br. Matthew recently died. (He was 82 years old and had cancer.) They gave him six weeks to live over two years ago. And, oh by the way, he refused medical treatment! Did you know Trappist monks are buried without a casket? Yep! They put the body on a piece of wood, cover its face, lower it directly into the ground, then toss the dirt in over it! All the monks shovel some amount of dirt. It's very unusual to see! A little creepy too! But from ashes we come and to ashes we return. The Abbot said the face cover is only because people find it strange to bury someone without a casket.

Mark, who used to be Br. Mark, decided to go back to the world. He was only 27, and I think he had women and relationships on his mind. He goes to college as a freshman. He was recently here with a female friend in a rowboat and was chased by a five-foot alligator around the lake. He said it just kept following them around as they rowed. They finally had to leave. See what happens when you double-cross God (smile)! Well, I need to hang up now. Talk to you later!

May God's mercy be with all of you!

Love,

Br. Rodney

PS The little booklet (enclosed) is another concert we have annually at the Abbey. It is called "Little Spoleto."

Welcome to Monastic Life! – Go To Sleep

Go to Sleep...

It may surprise you to learn that chronic sleep deprivation, for whatever reason, significantly affects your health, performance, safety, and pocketbook. The short-term effects are decreased performance and alertness, memory and cognitive impairment, stress, poor quality of life, occupational injury, and potential automobile injury. [3]

One of the things I noticed in years of monastic life was that monks seem to have feeble memory. They often confuse stories, facts, and events. It was not uncommon to be told the same story by the same person about a past event five or six times. It was not uncommon to find signs posted on the monastery grounds incorrectly or with the wrong information. It was not unusual for the brothers to feel uncertain about what was going on during specially scheduled events, nor was it uncommon for significant events to not get scheduled at all. I have even encountered circumstances where my mind seemed entangled with another monk's. He knew, but he did not know how. And I knew he knew but did not know how I knew he knew! What?

Then one day, I left my work area and traveled to the main workhouse, and when I arrived, not only did I not know why I was there, but I had forgotten the circumstances that made me leave my work area. I, too, had the dreaded "monk memory" disease. Another time, while speaking with the Abbot about another monk's life, he started laughing at my story. I had all the facts confused. I had the entire story turned upside down and inside out. I began to get concerned; did I have a memory disease?

Either the monks never noticed these improperly scheduled events, or they did not care, but for me, my suspicions took on a life of their own. I was a computer guy who used to struggle with self-diagnosis. I was already not sleeping and, after some time, began to have memory failures. I sometimes awoke to a cloudy mindset about where, what, and when around me? I mentioned my sleep deprivation to the Abbot, and he allowed me to have it checked medically. I had an overnight sleep test completed. The results indicated I was sleeping fine. I came home from the test and slept uninterrupted for two and a half hours straight. I was exhausted after successfully passing the "sleep test." After some time, I also had memory tests completed. All tests indicated my memory was "normal for my age."

While testing indicated my memory was normal, I could tell the people from outside the monastery noticed the issues I mentioned. They would correct the incorrect signs or laugh at the lapses, but they did notice them. And the fact that they saw it confirmed my suspicions that these circumstances were odd. For me, there were times when I would sleep for 45 minutes a night and then lie awake the remainder of the night. And at the point when I needed to get up, I would be on the cusp of falling asleep. I felt like I was being tortured!

I could seek an understanding of my issues through modern medicine. But the modern way is not necessarily the same as the monastic way. The monastic way is often rooted in religious history and spirituality. It is guided by a perception of reality developed by individuals over years or decades. It is not necessarily the modern scientific method of placing known symptoms together to discover or diagnose. The monastic way might use spiritual reasoning to determine a cause for the lack of sleeping (i.e., he is not sleeping. Will he get past this issue and go on to live a normal monastic life, or does his behavior indicate an outright rejection of this lifestyle?). And this "spiritual way" of thinking is one that a new person needs to get used to accepting. Often a spiritual conclusion might seem irrational to non-spiritual outsiders. To newer people, spiritual methods might seem insensitive as they may not immediately relieve the person of suffering or address the problem at hand. A person telling you to "pray on it" may come across as ignoring the problem. But it is helping you to turn your request to God. And learning that way is critical to Religious Life. In other words, with monastics, when the house is on fire, you don't always first call the fire department! Spiritually, the monastic response might seem utterly unrelated to the physical circumstances.

There are bells to start the daily community prayers and buzzers to give a warning of scheduled events. Usually, one person is assigned to sound the buzzer to warn the brothers of upcoming events. For a few years, I was that person. You see below a chart attempting to explain when those events occurred at different times of the day. Every little duty is a "little flower" in service to God.

Sample: Daily Prayer Schedule
A 5-Minute Warning Buzzer

3 a.m. Wake Up
6:25 a.m. Lauds
7:25 a.m. Mass (9:55 a.m. on Sunday)
        Terce: s occurs after Mass plus 10 Minutes
11:55 a.m. Midc ^Prayer
No Supper Buzzer - someone else
5:55 p.m. Vespers (4:55 p.m. on Sunday)
Possible Community Meeting (usually 7:00 p.m.)
7:30 p.m. Compline not 7:25 p.m.

Which Bells Do You Use?
(As one might guess, every size bell offers a different sound)

Vigils-------Giant Bell
Lauds------Giant and Large Bells
Mass-------Giant and Large Bells
Midday----Medium
Vespers---Giant and Large Bells
Compline-Medium Bells

Table(above): Daily buzzer and bell schedule

Angelus_____??? _____ and Large Bell

Table(above): Daily buzzer and bell schedule

This is a note of gratitude to the Abbot and the brothers for my acceptance to the monastery. It is a little creative, but it works for me...

$$F(MERCY) = \int_{\alpha}^{\infty} \frac{(\text{Hope}^{\wedge}2 + \text{Obedience} + e^{\text{LOVE}})\ d\text{MERCY}}{\text{FAIT}}$$

From: Br. Rodney K Odom
To: Our Lady of Methuselah Abbey

re: Gratitude

The Mathematics of Gratitude dictates that I thank you...I should abhor vanity, but instead, I made friends with it. On the other hand, the truth is painful and wounding, but it is the surest way to heaven. Jesus said that last part to Saint Faustina...he said the Way of the Cross is the surest way to heaven. If I could take a cab, I would take a cab, but I cannot. So let me try and prepare for wounds, wounds, and more wounds!

Thanks for all your help!

Sincerely,

Br. Rodney

Email Comments: *Mr. Leonard Goyke is a frequent, long-term, monastic retreatant and consultant to the monastery. Traveling all the way from Wisconsin, he volunteered his services. A retired scientist, he offered invaluable talents toward helping the monastery get its new businesses, including the mushroom business, up and functioning. He researched for Br. Mark to help him make business and technical decisions. He worked with me concerning the mushroom substrate purification process. We "cooked" or heated the mushrooms substrate (think food) to kill bacteria and molds mixed with it. The mushrooms use the substrate as "food." And without the cooking, they would have to compete for food with molds and bacteria. This email conversation below is about some of the testing Len created to maximize the mushroom growing process.*

Fm: Leonard, <leonard@gmail.com>
To: rod_odom456@yahoo.com

Mon, Jul 26, 2010 at 3:29 PM

Hi Bro Rod,

Please find out the water's pH before and after heating the substrate at 160 to 170 degrees Fahrenheit(F) and 140 to 145 degrees F. You and Antoine, keep up the excellent work. Also, another thing:

1. Try to cool the trailer roof.
2. Ask Vivian to let you try using a sprinkler that goes back and forth, not 360 degrees.
3. Please place it in an old tire, so it stays in place.
4. Place it on the roof of the trailer.
5. Check the temperature in the trailer before and after use on a hot day. If your plywood is already in place, do the same thing with the sprinkler in place.
6. Check temp under plywood before and after.

good luck,

Len
On Wed, May 5, 2010 at 3:00 PM,

Fm: Rod Odom <rod_odom456@yahoo.com> wrote:
To: Leonard <leonard@gmail.com>

We still have the columns for trailer four and five. I will check the columns/hoses for green mold. Mold growth is still a problem for us. Batch X17 was made. I threw out one of two columns because of green mold. We just received the liquid bacteria, but we ran out of the bits. I will tell Br. Mark you think we should add it and see if he agrees. We are fruiting [think: another generation of mushrooms from the same food, each generation produces fewer mushrooms] #12 for the 4th time, and 8 and 16 are now fruiting for the 3rd time. I moved everything to Trailer #7 to make room for Br. Antoine's stuff. We are throwing out so many mushroom columns because of mold, but we must have all the space we can get -- no time to play with the statistics -- so who knows when that will get done.
Rodney

'"May the Peace of Christ be with you always"'

Continued,

On **Wed, 5/5/10,**

Fm: Leonard <*leonard@gmail.com*> wrote:
To: "Rod Odom" <rod_odom456@yahoo.com>

Re: the final version

Date: Wednesday, May 5, 2010, 3:24 PM
Hi Br. Rodney,

Thank you for your follow-up work on the batches we started and your second report. Please examine the batch columns that had the black soaker hose in the center of it if you have the time. It was an attempt to eliminate anaerobic black or green mold. It would be interesting to note if it was batch five, which produced 33 lbs. of mushrooms. I hope you have substrate along with some mosquito bites as delayed-release bacteria. Did batch 16 have a third fruiting? Was batch 17 ever made? Thank you for keeping the mushroom test projects afloat. Any questions, please feel free to ask me anytime.

Leonard
630-945-1234 Cell

On Fri, Apr 30, 2010 at 12:03 PM,

Fm: Rod Odom <rod_odom456@yahoo.com> wrote:
To: Leonard <leonard@gmail.com>

I hope I can complete your follow-up work--

Welcome to Monastic Life! – Monk Or Hermit

Monk or Hermit

I read the historical lives of quite a few monks and nuns. I was not born Roman Catholic, and except for a few well-known Buddhist monks, all the people I read about are primarily Roman Catholic. Interestingly, I was not motivated to seek a monastic life by focusing on these holy people. I was inspired to leave it all behind when I read the life of Antony of the Desert. And while Antony spent some time with other hermits, the history written of his life is primarily one of him living a hermit's life - alone.

What I came to realize before I entered this monastery was that monastic life is a very social environment. However, it is predominantly socializing with other monks and religious. In my mind, because I entered Methuselah, I needed to stay at Methuselah Abbey and learn to be with my fellow monks.

The first monastery I ever visited, not including the Buddhist monastery in Thailand, was near Charlotte, North Carolina. The monastery in Thailand was not a spiritual visit per se, although one never knows with these situations. It was a visit by many sailors returning from the Gulf of Arabia on the way home to our homeport near San Francisco. It was part of a visitor's tour. The first purposeful visit was when I made a trip to Education Abbey near Charlotte; I discovered it was directly adjacent to a college campus. I saw no reason to go for another visit. I did not see or talk to anyone at the monastery. I could not imagine dealing with monastic life with so many people around. And, of course, my hormones in the presence of so many ladies on campus were too great a challenge. Years later, when discussing my visit with some monks who lived there at Education Abbey, I discovered the Abbot of the monastery was out of town the day I visited. I would never have met him the day of my visit. In any case, after sitting through their Midday Prayer, I left and went to the bus stop. And there, I waited for several hours to go back to Charlotte, where I lived. That monastic visit opened my eyes to some of the mysteries of monastic life.

It was during this period that I contacted Methuselah for the first time. Through Methuselah, I learned that the brothers of Education Abbey in Belfast, North Carolina, are Benedictine Monks and that the monks of Methuselah Abbey are Trappist Monks (O.C.S.O.) Eventually, I learned significant differences between the two types of monasteries' spiritual practices. Soon I realized that Methuselah is located on two thousand acres of forest. It was land donated for that purpose in Monk City, South Carolina. It was away from society. And to me, this forest made Methuselah a "real monastery!"

One of my biggest struggles in Monastic life was forcing myself to learn to be in a social group. And to socialize far more often than I ever had in my life. Some monks mention that they thought we should associate more often. I was just the opposite. I complained that we socialized too much. Being obedient to this requirement to meet the monastic social schedule was an excruciating period of change. Simply singing with the schola was a powerful capitulation for me psychologically. "I cannot believe what the Abbot was telling me to do! Was he serious?" Based on my response, you would think he was asking me to do something really outrageous like lifting a car on my own! But this situation helped me to realize how painful change is for some people. Being obedient to the Abbot and others had its challenges, but I was used to taking legitimate orders from people. Not being able to retreat away to hide from a social setting was an utterly new form of existence for me. I had many powerful episodes of anxiety, but I learned I would survive!

July 31, 2010

Dear Mary-Martha,

I hope all is well when you get this little note. It contains what I call my first concept paper. I attempt to explain to myself my understanding of what it is I believe concerning heaven and earth. I wish to understand my own "theology," but I try to do it in simple Christian terms (i.e., no long, complex, esoteric words). Fr. Thomas read it and said, "it is a good start," as in we all need to start formulating for ourselves somehow!

I saw your mom today. She is doing a lot of whispering and giggling. So she must be okay. Her hair looks nice lately (don't tell her I said that!) She is so worried about her "baby in Peru." She was hoping the bombing that took place would bring you home. I said no way. The Peace Corp goes through much worse. She chased me out of the library! I hear your dad finally swam to the bottom of the Gulf of Mexico and put a cork in the oil rig hole that is spewing oil [*a significant news event of the time, and her dad is a diver.*] All I can say is: so far, 100 days multiplied by 60,000 gallons a day. Do the Math! That is a terrifying situation both environmentally, legally, socioeconomically, and the list goes on forever.

We had a volunteer picnic, and your mom didn't come to get her 'thank you gift' – a metal thermos and lapel pin. Can you believe she blew us off! Well, it turned out to be fun, and we ate meat. Chicken! Umm Good! A sister-in-law of one of the abbey's employees catered. What can I say --- Best chicken ever!

I heard you were sick. Fr. Thomas offered prayers for you. Fr. Joseph offered a prayer for you on another Sunday earlier. I was thinking. Maybe if you didn't hang out partying all night and tried crawling into bed before four or 5 a.m. in the morning, you might feel better? Think about it, okay?

Any way-Be Good! Stay Safe! My prayers are with you and your comrades as well. The monks need you to bring them either an elephant or a giraffe back when you return. We need something to build our monastery visitor sales. Donations are a little tough to come by around here. I will eat a cheese sandwich for you in your absence. What do you like, Swiss or Cheddar?

I wish I had more to say. I am not used to writing some stranger in South America.

Sincerely,

Br. Rodney

P.S. We will have another Postulant soon, "Fr. Bartholomew from East Asia. He's 46. We expect him before Christmas. Being a foster parent to his baby turtles until he gets back. I am feeding them tiny slivers of lettuce and other rotten food! Being a parent is complicated!

Mr. Davenport was a beloved member of Our Lady of Consolation Catholic Church in Charlotte, North Carolina, and was highly supportive of my coming to the monastery. I asked the brothers to pray for him. He passed soon after. His daughter was amazed at how quickly his suffering ended.

Home Going Celebration
In Loving Memory
Of
Mr. Marvin William Davenport

August 30, 1931   October 10, 2010

Wednesday, October 20, 2010
1:00 p.m.
Our Lady of Consolation Catholic Church
2301 Statesville Avenue
Charlotte, North Carolina
Rev. Martin Schratz, O F M Cap., Pastor / Officiating

October 10, 2010

Note to the Brothers,

Marvin Davenport, a lifelong Catholic and lover of Jesus and Mary, is in his late 70's. He is a retired war veteran and an inspiration to our Lady of Consolation parish members in Charlotte, North Carolina. He attends Mass every day and is a member of the choir. Currently in hospice care and slowly dying of Liver Cancer, I ask please pray for him and his family's peace. Please pray, especially for his daughter, Marva, who is having difficulty dealing with his misery.

Br. Rodney

Gone Far Too Soon...

All I remember about the Watergate Scandal is that Congress was investigating President Nixon in the early 1970s, and because of that, "Sesame Street" was not on Public Television. I simply did not understand that Congress had to occupy all the TV channels. Grandma Ada Monk, my mom's mother (we were in Bell Arthur, N.C. at the time), could not explain any of it to my satisfaction. Every hour, I returned to her room to check and see if "Sesame Street" was finally on, and it never did show. It was President Nixon who ended the Police Action in the country of Viet Nam and Asia. I once spoke to my Uncle Bro (He was a Viet Nam Veteran) that the Viet Nam "war" was a Police Action, and he looked at me like I was ill! That is what it was called in our history books - a Police Action!

We did not remember much of the riots and protests of the war while living in Philadelphia. Though my father said, it did occur. We watched the movies about it growing up in the 1970s and 1980s. Among us in our family, the younger ones perceived my Uncle and my Cousin Jeff uniquely. They were older and Purple Heart Veterans of the War in Viet Nam.

But now, in his early 60's, my cousin was dead. Jeffrey Locke had a straightforward surgery, didn't feel well, called my Aunt Ruth (his mother) for the last time, and passed away. To this day, all I could remember about him was that he was a nice guy. He was always nice to me, and he always joked with me. Despite being an infantry person in a war, I noticed he had a soft side to his behavior. He seemed to have a unique ability to understand people's suffering. That was my comment to my Aunt Ruth and my cousins (Dana and Tarya): Everybody liked Jeff. I don't know a sole person in our family who did not think well of Jeff - everybody liked the guy! A death like that is challenging to fathom. We looked up to him, and for me, he was gone far too soon.

Despite his frustration with the brothers and their ways, Len desperately and persistently tried his best to get us to start being more scientific about our mushroom growing business. It would have meant less shooting from the hip (guessing) and more detailed data collection. I sent him a booklet of little writings as a thank you gift for his struggles.

Photo: Volunteer, Leonard Goyke, standing in front of the "new" mushroom cooking machine, 2014

November 19, 2010

Dear Len,

Did you know that on this date in the year 1686, **Robinson Crusoe leaves his island after 28 years?**

Yes, I bet you forgot!

Now I offer you this little collection of mine as a gift since I have nothing else to thank you with except a cheese sandwich. Let me know if you would prefer the sandwich!

Thank you for all that you have done for us and me since you have been here. You are quite an inspiration to me and many of the brothers.

Br. Rodney Odom, Postulant
Our Lady of Methuselah Abbey
Monk City SC 29333

P.S. I hope you realize we still need your help?

This little note indicates the start of my relationship with Saint Joseph in a way like never before. It bothered me that there were few icons of Mary's earthly husband in the monastery. Then we had a scripture class, and, in that class, I encountered almost word for word what an excellent monastic visitor told me of Saint Joseph. I assumed it was not coincidental. I believed it to be a unique encounter. And after that extraordinary encounter, I started paying more attention to Saint Joseph. I made it a point to clean his icons in the church, clean up around his "statues," and remind people when his memorial was coming. I engaged him with prayer requests. I made a novena to him to help me with a particular "thorn in my side." And miraculously, I never had trouble with the issue again. After that, my relationship with Saint Joseph was more real than ever. Loving God's earthly father takes nothing away from God himself it glorifies God.

November 26, 2010

Merry Christmas Joseph,

I wish to thank you for your note. I should add that if it were not Christmas, I don't think I am supposed to correspond with anyone outside my usual circle! I genuinely hope you don't mind. I don't want to cause trouble. I am still figuring out the rules here. I do send emails to some employees. So this communication might be okay? If you would tell Mary, I said Merry Christmas too!

I felt somewhat compelled to write lest you think I have something against promoting fatherhood. I don't. I have had the very same discussion about St. Joseph with a certain priest here. He has informed me that theologically Joseph is seen as a hidden life. He is not prevalent. On the other hand, We see Mary in scripture as having a prominent role in the coming of God's Kingdom (Book of Revelation). If you accept them as authentic, her apparitions worldwide certainly seem to support this notion.

In any case, I gave you those poems because I felt overwhelming gratitude that day we spoke in the refectory about the mushrooms and Mary's prayers. Those poems are the ones I like the most! I appreciated your kindness and sincere support.

But more critical for me (and my little writings) is that they are almost all "prayers" of gratitude, inspired by Mary (the mother) being genuinely present in my life. She is in every way my mother, but I might just as quickly refer to her as the 'Humble Servant of God.' She has given me a powerful tool to call on her for help; the prayer of the Holy Rosary. And she never fails to answer in some way! I am biased when it comes to my "Mom." But I welcome St. Joseph to be active in my life also. You ought to know that I didn't find her! She found me! And I am forever grateful at least to about 3 a.m.. in the early morning (smile) when it is time for Vigils. So don't be disappointed if my poems seem overly limited to Jesus and Mary!

Sincerely,

Br. Rodney Odom

P.S. Like a Baptist preacher once told me a few years back, it doesn't matter because it is all about Jesus anyway!

Part One

November xx, 2010

Dear Family,

Lesson on **Trappist Monastic Life:** What is Stability? In addition to the three most known vows of Poverty, Chastity, and Obedience, there is a fourth one of Stability. With Stability, we say that we will stay here in this specific monastery for life. We will dwell with this community that God has brought together until death. It might very well be the hardest of the vows to deal with and keep. At Methuselah, the monks pretty much stay within about one square mile every day, seven days a week. And most of that time is spent within about 750 square feet. So we eat, pray and sleep in a minimal area. We see each other every day, all day. And we have guests and retreatants that often attend the same prayers and Masses we do. So we see them frequently throughout the day when they are here. Though some experiences in the following paragraphs are facts occurring over many months, it summarizes in a mosaic to tell a story.

It is Friday near 6 p.m. when a small religious group enters the church for Vespers, the evening office prayer. They are a group of young adults and one older gentleman. After a glance, I guess that they are probably from a single church, and he is perhaps the group retreat leader. Most of the group looks to be in their late teens or early twenties. They are three women and four men. I look them over quickly and see no surprises or any apparent need for my help as I head toward my choir seat to wait and ring the 6 o'clock bells to start prayers. I have two minutes.

I look across the aisle at Br. James. He is a monk in simple vows; he has three years to go before receiving solemn vows. His choir seat is in the rear above the first row. He sits quietly with his head down in meditation. Br. James knows about my situation. He knows far too well about me. He and I almost had a confrontation as a result of my problem. Patience and mercy stopped him from coming at me with full anger and attitude.

It all started when they moved me closer to the church bell switch box because I would be the new bell ringer for community activities. So every day, eight times a day, he now had to look across the aisle at me and I at him. The situation became much more pronounced after that change. We entered the church together. If not by the same door, I would enter another one while, simultaneously, he came in another. We met face to face repeatedly. When he left dinner and walked back to his room, I headed to dinner to eat. We always passed each other along the way. After three of four days of these "coincidences," he was well past giving me strange glances, as he was now giving me strained facial frowns. One particular night I was sitting with Jesus in the chapel, but he came in after me. When I rang the bells to indicate five minutes to prayer, we passed again as I headed to my seat, and he went to his.

The first day it happened, it was odd. Then it became strange, and then finally just plain frustrating. Br. James was now angry and determined to stop me from "following him." He withheld comment every time, and I would innocently hunch my shoulders to indicate I had no control or explanation of why these encounters were happening. I continued to say my "Hail Mary's" repeatedly and thinking to myself, quick Mary before these people are ready to harm me! And she was fast! Thank God, another "evil-conspiracy-plot" defeated by a bit of faith and persistence!

But the 20-something-year-old female retreatant was not angry at all when this little quirk in my behavior started happening with her. She thought it was cute the way we kept bumping into each other. First, it was when entering the church. Repeatedly we arrived and entered at the same time. Then, for the second or third time that week, as I passed her on my bicycle on the way to work. Again, after breakfast, as I cleaned dishes from the retreatant dining area, and she was the only one left drinking the last sip of her coffee. It's was always a slight smile and a short giggle. Then a shaking of the head as she contemplates how weird a situation this is. I ask myself: Why am I constantly bumping into certain people in this manner?

Unfortunately, the fifteen-year-old who is on retreat with her parents the following week doesn't think it is cute. She is wondering why the creepy old monk keeps following her around the church, as she gives me a glaring dirty look and an attitude. Once, we had a guy from New York City as a monastic guest. He was here for three weeks during the fall of 2009. And when I started "following him," he became suspicious. He gave me a look as if I were up to something. But I wasn't. And my hunched shoulders and my opened hands indeed indicated my innocence. But that didn't stop these encounters from occurring. With him, it lasted about a week.

You see, they can go and come, but I cannot, and life becomes complicated when a married couple concludes you are following the wife around and need to stop or else! How do I know it is 'stop or else?' I do not know. But that look of hard suspicion and threatening stance from the husband sure conveys that communication.

To this day, it still happens. I am attracted to women, so it probably occurs more with them. But it also happens because they stare at me. It is so interesting: when I repeatedly look at them only to find they are already staring at me. They seem to express indignance as if I was the one who is constantly staring. My question is, why are they looking at me? What causes them to look at me? When I think I have learned to stop these odd encounters, it starts again. I don't seem to control anything about it. But I keep asking Mary for help, and I know, somehow, I am being strengthened by these weird episodes.

During Sunday Mass, Br. Carson thanked a group of people for visiting the monastery and asked God to bless them for their work in the area of paranormal research. So by now, I know, and the monks know. And I know they know. And they know I know they know. But in proper Trappist monastic form, they bear it without comment. Silence! Someone gave a little speech as prayer at Mass about accepting what God sends, etc.

I will soon send **Part two;** it should be interesting. Rewind your calendar about seven or eight years back until 2002 or so. I am still in the great city of Philadelphia. And imagine someone like me living in a neighborhood that seems like it is on some type of drug task force list. They are cracking down on crime. And me, well, I am home all day long because I drive a cab all night. Why am I home all day? I am running a micro-business selling software that I designed, coded, tested, and sold through my online web store. But I don't think it appeared that way to these people watching the area for criminal behavior. Imagine, if you would, what would happen if the police "task force" started following me around just based on some suspicion. What do you think would happen next after hearing the story I wrote immediately before this one? It is wild speculation on my part, but I assume I started following them around the same way I began following people around at the monastery. It is only in this closed setting can the behavior be isolated.

The following letter (Part two) deserves an introduction. It attempts to explain a situation that is a little weird. And it is written several years after the actual events occurred. So I am looking back on what took place and remembering my experience. I did look for notes about some of the things that I claim happened and found very few. The letter that I send you is not the writing of a mad man. Or even someone on mind-bending drugs, but an actual event that took place in the natural history of a human being. I still have in my possession an ink pen I bought on the very day I had an extraordinary experience that I thought was at least supernatural in flavor. And I keep it as a testament to that day. I suspect these events occur, but I don't see them with my physical eyes. Yet somehow, they still register in my mind as if I did. Thus, I am the only one who sees them.

Love,

Br. Rodney

Welcome to Monastic Life! – Can You Hear Me!

Can You Hear Me!

I think it takes a unique person to live the radical lifestyle change that the monastery offers and simultaneously deal with all the stress that comes with that change. We all enter this life with our naive ideas about it. Some people visit the monastery thinking that they will find angelic souls behaving perfectly. Some know otherwise. When I entered, I never expected the monks to be perfect, but for some reason, I did not expect the same run-of-the-mill issues as with the people outside the monastery. After all, was not this monastic sacrifice to learn to be like God? Trivial jealousies, insecurities, rumors, lies, revenge, and all that stuff that makes entertainment television so attractive were not supposed to be here in a holy place. Or was my expectation unrealistic?

I discovered that the monastery is merely a microcosm of the world I lived in before entering. And if people come into monastic life with certain imperfections, those imperfections will tend to dominate their behavior, no matter how long they are in this holy place. If I walk through the monastic front door with hyper-ambitious secular goals, most likely, that general psychology will continue for my remaining time on earth. In my case, I was on constant guard to tamp down my ambitious thoughts and constantly questioned my motivations for doing anything.

All our behaviors and mannerisms are an attempt to communicate some part of ourselves. And if we are listening to ourselves properly, we can learn what these behaviors are and how they speak to the world around us. Any form of feedback from others helps us determine how we are affected, including comments, language, facial responses, nuances in language, and even physical activity. Once, some monks visited from another monastery and left a thank you note on our bulletin board. And in the note, they thanked each monk by name. My name was suspiciously missing. Why was it missing? For whatever reason for doing so, could it have been because I purposely avoided socializing with them? Probably.

In another different situation, I remember feeling offense and jealousy brewing within me when the Abbot gave a speech thanking all the participants who helped, and somehow, he left my name off the list. Since I helped, I wanted a reward too! I had thoughts such as: "he left me out on purpose," "he does not like me," and even more. I could feel a level of rage in my mind as my thoughts cascaded into a bodily transformation ruled by jealousy.

And even more interesting was my detection of a counteracting mental process that was fighting to maintain proper composure. That part of me was struggling to have the proper response. That is, even if the Abbot did leave me out on purpose, I knew my response required more maturity and wisdom. And that part of me prevailed. I like to think I received help from God to form properly under stressful circumstances.

I was surprised by my reaction, and simultaneously, I was embarrassed because I didn't think I had such insecurities. But there they were, powerfully affecting my behavior. They quietly crept into my understanding of myself, changing my attitude and manner. And I had to learn to recognize it happening and, among other things, try not to let these poor tendencies destroy my relationship with others. I did not wish to be controlled by such thinking. There was literally a battle inside me as to what thoughts and feelings would rule my behavior. And though it only lasted moments, it seemed like forever. There were times this went on when I was not that successful in my struggles.

Rumor has it that somebody did something and caused such and such. I came into the monastery not realizing how rumors control people's lives. I thought the monks would not have such social practices. I was wrong. And while reflecting on it, I realized how much it flourished outside the monastery. Social drama like this was often the day's energy in monastic life. I supposed that it ruled so much partially because of the vacuum of verbal communication brought on by so few people talking. But I suspect that rumors and thus vain social drama resulted from a mental void of some sort. Perhaps our minds are formed in a way as to look for it and promote it for excitement.

There is a lot of spying and what I call "word-of-mouth, estimated facts" in monastic life. What is a "word-of-mouth, estimated-fact?" Let me explain by example. If I walk into a particular building every day at two p.m., people notice this tendency. But, what if today you see me some other place? You may think something unusual is going on with me. You might even think I am doing something I should not be. And what if you mention that you saw me to someone, and that person interprets what you say as: "He was probably someplace he would not usually be because he was up to some suspicious activity." The suspicion somehow morphs into historical fact. This type of thinking or reasoning is often the case in monastic life. And suspicious-eye thinking was not just in our monastery but also in the few other monasteries or convents I visited.

In a place where you might sometimes sell your birthright for a piece of chocolate cake, you must expect suspicious-eye thinking to come about. And this is especially true for the senior monks responsible for looking out for you and guiding you. Then, too, I believe that the suspicious-eye lends toward mistrust in each other, making everyone suspicious of the person standing next to them. We do not know who is watching and might discover us and our chocolate cake! The newer people are trying to build a "brotherhood" for their generation of monks, so this thinking is probably not influencing their relationship in a positive way. I also think it divides people's thinking. It brings about circumstances where I must behave like I trust my neighbor, even though I may be suspicious that they are watching and reporting.

The following letter portrays in detail what I might describe as my multi-part reality. I often divide my view of life into categories. One part is the everyday dealings like physical accomplishments and transactions, or anything that requires physical exertion. I call that "real life." Then there was the other stuff. These are ideas, mental issues, and experiences that seem non-physical. This world is just as real to me, but perhaps not to other people. This world is often influenced by books, movies, and emotional experiences. I am astounded by my simplistic ideas about life. As I live, I am forced to compare my reality to what goes on in the reality outside of me. The only appropriate word I can think of to describe it is fantasy. But my physical world followed my mental world. That is to say, the ideas of the mind affect my physical actions. And since a large portion of my reality is a mere fantasy, this becomes part of the basis for my life. If, for example, I think you are angry with me, I might behave differently than if I do not believe you are mad. And if you are, in fact, not mad at me, but I insist that you are, I am living a sort of fantasy of our relationship. In realizing this, I read the Holy Scripture with a different perspective. My personal truth and that of all people, as we live it, lead to the suffering and death of Christ. And because of the central nature of Christ to all existence, Jesus' suffering and death are an actual reflection of the purity of humanity or our "distance" from living what is actually true.

December xx, 2010

Dear Family,

Introduction

I was in my house at 1605 Roumfort Road for the last time. It was 10 years since I first moved in on the ground floor apartment. But it was the brightly-colored autumn leaf floating in the middle of the air that drew my attention now. It was about 15 feet or so off the ground. And it was retracing a giant circular pattern as it moved about its central point. As I watched in amazement, I realized it was Her. But my "scientific mind" was still looking for some cause for this strange phenomenon. Was this leaf attached to a spider's web? Was it caught on a thin string? After it blew away, I wondered what caused me to come to the window and look out?

Since the tree behind it was filled with yellow leaves, it occurred to me that I should not have noticed it in the first place; my vertical blinds were completely closed, and all I could remember seeing is a small amount of light as I walked up to open them and look out. I turned to get Gina, my neighbor from the upstairs apartment. I wanted someone else to see this, and as I did, the leaf floated to the ground and blew away. I am reminded of the following scripture:

He ran to Eli and said, "Here I am; for you called me." He said, "I didn't call. Lie down again." He went and lay down. Yahweh called yet again, "Samuel!" Samuel arose and went to Eli and said, "Here I am; for you called me." He answered, "I didn't call, my son. Lie down again."

Now Samuel didn't yet know Yahweh, neither was Yahweh's word yet revealed to him. Yahweh called Samuel again the third time. He arose and went to Eli and said, "Here I am; for you called me." Eli perceived that Yahweh had called the child. Therefore, Eli said to Samuel, "Go, lie down. It shall be, if he calls you, that you shall say, 'Speak, Yahweh; for your servant hears.'" So, Samuel went and lay down in his place. **1 Samuel 3:5-9.** (2)

In retrospect, I now understand how I made it out of Philadelphia safely and with my sanity intact. One day when my cousin Stacy called, I was ranting about a super-intelligent mouse in my kitchen. It left a trail of damage to anything I left out, yet, it defied all my methods to catch it. Stacy was silent for an extended period before she spoke. And her silence communicated so much to me. I think I left Philadelphia with most of my sanity intact! It was a long and challenging road, but my house was under contract for sale within eight days and transferred ownership in less than five weeks, and my car was donated a year earlier (September 2002). Most of my financial obligations were satisfied. And at this point in my little life, it doesn't bother me if people read this story and believe it. I am where I am because of the events that occurred. I am here and in no other place. They (the reader) will get out of the story whatever they get out of it. The problem with mystical events is that they challenge our notion of reality. Most of us would rather close the door on such occasions. Instead, we chose to act as they are all mischief or lunacy rather than accept them as a genuine part of the human experience. Still, the libraries are filled with books on people who have recorded such events. (The Christian Bible being a famous collection of such holy books.) Yet, so many Christians talk about the Christian Scripture as if it is a book of fables made up to help us cope with life's burdens and nothing more.

The Local Utility Companies

My last two years in Philadelphia were like being attacked by "reality" itself. I will explain the list of crazy events in this period to help you understand what I mean. Realize that for each controversy discussed, there are probably five others not mentioned. There is no room in this story to mention them all. Let me start with the least important areas. My home utilities suddenly started going haywire. Every three or four months, I called the telephone company because the phone lines would stop working, and the repair solution was always some event outside my house. The telephone company was responsible for those repairs. And they did not understand why it was happening. During this time, I received a letter from a law office representing the Philadelphia Electric Company (PECO) threatening to sue me. It was over an eleven-dollar utility bill they say I owed them from years ago. They said I had 30 days to pay, but my current electric bill was paid in full. When I called the local Public Utility Commission (P.U.C.) to report this unusual event, they told me they don't regulate electric utilities. Despite this, they did ask me questions about it and did take some general information. It seemed the gas company wanted in on the strange events occurring at that time. They began leaving shutoff notices in my door. This event happened on two different occasions. On another occasion, they parked a PGW vehicle in front of my house for 45 minutes. When I left to mail some packages at the local post office and returned, the car was gone, and there was another shutoff notice placed in the door. So I called the gas company and talked for about an hour. I wanted to know why they were leaving shutoff notices at my address when my gas bill was paid in full. The statement never had an apartment number, and this was a duplex with separate apartment utility bills. In other words, they would need to specify an apartment to "shut off" for the notice to make any sense. They said they would send someone out to investigate. After I hung up, I got an immediate phone call, and when I answered, the caller slammed the phone in my ear! It left my ear ringing. (I did not use a cell phone for most calls back then). and the slamming noise was excruciating. Now I was wondering who did that? The gas company sent someone out. The PGW employee explained that my meter number was confused with some other address. He stated that it was for a neighbor's meter given to me by mistake. Apparently, this type of thing happens all the time. Still, with the entire street or block of homes being twin duplexes with apartments that have separate utilities, there was no reasonable explanation for these for me or anyone on the block to get this shutoff notice.

The US Postal Service is not a utility company. But they provide a public service like the utility companies, and I was having problems with them too! I started getting unsealed mail. Some of my mail that arrived unsealed: bank statements, junk mail, letters, etc. And when I write unsealed, I mean just that: the envelope looked as if it was never sealed at all. Then one day, I found my upstairs neighbor's mail in my box. It was an opened credit card statement. It looked to me as if it were sealed at one point and someone had opened it. All this was too much for me to accept quietly. I wrote her a note about what I found and then I called the postal service and complained. They either found nothing, or they never called me back about what they did find. Luckily, I was moving from Philadelphia to become a monk, right? No! I continued to have problems with missing, opened, and lost deliveries for years after this craziness started.

In the eight or so previous years of living at 1605 Roumfort Road, I rarely ever received a phone call from anyone except my family and a few friends. I was one of those empty answering machine people - zero messages on most days! But in the last two prior years, I was getting political recordings, radio stations doing surveys, real estate investment salespeople, frozen meat salespeople calling, and more. But the most disturbing call of them all was "the hang-up." It was those machines that call your telephone, wait for a moment, and then 'click' - they hang up. And this calling happened all day long. I was so angry about these calls; I informed the telephone company that I would turn off my service if all these calls didn't stop...they didn't stop. So I turned off my ringer and stopped answering the telephone altogether. I started screening all my calls. A few friends tried to explain to me that this was normal! Fine for them, but it was not normal for me. And I wanted to know who or what was causing all these phone calls!

Then the Internal Revenue Service or IRS decided they wanted in on the craziness. For the previous six years, I filed my taxes electronically. But starting in 2002, I had to mail in my taxes. Why? Because the IRS could not confirm my correct birth year with the Social Security Administration. And somehow, this meant that they would not accept my taxes electronically. It seems that somehow my Social Security record changed. My birth date on file with the Internal Revenue Service was now different than the one I had on my birth certificate. It was now different from the one I celebrated every year and used to file my taxes electronically all previous years. I had to go into their office with proper documentation and prove what they had on file was wrong. I did it three times. My third visit was after I moved to another state. And only on the third visit to the Social Security office in Greenville, North Carolina, did they correct my record (and even then, they did so with great suspicion). And they were suspicious in doing so despite me having all the proper documents. But I pretty much had enough of "Big Brother" at this point and was not going to take any more crazy rejections of legitimate forms of identification!

In the 10 years that I lived on Roumfort Road, the only time I ever needed to call a utility company was after a bad storm. Now I was calling some utility or government office routinely.

The Neighbors

My neighbors were not all troublemakers. But with all the other unusual events going on, the few neighbors who were troublemakers stressed me to the point of psychological breakdown. One person, living across the street from my house, would put a nail in my tire whenever I parked in front of his. Once, when this occurred, he came to my door a week later to borrow tools. He behaved as if innocent. Still, this happened on three occasions.

Another guy moved into the ground-floor apartment next door to him. He lived there a short while, only a few months or so, but he had the odd habit of sitting on the trunk of his car and staring directly at me as I came from work every day. He never spoke. He just stared. Then one day, he was gone, and the apartment seemed empty. Soon after he moved, a bill collector called my house asking if I knew anything about him. I did not.

My neighbor directly behind me, who was home recovering from a stroke, was constantly digging through my trash. I assumed he was searching my trash because the city was fining him, and he thought I was reporting him. I found it curious that when I looked out the facing the backyard area, I found him searching my rubbish. Much earlier, I built a wooden fence around the little grass area on my property. And in conversation with someone else, I discovered he worked for the city. And, apparently, he had people inspecting my new wooden fence for violations. They found nothing unusual about my fence. I did an excellent job! And the woman driving the city vehicle left without any issues. I somehow came to look outside when that visual inspection occurred too! I did get a few fines (grass too long and the wrong type of recycled cardboard). For eight years, I never said anything to him about anything. We spoke, and that was it. Now, every time I looked out of the rear of my home, he was pointing at my house and talking to someone or looking through my trash!

Directly across from me (in the front) was another neighbor. One apartment was empty now because the guy living there left (apparently without paying his bills). The other was a lady who lived on the same floor next to his. I was told she was a consultant for the School District of Philadelphia. And her friend (a new roommate) was from Virginia. He said he met her over the internet. He came to visit for the summer and decided to stay. He spent all day on the phone with another woman in Maine who was madly in love with him. She wanted him to visit her also. The consultant wanted him out of her apartment as soon as he found a job. He found one at the local Home Depot. But he somehow managed to stay, and spent a good deal of the summer sitting on my front door steps, knocking on my door, or looking in my windows from across the street. Yes, I just happened to be looking out the window the same time he would be looking in from across the street. I guess he wanted to know if I was home or awake. I tried to explain that I was working (programming) and could not talk to him all day. He eventually moved. And so did his roommate, the consultant. I have no idea who those people were or if their story was true. Maybe she allowed him to stay all summer because she was afraid of him and could not force him out. Perhaps she left after he did to put some distance between them, but I never saw them again.

The Odd People Situations

It was clear at this point that the local drug dealers were very active. They murdered a neighborhood activist. No one knew who did it. There was a homemade sign on the block where he lived asking for any information on the crime. It seems that law enforcement was "sweeping the area clean." I noticed a bulletin indicating no more standing on corners or in front of storefronts on Wadsworth Avenue (the local business district). I was home during the day and went walking through the neighborhood for exercise. This activity got me a few stares. I minded my own business, and somehow was still a menace. Soon I had people sitting across the street from my house staring at me as I fixed my house up for sale. I had people following me as I walked to Home Depot for supplies. I had people following me to the local post office. When I worked outside painting, I had men in luxury cars pull up, sit in front of my house, and stare at me. When I went inside, they drove away. When I came back outside, they'd drive up, sit and stare. Maybe they were not drug dealers, but why stare at me? It got to the point where I was unsure who was following me or why. And I was becoming suspicious of everyone. Once I met a friend at an airport hotel restaurant to discuss my software design (we ate). A lady in a long trench coat driving a dark blue Ford Crown Victoria followed me there and then sat at the table next to ours. She listened to our entire conversation. When I left, she left. I didn't say anything to him about her. But I knew this was not the first time I saw her, and I realized then that she was following me.

My parents lived about four blocks away from my house. And I was in the habit of visiting them from time to time. It was not too long after one visit that my mother made it clear to us all that some people were following her around. I immediately thought of what was going on with me. We (my family) didn't believe her at first. To me, her stories sounded more outrageous than my own experiences. But eventually, I spoke up about what was happening at my house. I didn't say anything about it earlier because I thought, who will believe that strange people are following me around, opening my mail, messing with my phone lines, and all for no particular reason! One day, out shopping, I noticed a lady handing out 3-by-5 inch size sheets of paper. The paper read that the phone company is tapping people's phones. I listened to her and looked intently at her, and then said to her, "even if they are, how would you prove it?" She did not comment, but she didn't stop. I didn't believe her. I thought, why would they do that? After a while, my experiences became confusing. I couldn't tell who was just standing across the street from me and who was purposely trying to be annoying. What sort of shocked me was the day I was on a bus, and an elderly lady on the same bus and sitting directly in front of me began trying to take a picture of me without my consent. She was facing the front of the bus but trying to hold a camera up facing the rear. And she was trying to snap a picture of me. When I got up to leave the bus, I stared at her with a frown, and she froze. She avoided eye contact with me. But her facial expression was one of embarrassment. She knew that I knew that she knew, so forth and so on. Later, it occurred to me that maybe someone was following her too? Perhaps she wanted proof?

Another incident occurred while downtown in Center City. I was seeing a movie called "The Moth Man Prophecies". Before going into the theater, I went to a CVS store (a pharmacy) to buy a soda. two women came rushing into the store behind me and came at me, accusing me of following them. One retorted, "What are you doing down here? Are you following me?" I was utterly stunned. I had no idea who these people were. The second lady pulled the arm of the first lady, and they left the store. She said to her, "I don't think he is following you." It could have all been an act, but accomplishing what? These are all descriptions of actual events without exaggeration. Who in their right mind has experiences like these? Well, if you can believe it - I did.

The Law Enforcers

I walk into a store where I have been shopping for years. The people behind the sales counter know me. But today, they look at me in utter fear when just the day before they were smiling. I realize something is not proper. I turned around to find a man in a long dark trench coat staring at me with a very mean and nasty look. The cashier noticed him behind me, and it frightened them. So I purchased my items and just quietly walked out the door. I got into my car and headed to pick up my cab for the night. The next day it got a little scarier. When I walked to the supermarket, someone followed behind me at no more than 15 feet every single step of the way there and back. They never said a word to me. I didn't know them, and they didn't know me. After this event, I wrote a letter to the local city council representative complaining that the police followed me. A few days passed. Then a lady called my house from the councilwoman's office and told me "that this is what I asked for." The conversation was very, very brief; I hung up! While using the bathroom that same day, I said, "Jesus, this is crazy, what on earth am I supposed to do about all this?" Then I heard the following: "DO NOTHING." Was it Jesus who spoke to me? How do I know? I don't know how I knew; I just did. And from that point forward, I made every effort not to respond to this craziness or talk to anyone about it, no matter what happened. Only now am I reminded of Isiah:

*He was oppressed, yet when he was afflicted he didn't open his mouth. As a lamb that is led to the slaughter, and as a sheep that before its shearers is silent, so he didn't open his mouth. **Isaiah 53:7.** (2)*

Well, I was not quite a sheep. I was so mad about being followed in one incident that I doubled back and started following the people following me, and we were at high speeds. I suspect whoever this was, they were trying to induce me to commit a crime of some kind or react violently to their presence. Luckily, I calmed down, turned around, and went on my way.

The job of law enforcement is a serious one. If this was law enforcement or someone working with law enforcement, God help us all! Most of my direct encounters with the police were with them as people merely doing their jobs. A few seem to have a deep-seated hatred for me personally. But the number of those encounters was small. Most of the officers I encountered were professional and seemed to be genuinely nice people. I suspect that once you are on their radar, you are on it for a long time – guilty or not! And guilt or innocence is irrelevant. "Suspected people" are just people who have not been caught- yet. Whoever these people were, they did not have any reason to be following me. So in my mind, they were perverted and corrupt. And I suspect that when they do what they do, assuming people are guilty of something, it does horrible damage to public trust.

You are socialized to think one way, and now you are finding out it is a lie. I wrote my local politician and complained about being followed. They called my house and told me, "this is what I asked for?" So when I joined a gym at Stenton and Washington Lane, how was I to know that a local police officer was also a member at that same gym. And coincidentally, we went to the gym at the same time every day. We were often the only two there! And when I was stopping for pizza (in my cab), how was I to know another local police officer was already there eating dinner. One day, I drove to pick my taxi in West Philadelphia (I lived in the northwest); I had local police along my usual work route. For a short while along City Avenue, an unmarked car with a guy dressed as a Pennsylvania state trooper followed me, but he seemed disappointed when he noticed that I noticed him. They didn't do anything to me, but it scared me quite a bit. All I could think was, what was going on and how was I a part of it? It was as if I had become some sort of local "most wanted" person without having done anything wrong to be arrested. How could I tell I was known by the people I encountered? The physical reaction I would get from them. They look at me as if they just saw a ghost, or they would tailgate my cab until I left their area. It seemed that they knew my car (when I had one), and they knew the cab I usually drove. I rented number '32' from a private owner. I am sure that some of these events I remember were not proof of anything but were merely chance events with no relation to this conspiracy. But one time, I parked at the Rite Aid store to buy some items, and when I came out, a police car was parked in front of my car. The officer was inspecting my safety stickers. Was it a chance or a suspicious situation? What reason would he have to stop in a parking lot of vehicles to review my stickers? My stickers were legitimate, so why my car? But these things happen to others too! I had a guy (in the heat of the summer) get out of his car on a busy jammed street, walk back to me, look me in the eye, and ask me why I was following him? He was furious. And I could understand his experience, so I didn't think he was crazy, nor did I think he imagined things. It is easier to accept it as a reality when it happens to you.

But that's not all! I used to park at the central Amtrak station (30th Street Station) to pick up customers in my cab. And from time to time, I went inside to use the men's restroom. On multiple occasions over days, when I exited the bathroom, the doorway would be surrounded by four or five Amtrak police officers. And they stared at me. And I would look around at them and keep walking. I didn't do anything! It was a public restroom. I was just relieving myself! On another occasion near the Parkway area, I could not quite get to a urinal. So I parked my cab and ran for some bushes. When I finished, I looked down and what did I find? An entire underground (below street level) parking lot full of police cars and personal vehicles. And when I looked up, what did I see? A police car pulled up behind mine. The officer was on his radio (and doing what looked like a verbal report of some kind! I could only imagine what that must have looked like to him? I got in my cab and drove off. He followed me back to City Hall, where I parked. I didn't do anything (at least not that he could see). How was I supposed to know that the police had an underground parking lot there?

I had the habit of walking in the park for hours on some days. It didn't matter to me if it was cold, rainy, sunny, or snowy. I read religious and spiritual material on most days. I prayed and meditated. I had some extraordinary experiences by the streams, hills, and resting on those park benches. But now that I was "famous," I guess I was interrupting investigations going on in the same park areas. I was not welcome. And they (the police) made that very clear. But I paid my taxes like all the other people. And I was walking in the park before they started all this nonsense. So in my mind, I should continue doing the same thing! The drug dealers had already run me out of my neighborhood walks! So what's a daytime programmer / nighttime cab driver to do with himself? I used to be alone in all my walks in the park, and suddenly there were always people stationed in strategic locations. I could not take a wooded path and exit without someone standing there waiting and looking at me as if I were up to something (arms crossed). You might think the people being in these locations are a coincidence. I certainly wanted to believe that. But too many situations presented themselves such that that was not probable. I would have paid no mind to these people up to this period, but now every situation was suspicious. It was the facial expressions and body language that seemed so convincing.

Calling 911 (to report a crime or need for help) became a hobby for me. For the remainder of my time in Philadelphia, I must have called 911 20-times! My car was broken into three times, once right in front of my house. A neighbor saw it happen once and chased the person off. Again, somebody broke my window and stole a 15-year-old pullout AM/FM radio cassette player (was it even worth five dollars?), and again, my license plate was stolen. I'm pretty sure whoever did it was trying to get me towed. The city had a new program supposedly to help lower insurance rates. They were enforcing all traffic laws. And driving without a license plate was an immediate towing offense. I don't know why, but one day at an Automated Teller Machine (bank machine), it occurred to me to turn around, and I did. I looked at my car, and from the ATM machine where I was standing, I immediately noticed my license plate missing! A wave of paranoia and fear washed over me! With all the personal crimes together with the building fire, knife fight, missing child, car accidents, spousal abuse, couples spat, and the like that I encountered while driving my cab, I was always on my cell phone calling 911. But I could not say why I was coming across these events now when I never noticed them years before.

Try to look at the situation this way: If you were in law enforcement and a person "of interest" kept showing up in the same places as you when you were off duty or in the middle of investigations or whatever the term would be, would you look at it as a coincidence? I would not. So when my buddy (in Maryland) and, sometime later, another friend of mine in Virginia told me in telephone conversations that the state police were following them, I thought maybe I was the cause. But I didn't say anything to them about my situation. But I was the central person in common to the strange events.

Plus, it would be too embarrassing to talk about with them. No! I wanted clear and undeniable evidence that these situations were not coincidental. That meant collecting more mental evidence and saying nothing to no one! I didn't need many naysayers telling me I was crazy and causing me to lose focus. But these were the few people I called on the phone, and now it looked like my phone records were involved.

Internal Revenue Service

When I sold my duplex on Roumfort Road in Philadelphia and filed my taxes, I filed one of the forms improperly. I got a call from the Internal Revenue Service (IRS.) and received a phone audit. My refund had not changed after I filed the change to my taxes; however, I was in Greenville, North Carolina, and they now wanted me to come to their office in Philadelphia for an in-person audit. I informed them that I was no longer in Philadelphia. The guy on the phone requested that I mail a note from North Carolina to prove my location. So I did. But after he received it, they contacted me again. He informed me that that was not enough. This nonsensical interaction lasted for months, and eventually, I moved to Charlotte, North Carolina. When I contacted the IRS from Charlotte, the issue was still not resolved. This calling and finding no progress in resolving my issue were undoubtedly a form of harassment. My taxes were not that complicated! After my last call to them, I hung up the phone and prayed to Mary, the Blessed Virgin. I told her I have no idea what was going on with the IRS., but I do not know what I am supposed to do. And I offered it to her to deal with in her way. I never called the IRS. again, and I never heard from Internal Revenue Service concerning that matter.

Banking

While I was in Philadelphia, I had a checking account with a small local bank. It was a very personal bank, and the fees were much lower. But about a year before I moved from Philadelphia, I opened a personal and business account with a larger bank. I had a challenging experience with the previous bank, and the experience was enough reason to move my account.

By the time I moved to North Carolina, I was banking by mail, and all was fine. Eventually, I opened a local checking account in Greenville. And I did my banking locally. But by the time I moved to Charlotte, North Carolina, banking by mail with the bank in Philadelphia was not working out. I needed to open a savings account. So I tried to do so by mail with my bank in Philadelphia. When I received my savings account by mail, the account package was open, probably searched, and all the pamphlets and personal papers were held together by a rubber band.

This is what happened that day: when I went to the mailbox to get my mail, the postal delivery person was still there. When I opened my postal box and pulled out my mail, I saw my banking package had arrived. It was opened. All the documents were wrapped in a rubber band. I looked at it all and looked at him. He looked at the packet in my hand and kept right on stuffing mailboxes. He never said a word. Then I realized someone searched my mail and wanted me to know it. I called the bank, reported the packaged had arrived opened, and told them not to open the account. I opened a new savings account in Charlotte.

Surveillance

I have never been someone who goes out and gets involved in "things" around me out of a need to be active. Nor was I ever someone who socializes much. And as a result, one might conclude that I was out of touch with the world around me. But I would argue that many people would be just as surprised at the level of surveillance in our society as I was and am. We have it taught that we "live in freedom," and I always assumed that included freedom from being watched and observed by strangers. And because of the direction of technology and the mass collection of data, all that surveillance is already worst. It will penetrate deeper and deeper into our personal lives. When I was working for a large health insurance company as a user of mainframes back in 2001, I concluded, in my mind, that societal privacy was a figment of people's imagination. And the events I experienced and write about now only confirm my thoughts on the subject: Freedom and thus privacy is a product of the human condition. But it is not a real possibility. It might seem noble and necessary to "go after it," but it is not an achievable goal for human beings.

Jesus then said to those Jews who believed in him, "If you remain in my word, you will truly be my disciples, and you will know the truth, and the truth will set you free." They answered him, "We are descendants of Abraham and have never been enslaved to anyone. How can you say, 'You will become free'?" Jesus answered them, "Amen, amen, I say to you, everyone who commits sin is a slave of sin. A slave does not remain in a household forever, but a son always remains. So, if a son frees you, then you will truly be free. **John 8:31-36**. (14)

The current direction of data collection will probably eliminate the fantasy of privacy and freedom. I think that has tremendous implications for nations and societies in general.

I learned as I see differently: I did not know that there are people in some neighborhoods whose sole purpose is watching and keeping tabs on what others do. I did not know that people are hired to ruin other people's lives with nuisance activity. In the short time from 2002 to 2020, I experienced near-continuous nuisance and privacy violations in my personal life. I observed countless "investigation activity" that, in my mind, was simply a waste of tax dollars. I saw the collection of many of society's organizations come together in a nearly seamless way to collect and relay data on people's whereabouts and actions. In the various cities where I lived in those years, I witnessed public transportation, library, postal delivery, government, banks, and landlords used to collect and process personal data, all in the name of verifying suspicions of criminal behavior. All this has been going on in society until 2002; the difference is that I was now aware of it.

In some neighborhoods in Philadelphia, you cannot walk in a local business without being watched with suspicion. If the people do not know you, they view you with suspicion. And it is not because you are an imminent threat physically, but because the people are not sure of your purpose. What are you up to and looking for in their pizza restaurant? What kind of car are you driving? Why have they not seen you before? Do you know them from somewhere? Why are you suddenly buying pizza here in this store? I used to think this was all an unhealthy paranoia. I now perceive these people as a "group psychology" experiencing the post-traumatic stress of repeated privacy violations.

Some Conclusions

Here is what I have found to be entirely accurate. This story, at a minimum, is too absurd not to be told. But if what I have written is as precise as I think, it is reasonable to do more than stop and think. Is Jesus talking to a cab driver/programmer from Philadelphia? Although I sensed that I was to "do nothing." And to be honest, nothing I did try to do to stop these events did any good. There was no response from the Public Utility Commission, the US Postal Service, the Social Security Administration, or the local political offices. In the end, all this activity is a distraction. It struggles to test your ability to stay focused on God amid great turmoil. Without a focus on Christ, I am lost.

But what was important was that I took the time to collect empirical evidence in my mind as I thought about what I believe. With the grace of God and mental verification, I maintained my sanity as events got worse and worse. And it is based on the logical processing of empirical evidence that I could accept this strange reality suddenly occurring all around me. I knew then that I did not imagine the situation. After some robust and revealing news reports, I learned a few years later that opening people's mail and mail showing up missing was a problem for the postal service. But the postal service doesn't advertise this issue. This is likely the reason why so few people would ever believe me when I say it happened to me. Neither my mortgage payment nor my student loan payment showed up that month. Yet, I distinctly remember mailing them together and which mailbox I used. In another situation, I walked up on a plain-clothes police officer using a badge to threaten a postal delivery person. This officer wanted to see the mail before it was delivered. The post office has its federal rules, but that didn't stop a scared delivery person from showing the mail to the police officer. I did see a report on the local news about a new device that people were using to capture mail before it drops in the mailbox. Hearing that truly made me uneasy. But it might explain why my mortgage and student loan payment never showed up as paid on my accounts that month.

By the time winter of 2002 ended (early 2003), the company where I rented my cab disclosed that some of the cash I was collecting was routinely marked. When they told me this, I simply threw up my hands. I cannot control what people use to pay their fares! At that time, cab driving was primarily a cash business and customers paid in cash. I deposited my paycheck in cash. Cab drivers rented their vehicles with cash. The company checked all the bills they received from cab drivers for authenticity. I thought "marked bills" are related to tracing illegal transactions. Who knew the taxi business was so complicated! During this period, I started blacking out while driving my cab. I had three accidents. two accidents occurred in one night. So I stopped driving the taxi and obtained a temporary job in New Jersey grading state achievement exams. The job lasted several months. Then someone started calling that office where I worked. The people at my job concluded they were trying to get me fired. But I had not lied on my application or other papers I submitted, so (apparently) they had no grounds for any type of termination.

Later in the fall, shortly before I left Philadelphia, I was on my way home on the bus, and as I stared out the window, I heard the words "ANYTHING YOU ASK." There was a soft, peaceful, but serious tone to the voice. And I could feel the presence of someone I thought as Jesus staring at me (in my mind). And a chill of joy went through my whole body. I became tearful inside. I thought to myself, "I must be doing okay, amid all this crazy stuff." But then I didn't know what to say! What do I ask? So I said nothing. I thought to myself, "What if I ask for the wrong thing?" After years of thinking on the encounter, I concluded "anything you ask" means to pray for help for my family, my world, and its contents. Jesus was giving me instructions. I was to pray for the coming of The Kingdom. And only now, after years away from it all, do I realize that I shouldn't ask from behind a mainframe computer terminal. Or from behind the wheel of a cab. And so, the monastery is where I decided I would focus myself to "ask." But I had to get there first!

When I moved to Charlotte, North Carolina, I thought back on a few events in Philadelphia that influenced my understanding of life in a very poignant way. She was 25 years old, and her body set afire in a dumpster in the early morning. His was rolled up in an old rug and left behind some people's houses not five blocks from my own. They were visiting friends and ended up riddled with bullets one corner from my house only a few months after I sold it. And they were up and down Broad Street: the faces of missing children. I used to see them every day as I went to work or rode the buses in the afternoon. There was a war going on, and somehow willing or not, I am part of it. In Greenville and Charlotte, it became clear that this war was very physical and quite spiritual and, therefore, very much eternal. What comes to mind repeatedly concerning all of this is this following scripture:

After that I saw another angel coming down from the sky. He had much power. The bright light that shone from him lit up the earth. He called in a loud voice and said, `The big city of Babylon has fallen down! It has fallen down! Bad spirits live in it. All bad spirits hide there. And all kinds of dirty birds that people hate hide there. All the nations are broken down because they are full of its wrong ways. The kings of the earth have joined with it. The traders of the earth have become rich because of its wrong ways.

Then I heard another voice from the sky that said, "Come out of it, my people, so that you will have no part in the wrong things it does. Come out of it so that you will not have the big troubles it will have. Its wrong ways are piled as high as the sky and God has remembered the wrong things it has done. **Revelation 18:1-5.** (14)

2011

Evolving Uniqueness

As I fiddle around in the world of the physical,
I re-discover the world of the mental.
Over and over, I explore a deeper, unknown
Notion of this place that I am.

Sometimes I know I am blindly stumbling in the
Dark basement self.
Down here in the basement, I reunite in recollection.
I am dust-covered and long forgotten, timelessly ignored.

Having morphed and transitioned back to the physical.
With a new mental lens for living my realty.
It's an altered, innovated human journey.
Everything is the same, yet all is distinctly different.

Fascinated and thrilled, this growing kinship, with myself,
I return down within to those same sources.
Incapacitating fear, surmounted by hope,
I pursue precious gems useful for knowing God.

Chapter Introduction

From 2011 to 2013, I accepted and adjusted to many new aspects of life, both as a new Roman Catholic and a new monk. One different perspective I needed to develop an eye for was iconography. The term 'icon' seems to represent so much of Christian, Roman Catholic, and monastic life. *A religious icon is a sign (a word or graphic symbol) whose form suggests its meaning. Paintings, pictures, statues, stained windows fill Roman Catholic churches. Their purpose is iconic. It takes what is well known and points to significant religious or spiritual values, which are very likely unseen.* (5) And it is the thinking of life in terms of icons and symbols that occupied my efforts. In all my experience with churches, I simply never realized the purpose of these essential tools.

Since I am not a trained theologian, I feel uncomfortable writing about some subjects. However, suffice it to say, it is an immense effort on the church's part to get followers to point their minds and hearts in the proper direction. One "picture" can tell a story and offer different aspects simultaneously. And ideas about God, death, heaven, hell, purgatory, and sin all have an in-depth history demonstrated using icons of some sort.

Religious debate abounds. Many books authored by informed people of the church are collecting dust in libraries worldwide. Most people do not read them. There are biographies filled with people whose life experiences demonstrate what is true about church teachings, but in our dual lives, we believe and do not believe simultaneously what the church has to say. The church teaches as fact the miracles Jesus performed in his life here on earth. From my experience in discussions with people both in and out of monasteries, people still debate whether Jesus fed thousands of people with a few fish and a piece of bread. Some say the story is all symbolism, and some say the story is actual. My experiences indicate God can pretty much do anything. It is his reality to do what he pleases. To me, God dwells in the heavens; he does whatever he wills. Still, hidden within me are real doubts and ill-formed conclusions that hamper my progress in my relationship with God. My mere presence in the monastery lifestyle has helped me reform my being to accommodate the Church and its teachings and make many discoveries!

It has helped me see or experience the Sacred Heart of Jesus, the Merciful Heart of Jesus, the Virgin Mary, and her earthly husband, Joseph. It has helped me understand many of the struggles of the Saints. It has dragged me kicking, hollering, and arguing away from my understanding of death, heaven, and hell, as well as purgatory. For instance, I now understand death as both literal and iconic. I no longer see death as something I should run from or avoid; I have learned that death is an icon for a great mystery of light in my short stay. But it is also a dark, scary place when I am struggling with it in the wrong way.

When I changed from Postulant to a monk in Simple Vows, I changed my name from Rodney to Anthony-Maria. Anthony for Antony of the Desert and Maria for Our Lady of Guadalupe. It was reading about Mary that led me to Catholicism. Inspired by and meditating on the story of Guadalupe helped me learn about Roman Catholicism. And though he was a hermit, reading about the Life of Antony led me to monastic life. This is what my mind could accept at the time. Having a new name and getting used to hearing it is oddly transformational. And I always find it interesting to hear why another person chose their new name. Family and friends often struggle with your new name and usually have a superficial notion of why. Mine never stopped calling me Keith or Rodney.

January 16, 2011

Hi Mary-Martha,

This is Br. Rodney from the States, offering you a big HELLO! I hope all is well. And tell all the girls you teach Br. Rodney said "hello" and "behave properly and do their homework." I've got pictures from the slideshow of all the children, so if they act up, I can identify them via satellite, then I will air-drop smelly, used tire sandals on them! When you get your email address, you can communicate with me using: *Rodney@Methuselahabbey.org.* I look forward to hearing from you. Remember, I gave you strict orders for you to stay safe! Now, I hear from your mother that you have sprained an ankle! If this were the military, you would have to go On Report for disobeying a lawful order! Lucky for you, you're in South America, or I'd have to have you put in the brig awaiting Captain's Mass. Ask your dad what that means!

What is going on here in the States? In the news From Methuselah Abbey:

A U.S. congresswoman of Arizona was shot along with 18 other people at a supermarket in Arizona. nine shots were fatal, including a nine-year old girl. She (the little girl) was there at the supermarket to learn about politics. The gunman shot everyone as the congresswoman gave a public speech to an audience in the parking lot. Based on the available information, a mentally ill guy decided to kill everyone because he disagreed with her politics. Everyone across the nation was praying for the congresswoman, Gabrielle Gifford. According to the local news, this is only the sixth time a congress "person" is a target in an attempted or actual assassination. Anyway, her injury was through the left part of the brain. Doctors thought there was little chance of recovery. But each day, she is making improvements. By now, she can probably sit up and speak. One day recently, it is told that she said, "Where is that Mary-Martha!"

The floods in Australia are terrible. Waves of water on the highways, sharks were swimming in the streets of small towns. The weather is CRAZY! Some towns are cut off from every form of transportation except helicopters. Warned to leave, some still refused. In any case, I think people who say global warming is not a "real thing" better wake up!

I included a prayer for Methuselah in this letter. I want you to pray for us when you get a chance. We have high hopes for the future. But we need more help! Titus came back from Maine, Matthew is back from D.C. (but mentally, he is somewhere else as he recently separated from a long-term romance). Randolph has to take care of some personal issues, but he may move to Charles City and become an Oblate. He wants to be free to compose music, which, apparently, prevents him from becoming a monk. So he will probably be leaving for home at the end of January to go home and take care of business!

Your mom put some extraordinary chocolate in the library! And my name is written on each little piece! Oh, the joy! She loves me! She loves me not! She loves me! It's Hershey's. She thinks I am so silly. I told her the Abbot threw a book at me and hollered for me to 'get out of his office!' And She thought I was serious. Apparently, this was a norm when she was a Religious. She mentioned to me, in conversation, that you were bit by a snake some time ago at Methuselah. Wow! You better be careful, Miss Lady! Try not to start trouble with the locals, okay?

I did my second solo in choir (schola). Many people told me that I have an excellent singing voice. So you might want to stay clear of me. Also, I told your mom that I have your harp music compact disk. I was supposed to make a copy and never did. I will give it back soon, I promise! Don't be angry with me.

The Abbot is going to Rome soon, and he has some other travels. So Fr. Thomas will be in charge for quite a bit this spring. My sister (Kim), her husband, and my mom will visit in April for the first time. I will show them my hat (that you gave me). The people love that hat! Anyway, time to go! I need to use the treadmill. My prayers are with you, Mary-Martha. We all think about you - for the most part. Seriously though, it was good to see you. You are taking excellent care of yourself, and please keep it that way.

I know now why I write these letters. I knew before, but now I am much more conscious of it. And everyone enjoyed the slideshow.

Sincerely,

Br. Rodney

P.S. We have had (2) 12 inch plus blizzards in the northeast since January 1, 2011!

She came with certainty at least once year. She usually assisted at Christmas events. Mary was a doctorate in theology. From what I can see, she lived as something of a hermit. I often thought she was more monastic than the monks! Somehow we connected about some poems I put in booklet form. And this is correspondence about some she wrote.

January 20, 2011

PO Box 4321
Riggy, NC 12345

Dear Mary,

I hope all is well with you. I know you are a busy person. So I will try to make this note short. We miss you here at Methuselah. Fr. Matthias has removed all the Christmas decor. The season is gone, and we look toward St. Valentines' and St. Patrick's Day.

Now about the poems you sent. I was happy to read someone else's similarly life experiences. I have an entire book of writings I would like to send you, but I don't want to burden you. First, let me say that I am not a professional writer if you have not figured that out! And I tend to write with no regard for anything except the most basic rules. And more than anything, I try to express myself modestly. If I feel myself getting complex or overthinking, I immediately know something is wrong with my writing. I need an almost child-like sense of ideas as in: "Jesus loves me this I know, for the bible tells me so!" Though sometimes it does get complex.

Having read what you have written, I must say you must be a bit of a mystic. And with all your background, you must know about mysticism. I liked "The Words" and "True Communion." You guessed it! It seemed to me that I understood what you intended to communicate in those two poems. Generally, I can design a puzzle, but I cannot solve one. And to me, "In the Light of Communion" was something of a mystery. And that is even with the explanation you offer. And just like yours, my poems tend to be inspired by personal events.

Not that it is any of my business, but you seem to be more of a monk than the monks. Your writing appears like prayer or meditation. And it is apparent to me that you are in touch with so much more. Here, if people notice anything, they rarely, if ever, talk about it openly. I have had a few curious experiences, but most are not visual. I do experience an interesting inner life, but primarily auditory or dreams.

I have only one question: In that particular poem, how will you "join Him on the Cross?" Because that question was significant, or it would not have been asked? But I guess that that is not my business either. Is it? I suspect that that is between you and Jesus.

I will eventually print some of the stuff I have and send it to you for your amusement. Until then, please take care and stay away from the bears. (Mary once told me a bear came up to her while she was doing yoga and her dog barked until it ran off!)

Poetically sincere,

Br. Rodney Odom

January x, 2011

Dear Joseph,

My buddy Fr. John just passed away. He graduated with honors. At 88 years old, he led what seemed like a full life. In this picture, he lost a good deal of his skin pigmentation due to vitiligo. When he died, he had Parkinson's disease, but this did not cause his death. A short history: He was the son of three generations of Baptist preachers in the South Carolina area. The church they founded is still alive in the Charleston, SC, area. But he said one day, his father came home and told his wife he had converted to Catholicism. And so, the whole family converted to Catholicism. And the younger (Fr. John) became a priest. He went north to the Boston, MA area to enter the Catholic priesthood because the southern society was not yet ready to ordain an African American man. Fr. John first entered the monastery but left for 10 years during the Vietnam era because of illness. While away, he served as a chaplain on a local Air Force base. Father was very active socially and in the civil rights movement. And he ran for mayor of North Charleston. He came back to the monastery in the late '70s and eventually gave up practicing priestly duties at the monastery to (as he put it) "seek a closer relationship with God."

I found Fr. John to be very explicit, and some would say outspoken. I appreciated that about him. Close to the end of his earthly life, he died once (no pulse for quite some time) and then returned to us for a few days. He said to let everyone know that he did not see any white light. And then he finally went home. All the monks took time sitting with him as he slowly passed away over days. He apologized to me for not spending as much time with me as he would have liked.

Photo: Fr. John and I in the Solarium of the Senior Wing, several weeks before I was told of his impending death.

(What I have written next, <u>Just My Imagination, Once Again</u>, was my experience of Fr. Leonard after he passed away, the funeral mass was over, and I was back in my room.)

Sincerely,

Br. Anthony-Maria

Just My Imagination, Once Again by Br. Anthony-Maria

Based on my reading and learning here at Methuselah, I write the following: With the Ascension of Jesus into the Heavens to be at the Right of the Father, we as followers of Christ have already received the gift of heaven; 'The Gift of Heaven' being the fullness of life. And we begin to experience this increasingly as we follow even closer the "Way of the Cross." I guess that's how "seek and ye shall find" and "ask and ye shall be given" is possible! Heaven is waiting for us to reach for more life. In monasticism, participation in the "heavenly" is routine through prayer, meditation, scripture, Lectio (prayerful reading), and Holy Communion. Considering these facts, I try to document a particular supernatural experience.

I met Fr. John in 2007 on my first visit to Our Lady of Methuselah Abbey (Monk City, SC). Fr. John, 86 years old, lived with both Parkinson's disease and a condition in which he lost skin pigmentation. He said, "This is all that's left!" He was otherwise alert and capable of using a motorized wheelchair to get around. Fr. John learned he was "meant" to be a priest through his paternal father. When he was ordained, it was with the Holy Ghost Fathers in Connecticut. The southern states were not prepared to ordain an African-American at that time. He was a very active person as a priest, social activist, and U.S. Air Force chaplain during the Vietnam era. He was busy all over, including Harlem, NY, Charleston, SC, and other areas. But this little story is not about his life as enjoyable as it seems to have been. This story starts with his transition from this life.

Fr. John was my self-appointed buddy when I started visiting Methuselah. He looked out for me from his wheelchair, his eyes always watching. He would tell me, "try not to make so much noise when collecting the dishes," and in the refectory where we ate, he would say, "don't go into the serving area using the out-door even if other people are doing so, you are not supposed to do so." A continuous flow of these tiny bits of advice helped guide me into the abbey culture. When I arrived at Methuselah for the last time (when I arrived to stay), he told me that he pestered Jesus day and night for me to come to Methuselah. And before he died, he spoke to me about his regret that he did not spend more time talking with me. I had a fondness for him. So I had a modest goal in my mind. I wanted to take a picture with Fr. John before he died. I told no one about this goal. I assumed he would die before me! But as schedules were at the monastery, when would I have time to take pictures? Frankly, based on his behavior, I figured Fr. John had a few more years before he would pass on to the fullness of life.

However, while leaving dinner (the noon meal) one Saturday afternoon, I walked alone toward my room via the Senior Wing of the monastery. As I walked, it was made known to me that Fr. John would die soon and that I should hurry and take my pictures. How was this information made available? I heard a voice in my mind like my own self-talk, only I didn't identify it as my voice. I breathed a sigh as I proceeded down the passageway; I believed what I heard. And when I saw Br. Thomas, the informal "monastery photographer," I arranged with him to take pictures of me with Fr. John as soon as possible. Sunday the next day, around the same time, Br. Thomas was available, and I had already arranged with Fr. John for all of us to get together. When Br. Thomas went to Fr. John's room to help him dress, he was occupied doing something important. So Br. Thomas instead went to get the camera from his room, and I waited outside Fr. John's room for them both. Fr. John called me in his room to help him put on his habit (think religious clothing). And after we proceeded, using his walker, across the hall to the Solarium to meet Br. Thomas and take a few pictures. The sun was very bright through the windows, and it was a perfect day for using a camera inside!

Before taking pictures, Fr. John jokingly asked Br. Thomas if he was going for "the stupid" or "crazy look?" and we laughed. Fr. John was often a joker, but when he was serious, it was apparent. Some people didn't like his bluntness, but I admired it very much. We took about five pictures together, and since it was a digital camera, Br. Thomas left and emailed them to me immediately. Fr. John returned to his room somewhat baffled as to why I made such a big deal of taking pictures. He stopped and looked at me intently as he walked toward his door. He didn't say anything. I stared back at him. I never mentioned what I experienced or heard in my mind. I thought that would be stupid; what would happen if what I heard was wrong? But I figured he had to look at me like that for a reason. He knew something was afoot! In any case, he proceeded into his room.

Over the next week, Fr. John came to Offices and Mass as usual. And because I was expecting him to pass away, I became impatient. I was not hoping he would die, but I wondered why he didn't look or act sick? What was going on? Why was I told he would die soon? What did I hear in this head of mine? After a second week began and was half gone, I assumed that I misunderstood or what I heard was wrong. But then three days passed, and Fr. John didn't come to Mass or any of the Offices. I thought that was normal because his illness made him weak from time to time. Then the Abbot announced his condition: he was bedridden. He said it was severe, and he probably didn't have much time left, perhaps less than a week. The monastery contacted his family.

I began visiting Fr. John in his room. He was very calm about the idea of dying. He talked in a usual way but was eating less and less. He spoke of death as if he were reading about it in a magazine. His family began to arrive to be with him and talk to us. On my last visit, he kicked me out of his room. I knew it was not personal. He was receiving many visitors, and he needed time to be alone. Nor did he wish to be a burden or have people "standing watch" over him. So I hovered around his doorway outside the room. Whenever I passed his room, his sister assured me he was okay. Fr. John passed away during Vigils (between 3 a.m. and 4 a.m.) on December 5, 2010. Br. Mark started the Toller bell (slow constant ringing of a large bell), and we all knew that a monk had passed away. I was about to go into my room when I heard it. I turned around and immediately started praying the Divine Mercy Chaplet. He was dead (for the second time). All the brothers gathered in his room. The Abbot began the prayers. Soon after, the body was sent away for funeral services. It was returned prepared for burial some days later. We had Midday prayer and started a vigil for his burial. We read Psalms and prayed for him. The monastery had an information bulletin board where people signed up on a list to sit with the deceased. The sitting required at least one person every 30 minutes until the funeral. And when the list was slow to fill, I filled in my name in almost every blank spot.

His family continued to arrive through the next day. The funeral was to be in the afternoon of December 9, 2010. But after Lauds (morning prayer) that same day, I went back to my room. I was feeling very gloomy inside. I was naturally contemplating life and death, so I sat at my desk to write about my feelings and the experience at Mass in my journal. That's when he spoke to me. As if standing behind me, he said, "thank you for your prayers." He continued to speak, and I sat there calmly, listening. What else was I supposed to do? Then he said, "God loves you very much..." And when I heard this, I immediately put my head down on my desk, and tears of joy poured from my eyes. My sadness was gone instantly. At this moment, I felt something going through my mind - it felt like a slight breeze of wind tickling my mind and scalp. So I began to write.

By now, the tears were pouring onto my paper and smearing my ink. You see, I had a little poem in my mind for months and could not find a way to express it; however, it would not leave my thoughts. So after a late-night novena that I was praying for someone else, I also asked Jesus to help me write the poem for the Christmas holidays. Before I asked Jesus for help, I had five different versions of words, each speaking about some aspect of a bigger idea. But, individually, they were incomplete. It was weeks since I asked Jesus to help me write this poem. But during this encounter with Fr. John, I wrote down 95 percent of what would be the final version of the poem in a matter of 10 seconds. The current version used all my mental ideas. But this version was linked together in such a way as to be expressed in new and unusual dimensions. Then Fr. John said, "I have to go now." And my experience was over.

After I read what I wrote down, I thought, "Wow! I wrote this?" I was filled with pride and simultaneously baffled by it all. I felt like a kindergartner showing his parents his first excellent test score! I read it repeatedly. It was beautiful to me. And even though I asked God for help in writing the poem, it occurred to me after asking that, perhaps, God might not be bothered with my minor poem problems! After this situation, I thought to myself, "God is really, really nice and seems intimately involved in every little struggle I have." And from then on and for days, I was happy and filled with joy. I took every moment I could to finish polishing the ideas I wrote down. And every single time I looked at Fr. John's body in the church for the remainder of the day, I smiled because it seemed to me, he was okay! After an experience such as this, it is hard to understand how I might still wonder about an after-life. I feel confident that this was a special grace from God to strengthen my faith and perhaps pass the story on to others that might also believe that God is waiting! The poem I wrote is next (I always tear up when I read it):

Tears descend from soaring heights
Like a rain dropped from clouds on high
Announcing the opening of a symphony
Beyond the imagination of all creation.

Across the cosmos
Countless twinkling stars share the news
Outlining the dark vastness
Of an invisible, omnipotent presence.

Conducting as designed
Teaching oceans and seas
A moon plays its small part
Orchestrating a hypnotic percussion of calming meditation.

Leaves of trees
Play the keys of the wind
With flocks of birds dancing on air
As to a whispering joyful love song.

So many flowers exploding in colorful climax
Plants delicately direct every sort of creature
A diverse crescendo of soulful instruments
According to practiced instruction.

And how dare I casually critique
The greatness of it all
Me a mere conduit of bizarre tales
Offering a far too limited opinion.

But for now, a halo is set
As the fog rolls in on our cathedral lights
For a mesmerizing golden glow
We, too, participate in this prayer!

I am wrapped snug and quiet
In the solitude of a dark, empty church
Captured willingly by its Grace
And oh, so grateful*1 for its infinite Mercy. [20]

Welcome to Monastic Life! – Learning To Share

Learning to Share

Having spent most of my life in and about the "hard concrete" of urban life and relatively little time exploring the depths of nature or living in a forest setting left me entirely lacking in the actual nature of life on earth. Let's face it, documentaries about wild kingdoms cannot teach a person but so much. So living at Methuselah in the middle of a forest was a real awakening for my entire existence as a human being. My previous experiences with other life forms were limited to what you might find in any large urban area. For me seeing a deer crossing the road was an eye-catching situation. It is true that when I was younger, I visited my grandparents every year, and they lived in relatively rural areas where you could easily see more than a squirrel. But a week or two there where they live did not teach me what living in a forest firsthand, every day, all day for years can teach.

And to suddenly be exposed to squirrels that want to play games with you and snakes that want to eat other baby creatures was very new for me. To find turtles on the road after a rainstorm or wake up to giant flying "Carolina Cockroaches" crawling the walls in my room took a bit of time for adaptation. I relearned the word "brood" after discussing some wild turkeys passing by our room one morning. I now know their talons are almost deadly, and their mostly breast meat tends to be tough.

I lived with strangely colored beetles that never moved, and then one day, they were gone. There are always little Geckos crawling all over in various places at this monastery, even inside buildings. And while they are not threatening creatures, I always thought they would get caught in the building, dehydrate, and die. Senseless death bothered me. My biggest challenge in all this was to learn to see all life as equal. I needed to learn to see all life as having a right to exist as I see myself as having that same right. I struggled to overcome my need to "kill it" because it was creepy-looking or perhaps poisonous. If it was not a real threat, I needed to learn just to let it be.

Once while spraying a tarp down with fresh water to clean it, I killed a field mouse. Some of the spraying water hit the mouse, and just that quick, it was dead. I thought about fragileness for a very long time after that. Here I learned that life could be far more fragile. And it occurred to me that if I thought the field mouse's life was fragile, there is probably life that sees me as weak as well. So I thought to do unto others as you would have them do unto you!

Over the years, I learned to walk past earthworms and other slithering creatures making their way across the "hard concrete" walks to get to another mud hole. I tended to stop and help them. But finally, I told myself: Nope! Assisting worms is not my purpose here. Worms have their little struggles, and I have mine. I learned that flies are not just a pest when flying about you. They also bite. Wearing a hat of some sort when out walking or exploring became the norm. Here I learned that yellow jackets could make a nest in the ground and I had better not step on them lest I find myself running. I am still puzzled about how a wasp knows the difference between the tractor and the person driving when stinging. And while I knew well about the tiny fire ants before I came to the monastery, it took quite a few reminders not to plop down on the dirt to rest my feet without looking first. How would I respond to a big thing smashing and destroying my home?

I learned to accept that snakes like to eat baby squirrels and baby rabbits. I had to admit that that was not bad; it was just the thing that snakes do. And while I like the squirrels, I didn't fight off the owls who decided to feast on them in the area where we lived. I had to learn that every snake was not "pure evil," and most snakes wanted nothing to do with me. I had to learn not to kill them on sight but to find a way to get them out of the way so I could get my job done.

And while I like watching the alligators, they are one of the few creatures I worried about as genuinely life-threatening. They can be large and ferocious. Once they reach maturity, they don't move out of the way; I must go around. You can spook them, but they can hunt you as well. All of this and more taught me to value life differently. I learned to appreciate life in a way that was not so people-centered. I learned to share.

January 30, 2011

Dear Mary,

Thank you for the Relic. I felt I must write this note (though it is a long time coming) for two reasons. One is to say Thank You! And the other is because of my history with Padre Pio (Saint Pio).

Please understand that I was not born Roman Catholic. I started attending a Catholic church in late 2006 in Charlotte, North Carolina. I converted officially in Easter of 2008. However, I began reading about Padre Pio in the year 2003! This reading took place well before I even thought about Catholicism. And while I did not know it at the time, he is one of my inspirations for the type of monastic order I knew I would enter. His was different than the Trappist, but his version of the Franciscans lead me to a monastic order of offered deeper contemplation. Antony of Egypt, Padre Pio, Teresa of Avila, and now Saint Maria Faustina Kowalska. I knew about Saint Faustina before I ever thought about Catholicism. Some stranger in Philadelphia, Pennsylvania (my family is still there) saw me getting off the subway one night and gave me a pamphlet about Divine Mercy. I looked at it and thanked him gratitude. And he said, "I knew it was you." And he walked off into the night. Always another mystery in this new little world of mine.

Reading about their lives has changed my perception of reality altogether! I am guided toward some "yet to be determined" goal. Sometimes I look at the rosary beads, and my heart fills with warmth and awe. Frankly, I didn't even know what a relic was until you sent it to me, and I researched online. And there my heart went again. Now I am scared to carry the Relic because I am afraid I will lose it. I tend to break things like this(smile). I am strong but clumsy.

In any case, I am authentically grateful for you, and you're generosity!

Sincerely,

Br. Rodney Odom

Postscript: I insert a personal prayer request with this note. Pray for us! (The monks started a daily prayer for the monastery, and we're asking friends and benefactors for their help.)

Lessons From Inside By Br. Anthony-Maria

I was very fond of a young woman who regularly visited the monastery. And, as always, I looked forward to seeing her on this particular visit. But this visit was different. As I hugged her, I was left astonished. The instant I embraced her to enjoy her presence, my Guardian Angel spoke to me! For me, it was a rare form of communication. It was not a mumble. It was clear, and it was exact. Consequently, I took it very seriously, and as I heard the voice, my body froze for a moment. I didn't ask who? I heeded the warning. What my Guardian Angel said to me was, **"You are taking another man's wife."**

Now, to be explicit, I enjoyed seeing her, but I had no conscious idea that "taking another man's wife" was what I was doing. And based on that communication alone, I came to a deeper understanding of many related biblical topics. And a much deeper understanding of what it means to be human.

For some reason, I immediately thought of King David and Bathsheba of the Jewish scriptures. When I was younger, I wondered how David could admire a married woman from afar and insist on possessing her and not realize at the very moment that what he was doing was inappropriate. I figured he had to know the Ten Commandments! But I did not quite understand David when "judging" him as law-abiding. The scriptures make David to be essential. Also, in the story of David and King Saul, I saw in his behavior depth of being. When King Saul came after David to kill him, David captured King Saul and did nothing to him. He allowed King Saul to go free. He went out of his way to let the king know he was not after his throne.

I always interpreted this as a person who was not displaying blind ambition. I considered that a positive quality. Also, it indicated to me that David had regard for Saul's holy selection as king. Thus, to me, he seemed to fear God. So when he took another man's wife and had the woman's husband sent to war to be killed, it seemed to me to be out of character for David. But it never occurred to me to seek a more profound understanding. From that, I came to have a sense of Abraham's fear when he purposely told people his wife Sarah was his sister. Initially, I judged him to be a little strange for such behavior. Yet somehow, I could see how he truly feared being killed due to her great beauty.

Based on my reception of that one clear communication, I came to a deeper understanding of the nature of sin, human existence, and certain biblical scriptures like Psalm 73 and others. It makes me realize that human beings have deeper behavioral aspects and are often silent and powerfully influential. That more profound nature will go after what it feels it needs to fulfill itself. And sometimes, how it goes about fulfilling what it needs is inappropriate. An individual may not be consciously aware of their deeper motivations. It becomes plain to me how easily I fall into an unacceptable situation. And by the time I am aware, it is too late; too much damage is done. In other words, if I am slipping, I usually fall before I realize I have lost my balance; I only react to losing my balance after it is too late or too painful to recover.

I also came to a deeper understanding of the early chapters of the Book of Revelation. I see how the people of the various churches slip in their relationship with God. Even to the point where they don't know how far they have fallen. Their behavior is so far off the mark that Christ himself must intervene to direct the situation personally. Thus, a group of people can decide to take an explicitly wrong action, know that the action taken is improper, and proceed because the moral objection is sublimated.

It seems that the momentum and dynamics of the decision-making process are often subtle. It is like waves in the ocean. The surface wave is what we observe, but there are many more beneath the surface we cannot see. And they are the cause of the wave above them. At times the human mind seems to process in the same way. As all the factors of the mind's decision are considered, there is a silent tug-of-war going on. I make the poor choice and do not know why! Somehow, the moral element is sublimated to some other overwhelming mental influence.

I see so much going on with being human. And it seems to get even more complicated when it comes to a group situation. Taking time to focus attention inward seems a requirement to be human. Maybe we ought to struggle a little more against the social tendency to depend only on each other, seek comfort only in each other, and duplicate only what others are doing. Even without each other, we are never alone. So if we focus on overcoming anxieties and fears when there is nothing to do, nothing to say, and to be present with those feelings can become adversity processed with God's help.

I often unconsciously create distractions and more "meaningful activities" instead of God in daily life. Here, my experience with taking the time to look toward nothing and wait for nothing has been enriching. Sometimes I ask myself, "self," what are you doing and why? Can you hear God calling you to sit and be quiet? Or are you running from something out of fear? "Self" what is your true motivation for doing what you do? Is it truth, or is it fear? Are you seeking peace or avoiding pain? There are times when all I know is I have to stop moving and settle down. No more creating barriers to this process of "relationship with God." I sense that this practice must take place and is not optional. And to me that I can know this is a gift. It is learning and knowing that nothing is more important than the healing presence and power of the Spirit. This knowledge wins the tug-of-war to sit and let me be one with the creation and creator. In my mind, I need to be more like Mary. And less like Martha. I struggle to get "all of me" on the same footing.

And yet still, in life, a fighter pilot amid battle can't stop. The pilot must keep their focus on the action at hand. The person driving the car must keep moving safely. The person supporting the family must remain focused on doing so correctly. Curiously, one communication of "you are taking another man's wife" brought about such enlightening insights. I have come to realize that while I need to stay focused on Christ by both action and word, my "safety" is not dependent on me or any other human being!

I have realized that my mind is not best when constantly socializing or jumping from activity to activity as the multi-tasking world requires. To stay focused in this way, I cannot let life overwhelm me too much. When I go too far with activities, I am easily divided and thus just as easily conquered. Trying to do too much has already cost me! I risk, again, losing my orientation and having no way to know which "way is God."

Other distractions stop me from seeking God. Sometimes fear or anxiety stops me. When I settle, I realize something is wrong, and I return to the Source for help. So you see, for me at least, what remains of this life of mine is my chance! My ambition for earthly things is quietly converted to desire for seeking God. And my responsibility is to sit and wait, to explore the inner way of my being. I must lean on my inner world more and more. In doing so, I fulfill my ambition in ways I know not! My job is to judge the outside world accordingly and block those issues that are not likely to help me much in an inward way. I don't take so many cues from the outside world anymore in my job. I must map out an inner path to freedom by observing the chains that keep me earthly and praying for Jesus to break them. My job is to ask and keep asking for Jesus to put all chains or enemies under my feet. It seems that then -- and only then -- have I fulfilled my life's intention.

Below is a short note to my former managers and coworkers of Frito-Lay, inc. in Charlotte, N.C. After meeting some people at Methuselah, it occurred to me that the world is full of coincidences indicating how connected it is.

January 31, 2011

Dear Mary-Martha,

I am now living here at Our Lady of Methuselah Abbey. I just wanted to let you know that Henry Lucens, who was President of the American Congress of 1778 and signer of the Declaration of Independence (the one that brought about your freedom from Great Britain and the King of England), was the original owner of this former rice plantation and his entire family is interred here. His great, great, great, great (not sure how many) nephew regularly visits as a retreatant. He knew and often went yachting with H.W. Lay, for which the company Frito-Lay, Inc. is named. He said Mr. Lay died of a disease.

I just wanted to say hello and let you know that I have connections if you ever decide you want to "work in the rice business." Just call me; I might be able to help (smile!)

It may cost you a few cases of sausage and cookies, but we can negotiate that later. Happy New Year!

Sincerely,

Br. Rodney Odom

February 15, 2011

Dear Mary-Martha,

I received your letter. So happy to hear from you! The envelope was odd, but I guess that's the very delicate nature of airmail paper. It took a month to get here. I see you went to Amsterdam or someplace like that on your way to South America. I said to myself, this letter is screaming Soap Opera style story. How would the storyline go? "Her plane landed in Amsterdam, she had lunch and talked business over coffee and relaxed with a view of the canals. She would have to be back in the States by evening to take her daughter to the ballet." So I hear you climb mountains now? Well, all I can say is keep at least one leg and one arm on the ground/wall/cliff at all times. Your poor mom is freaking out over here (Quiet! don't tell her I told you!) I said to your mom, "I thought Mary-Martha hurt her ankle?" She answered, "She did." So then I asked, "so-how can she climb a mountain?" and she said, "This is what kids do nowadays (throwing both hands up)!" Anyway, we know you are responsible, but your poor "mommy" is at home worried. So give her a little break from all the action-movie stuff, okay? I worry about her. I didn't mention to her the U.S. Congressional investigations into the rapes occurring with Peace Corp volunteers. She already thinks you might get kidnapped during the elections there!

She bought the monastery pizza before Lent! Wasn't that nice of her? (The brothers had a tradition of eating pizza on Fat Tuesday, the day before Lent. Who doesn't love pizza!) I will be doing a 60 day fast of sweets for 20 days plus Lent. Wish me luck. I don't want to be controlled by chocolate for the remainder of my life. I discovered in this monastery that I am ruled by so many things I would never have guessed were possible. So at times, life is an all-out war against my nasty habits. I concluded that we yearn for so many things but never know until they are gone! Next is fasting from pizza. Oh, the pain and agony ahead (smile!)

January: One of Methuselah's very active volunteers (Gail) has a son sailing from Guam to Asia. And their boat was three and a half days overdue to a Filipino port. It turns out they lost power and were adrift. It is on all the news channels and in newspapers. The only woman on board had a cell phone, and when they came within range for its use, she called her husband with their exact latitude and longitude. In the meantime, two helicopters and three airplanes failed to turn up anything. They did eventually find them alive and healthy. It is terrible all the stress mothers go through worrying about their children! But all the brothers like Gail because she is friendly and sews all our clothing for free. The coast guard out of Guam complained that the people did not adequately prepare for going to sea. They had no emergency communications, no extra food, etc. So you ought to remember that Missy, when you go off climbing giant mountains and things like that. Stop having everyone worried from all your crazy stunts.

Update: Pontius Pilot left us. (Pontius Pilot was a candidate for monastic life at Methuselah. He visited several times and expressed serious interest in monastic life.) He is from the Washington, D.C., area. He had some personal financial issues to deal with before trying to enter. My guess is he won't be back. Another monastic guest is month to month until he leaves forever. I mentioned in my last letter that he wanted the flexibility to compose music full-time, and thus he won't enter Methuselah. He says he wants to stay here longer to take care of personal business before moving back. The guy from Croatia is disgusted with monastic life. He's going back to Croatia. We think he is just not ready. That leaves Fr. Bartholomew and me as Postulants. I feel I am here to stay. I am older now, and this way of life is my "career." If I were 10 years younger, I might find something else more interesting, but this is my only real goal in life at 45. In life outside the monastery, there are many attractive distractions. Still, seeking a closer relationship with God is my sincere and authentic focus (in or out of the monastery). As of this moment, I think of the life I left behind as over.

Miguel from Mexico is starting as an observer again. He was here for three months earlier this year. But, at 20 years old, he is still discerning a call. He thinks he wants to be a priest. He can be both monk and priest. Your mom told me you are exploring Religious life. I can easily see you as a Religious. Whatever you decide, I think someone with your presence is hard to find, and any organization would be lucky to have you. I mean that sincerely. That is one of the reasons I write to support you.

We have a theology class with a priest named Fr. Paul. I think he is semi-retired and staying at the monastery [he passed away about year after I left the monastery, May He Rest in Peace!]. He is a well-known theologian. Through him, I am learning words like hamartiology. We have six chapters to read and two papers to write, and it's all filled with words like hamartiology – Oh, please have mercy on us! I hope I spelled it correctly.

Ursula retired. I miss her already. We had a special retirement dinner at the store sponsored by some volunteers. We had meat and pie and all other kinds of tasty things! I took a few pictures with her. She is good to us, and it is too bad she left. She said, "I just realized I am not 35 anymore, and it was time to stop working so much." I think she is about 70 years old. Your mom was not there, but they are close so that she will see Ursula regardless of parties with meat and pie. Angel runs the store now. Angel is intelligent and experienced, and she can handle it. I think until it tires her out, she will enjoy the job. She also gets some help from volunteers.

I guess by now, you have heard that the governments of Tunisia and Egypt are overthrown! According to the news, the police were harassing a street vendor in Tunisia, and (from the stories I read) he was so impoverished and unable to support his family he set himself on fire. People used YouTube, Twitter, and Facebook to spread the news worldwide. Soon after, unrest spread throughout North Africa and the Middle East. After eighteen days of protest, Egypt's Mubarak is now gone, and there is unrest in Syria and Iran.

By the way, don't be sad. Your mom told me you two made a pact. It's sweet, mommy-daughter stuff. She loves you a lot! Also, I know you have email troubles and that your insufficient email account fills quickly.

Warm Regards to Mary-Martha,

Rodney
Rodney@Methuselahabbey.org

1234 Methuselah Abbey Rd
Monk City, SC 29333

Welcome to Monastic Life! – So Many Abbots

So Many Abbots

When we visited the Sisters of Mercy Convent in Belfast, NC, we had two sessions with the Abbot of Education Abbey in which he spoke to us about monastic life. And in one of the sessions, he spoke of the number of Abbots in a monastery. He said people think there is only one Abbot in a monastery, but that is not always so. He said sometimes there are sixteen Abbots in a monastery. He spoke symbolically about how we as monks tend to become our own self-designated Abbot and start to make decisions for ourselves and others around us. We begin to take on the Abbot's role informally based on our own choices.

When you have not entirely included in your thinking that you, in the practice of obedience, need permission from the Abbot or someone formally designated by the Abbot to act in some way, you will eventually take on the role of Abbot.

It is not uncommon for someone new in a monastery to "decide the direction" when someone really needs to contact the Abbot and obtain guidance and permission. For example, take the case of spying. The Trappist monastery's teachings indicate that when I see you doing things that are not with the monastery's rules, I should, at the appropriate time, inform you that your behavior is not proper. The teachings do not indicate that I should set up a scenario where I can collect evidence of your wrong-doings and then tell others that you should not be doing such things. The teachings do not indicate that I should, on my own, try to teach you a lesson about violating the rules of the monastery. But this happens, and it happens often.

Security is another example. I always had a problem with my appetite. And it was not uncommon for me to go and eat when no one was looking. But the people in charge of the meals never came to me and said, you are eating when you are not supposed to be. They never told me to go to the Abbot and talk to him about my issues. Instead, it seemed they approached me as if a criminal. And I was "reported" to the Abbot in scenarios such, "he was taking cheese without permission."

There are so many situations where a person can "assign themself" Abbot and take upon themselves the Abbot's responsibility. In situations like these, we do not guide the new person. The Abbot is not adequately informed of problems in the monastery, and the "investigator" is again designating himself as Abbot. I suspect this contributes to the chaos in the organization in an unhealthy way.

March 20, 2011

Hi Mary-Martha!

Or should I say, Sister Mary? I had to write to let you know that the Canadians have undercut the prices of your erectile dysfunction pills! And if you don't lower your price, I will take my business elsewhere (smile!) I have a junk email promoting fake medication coming from your email account address! Someone has access to your account! **Update:** My Lenten fast is doing quite fine, thank you- especially since your mom cut off her "secret" library chocolate supply - !@#%& ^%@! Why are all the secret candy suppliers Catholic! Also, we do not elect a new Abbot for another year and a half. That is quite a while! If I could mail you a few Twizzlers, I would. It might help you feel better. I enclosed in this letter chapter three from a book on dreams. It will guide your thoughts as you experience life there—my advice: Pay attention to your dreams. Dreams help you understand the life going on around you and within you. I hypothesize that some parts of you (us) don't have access to a mouth, ears, or other senses. And those parts express themselves in different ways, like dreams. They are calling out for attention - our attention. So write your dreams down for later interpretation. I think "you" or "your dreams" communicate to you more clearly as you learn to communicate with yourself in this way. I always get another brother here to interpret mine. Like Joseph of the Jewish scripture, sold into slavery, he interprets dreams well and immediately. Also, for your reading pleasure, I include a copy of a theology assignment from one of our classes. I thought you might need some help getting to sleep (smile)!

Now, to get to the fascinating letter you emailed! I give you my opinion. Based on my experience and what I have read in books. So that's all I will offer, but it might be helpful. You and I share much in common. I am not as social as you seem to be, but the comments you made might very well have been coming from me!

I say, welcome to the world of contemplation. Welcome, O wonderful Mary-Martha, to the darker sides of the force. Welcome to a taste of the inner world that will get louder and louder as you spend more time alone. All I can say is no matter what thoughts come up, stay focused on Jesus!

When I first came to Methuselah, I used to look forward to being off on Sunday when we would not have so much activity (no work). But then came Monday morning! On Mondays, I found myself surrounded by dark feelings, a sort of mental grayness or sadness. Whatever you do, please find a way to tolerate this mental haze until you can read more about it. Don't think of it as something wrong with you! Here is what one religious psychologist said: Depression (if that is what you are experiencing) results from repressed anger. Anger naturally occurs when you frustrate yourself. Frustration occurs when you are denied something you want or have something you love / like taken away. Allow these feelings until you learn not to repress them anymore. I find it goes away with meditation. I would email you some stuff if I thought you would ever get the email? So I won't.

So in other words, and in a certain way, depression is good. All this is a sign that you are paying more attention to your inner world and your emotions, and now you can act (meditation). I recommend starting a meditation routine. I used to say the prayer "Hail Mary, full of Grace" when I first woke up in the morning. It was my prayer to help me deal with my mental state. Waking eventually got better with time. I believe yours will also as you learn to allow yourself to be deprived of certain social situations [In her case, the condition never improved.]

Sadness is less of a condition, and I suspect, is more temporary. I wish I could comment on social networks, but I have never had the problem. I have never needed to socialize with more than a few close people. Sadly, television was my company. And while I did have "social activity," it was usually alone or forced (with someone else). You seem like a nice enough person. Ask someone whose opinion you trust why they don't socialize with you. But be prepared for the truth. And keep it private. If they think you are "too religious," you should learn to do without frequent socializing with these people. Mary-Martha, I hate to say it, but you seem to have a specific drive toward authenticity that others don't seem to have - at least from what I can see. So it is up to you to build the determination and focus on tolerating these discomforts until your heaven "or joy" breaks through to you in a more pronounced way - opinion only. Meditation, Prayer, the Eucharist, and Scripture are my primary focus. Other good books (not the Red Shoe Diaries) will help you understand your serious plight.

Many people are down on marriage nowadays. Be careful about writing off marriage. If you were here in person, I would tell you my more intimate thoughts. But remember, marriage is a Sacrament. It is meant to bring you closer to God. With the right one, it should be very, very meaningful.

Listen to your dreams, pay attention to your habits, and read. What do you read already? What you do already is what you like and might lead you to a vocation. Also, acquire a decent book or audio on Christian meditation. I would send you what I use, but I don't know how or if you have a Compact Disc player? Oh yes, don't let the energy of youth keep you from focusing and staying in one place for a lengthy period. Your choice of the Peace Corp was for a sound reason. And to me, it sounds like your answers are coming to you. These feelings are not all pleasant feelings but accurate indicators to help you. Don't let your energy prevent you from tolerating the Journey. Nowadays, people don't have to get married, and they don't have to do the same job for 40 years. There is an entire trainload of career opportunities for younger folks. But it does not mean that marriage and lifestyles of this sort are not for you. Develop these skills: Focus (on Jesus) in the face of discomfort and pain. Determination (get an excellent but tedious habit like building houses with toothpicks to overcome inner resistance to focus, and use it to develop a listening heart. (With Grace from God, the quiet and solitude of your situation will do it for you.) Your guardian angel and Mary will take care of the rest. Also, pray the Rosary all the time because Mary will come to your aid when needed.

I was pleased to get your letter. I like to hear from you. Don't sweat over responding to me now that I know you receive the mail that I send you. I am okay...be good!

Sincerely,

Br. Rodney

April 16, 2011

Dear Mary-Martha,

Happy Belated Easter!

When I talk to Father T. about your mom, I always call her Ann, but he corrects my pronunciation. I say if she keeps buying us pizza, it can be Princess Ann! Now let me start this letter by stating that I wore the banana hat for the first time one Sunday as I went walking/exercising. It was outrageous. Cars were slamming on brakes as they passed by going to the flower gardens. People wanted to reach out and rub my head. On a less exaggerated note, I do think it is a lucky hat because I spoke to one of the guests as they were leaving to go to the store, and they asked me if I needed anything, and jokingly, I said, "bring me a bag of double cheeseburgers!" That beautiful lady and her mom came back and left a giant grocery bag filled with 10 double cheeseburgers - all for me! She wrapped them in a gift bag. I thanked her kindly, and again I was the envy of the monastery! The Prior let me have them. Everybody had a unique angle to try and get one of my burgers, but I just growled and showed my teeth, and they left me alone. All the monks eventually backed off. It is the way of the jungle!

I have not seen Mrs. Ann in a very long time. It's been about a month now. She sends an email from time to time, but that is about it. One day I told her that "I had my eye on her because she was always up to something!" I said, "all you Monk City people are always up to something!" After that, she stopped speaking to me? I don't know what happened. Well, she came into the library for Holy week, and I gave her a big hug. I told her some woman in South America ordered her a hug. So when I came back from work at lunch, she was still there with the puppy. And she got another hug. Then someone else came in, and she received another hug from them! Then the dog started growling at us. He was jealous and wanted all the hugging to stop. The little doggie is adorable! But when I came near him, he growled at me and rolled his eyes at me! I was hugging his mommy too much!

We have had two tornado watches and several bad storms. 40-something people were killed across the south from the same storm system. There were more tornadoes in just three days in Raleigh than expected in that whole month. One day, we were on a tornado watch several times until 9 p.m.. A tornado killed a father and his baby daughter while sleeping. A tree fell on the house. In another case, a tornado killed a mother and her son as they crouched in the corner of the house. Another tree fell. And that time, it happened during daylight hours. There were some positive stories too! A Lowes Home improvement store became a shelter. The people looked out the front door and saw a funnel cloud coming directly at the store. The manager quickly gathered everyone to the back of the store, where the walls are cinderblocks. The tornado proceeded to rip up the other parts of the store, and no one was hurt. The weather is wild now. Floods, tornadoes, and earthquakes, you name it, it is happening. Your mom ought to be worried about us, not you!

Up north and in the Midwest, they are getting horrendous rainstorms and the like. Rivers are overflowing their banks. But this is nothing compared to Japan: 9.0 Earthquake. 30,000 people are dead or missing, and whole towns are washed out to sea because of the tsunami that followed. Man-o-man is the planet 'Earth' going crazy! By now, you must have heard of the nuclear emergency in Japan. It is still going on because the tsunami ruined a nuclear plant. A guy's bodily remains washed up in California all the way from Japan! And low levels of radiation are now being detected in the U.S. due to global drifting air masses.

All is well here at Methuselah Abbey. Br. James is in Canada, but he should be back in six weeks. We are readying for Eastertime. But it will most likely be over by the time you read this. This year, I mailed 50 Easter cards to various people in my social circle. Being the Best-Looking Monk 2008, 2009, and 2010 keeps me very busy. And now, with the banana hat you gave me, there is no stopping me! We have many guests here for Easter. Fr. Mark gave us an excellent meal for the Last Supper. Just my opinion, but I think Jesus would have been quite satisfied. The Abbot is back from Columbia (visiting our Trappistine Sisters). One of the sisters made every brother a bookmark. HNO Rodney is my title: that means Hermano Rodney.

Please be careful. The news talked about two men and a woman hiking in the mountains near Iran. They didn't do anything wrong, but what these hikers didn't seriously consider was the behavior of the governments in Iran. The three were spotted and arrested. Now two are on trial as spies. A single woman alone there is not the same as a single woman alone here in the United States. In the end, you must live your own life and live it with the consequences.

As a follow-up to my last letter, I wanted to make additional comments (you never know when I might say something useful): First, I will pray for the girls in the school you teach. I love children, and I wish to help in my little way, but my prayers help in a better way because God has a different set of values than I do, and he can do a lot more than me by myself. I included some Christian Meditation techniques in this letter. I decided to send a hard copy for reuse. Very simple but helpful if you use it. There will be a test next Christmas on your progress! Also, on your general emotions that you notice when you are alone, I can say this is the opportunity of a lifetime for someone raring to do inner work and journey through self-discovery. I know you like to explore the outer world but don't waste this opportunity. Should you come back here, you may never get another chance like this one. Life here operates far too quickly and noisily. Even here in the monastery, it is hectic, and "being alone time" is rare.

Some of your social issues associated with talking to people on the phone, etc., are at least partially due to your own "self-talk." I say if you can overcome the fear of leaving Monk City and going all the way to Peru, South America, you can undoubtedly face your inner voices that say, "don't call and talk about anything with anyone." This kind of self-talk can be just as harmful as it is helpful. But you must be aware of it to be indeed free. Please, no bungee jumping in Peru (you don't need that kind of freedom), but ask the nuns or other more experienced women how you should go about socializing to eliminate some of the blind risk. It seems to me most of the risk in your situation is in what you don't know and not in what you do. People can tell you the best way to get around safely so that your mother doesn't die of worry.

And as for a vocation (and I'm not too fond of that word), as you learn yourself, your career will emerge. Saint Teresa of Avila wrote something similar (I don't remember exactly), but she wrote something like, if you don't know what you are meant to do, you have not yet learned yourself well enough. If you discover yourself haphazardly, so you will emerge randomly. If you learn purposefully, so you will emerge in that way. Meditation and prayer (ask and keep asking) will lead you the best way.

By the way, nowadays, there are plenty of Sisters who lead everyday lives "outside" the convent. They serve God in regular clothing, run hospitals, teach university classes, etc. but go back to group living at the end of the day. I don't know the history of the change to regular clothing. On the one hand, you are not supposed to be of our world (in it, not of it); on the other hand, you don't want violent treatment because of your differences. Just for your information, convents and monasteries purposefully lead dull, boring, repetitive, trivial lives. In these activities, you discover God in the fine details of life. But one should not live that lifestyle without regard for purpose. Now- I am inquisitive? How can you be someone other than a Nun, Contemplative, or lead some other type of Consecrated life and "give yourself completely to God?" I know it is possible, but please answer the question. I suspect with your heart being the way it is you will soon "fall in love." And that brings with it a whole host of other issues, especially if it is with the "wrong" person.

Vivian, the horticulturalist, is retiring in June. As you might know, we closed the Native Plant operation. I will post your address on the board, ask the monks to pray for the girls, and tell them you said hello! Maybe I will get a letter-writing competition! Competition be darned! It doesn't matter; I will forever be the best "letter-writer-ever"!

Be cool-- much love--stay safe,

Br. Rodney

Welcome to Monastic Life! – Which Opinion?

Do I accept the Mainstream Opinion, the Monastic One, Both or Neither?

In the year 2020, the greater society had many issues that influenced monastic practices. I am outside the monastic life and reflecting on my own experiences. From an outside social perspective, monastic life seems rear-facing. I assume it is that way because it appears to outsiders as very traditional. They see the monastic purpose as for an old-fashioned time that passed a long time ago. The actual practices are rooted in the repetition of ancient religious traditions. But it is focused on God, and God does not change. We change to orient to God. Thus, God is never out of date. Change is a unique circumstance that requires much prayer to process comfortably in monastic life. But monastic life is supposed to be an introduction to the heavenly way:

Yahweh passed by before him, and proclaimed, "Yahweh! Yahweh, a merciful and gracious God, slow to anger, and abundant in loving kindness and truth, keeping loving kindness for thousands, forgiving iniquity and disobedience and sin; and who will by no means clear the guilty, visiting the iniquity of the fathers on the children, and on the children's children, on the third and on the fourth generation. **Exodus 34:6-7.** [2]

I said, "My God, don't take me away in the middle of my days. Your years are throughout all generations. Of old, you laid the foundation of the earth. The heavens are the work of your hands. They will perish, but you will endure. Yes, all of them will wear out like a garment. You will change them like a cloak, and they will be changed. But you are the same. Your years will have no end. **Psalm 102:24-27.** [2]

While in the monastery, I encountered gender, racial, ethnic, sexual orientation, child protection, and inter-religious issues in some form. The monastery must maintain its "god-oriented" direction amid these intrusive, socially significant, evolving human issues. And how to do this properly is the subject of much conversation and prayer.

The mere separation of genders is a huge social issue today. It was not as much an issue in the past. And while many Religious see separation as an opportunity for self-denial, non-religious see it as an opportunity for gender discrimination. Female guests of the monastery give "speeches" during Mass because of gender limitations associated with homilies. They do not provide homilies as a priest would. This difference is a source of tremendous social friction for some people. The brothers recognize their frailty when dealing with gender. The brothers do not talk openly about it, but their behavior changes when women are present. I assume defending their hearts as well as their thoughts is a priority. And some visiting women take offense to this way. Gender equity is a prevalent theme nowadays. Society says you are not allowed to behave as if there is a difference.

As an example: we allow conversation in the kitchen for important business. Once a woman, and frequent volunteer at the monastery, offered to cook for the brothers when the cook was absent. It was a Sunday, and I happened to walk past the kitchen and glance inside. There she was surrounded by five or six monks, all talking and helping her out in the kitchen. She did not need that much help, and she knew her way around our kitchen. We glanced briefly at each other as I looked inside. Her facial expression indicated to me that she thought her presence was disruptive. She knew the support the brother offered was extraordinary.

We have new rules imposed on the monastery because of changes in the greater society's laws and direction. There is a greater social emphasis on child protection. The monastery is now certified as a "child-safe" zone. This new way limits who can permanently live at the monastery. Gender orientation is more prevalent in society. While gender orientation has been an issue inside the monastery for a long time, it has never been dealt with as openly as today. For example, the greater society now allows same-sex marriage. The monastery members must interact with all the people who come to the monastery in the same acceptable way. Having same-sex married couples visit the monastery presents a dilemma for some monks.

Society is constantly changing. But not all of it is changed for the better. Sometimes guidance is not clear. Sometimes direction is in contradiction to circumstance. Sometimes change comes from popularity and has nothing to do with holy righteousness. Sometimes change is forced. When the monastery voted to institute a Desert Day (except Compline, all community prayers are canceled in favor of personal prayer and contemplation). One of the senior monks protested. In his mind, we were neglecting community prayer. And while he was visibly upset about the change, we voted for the "Desert Day" anyway. I sometimes wonder if we were wrong to make such a radical change in the face of a long-held tradition. Then again some of the older monks remember the days when community prayer was divided between monks who labored and monks who participated in choir. They often say they did not become a monk who sings. They changed.

I learned much at Methuselah about the kindness of strangers. Br. Thomas' mother is an author of religious writings. She guided his foundation of faith, and here she was trying to help me a new catholic, even without my knowledge.

May 15, 2011

Mrs. V. Mary
333 Jerusalem Road
Sparkling Gems, City 12345

Dear Mrs. Mary,

Some time ago (quite a bit, if I recall), you purchased a subscription to Magnificat Magazine for a certain Postulant Rodney Odom of Our Lady of Methuselah Abbey. That person would be me! Since then, I have discovered that it is an excellent, high-quality gift not found in just any walk of life. I thank you for this gift. As people often say, it is better late than never to start using and reading this as a new member of the Roman Catholic Church.

I initially thought it was the Abbot who purchased the subscription for me. Back when it first started coming in the mail, I thanked him. Since he had no comment about it, I never confirmed that he purchased it for me. And with Abbots being so busy, he could have easily have forgotten he did order it for me. Then last month, I received one with a Spanish language cover, which made me look at it in more detail. In doing so, I discovered it was Br. Thomas's mother who purchased it as a gift. Ay Dios mio! Woe is me! What have I done!

Anyway, I have entered you as an applicant for the **Methuselah Abbey Double Cheeseburger Award** for your kindness. It is very prestigious. But I must warn you that it is very competitive. Even Pope John Paul II is one of many submissions who only made runner-up.

Sincerely,

Br. Rodney Odom

May 20, 2011

Dear Mary-Martha,

I am oh-so-sorry to hear of your illness. I was distraught. Not just because I was concerned for you, but also because your mom is something of a "dramatic." She had us thinking your life span was much more limited than we prefer (smile). But at least you made it back from Bolivia okay. And as I told your mother, there was a reason you didn't fall ill with a bunch of total strangers. We pray for your continued health. Please be proactive when you have a chance. I was hoping you could read up on issues associated with malaria. (I sent some emails. Yes- more emails from Br. Rodney.) Don't be like so many of us who are not thorough during severe illness, only to find out there is far more damage than initially thought.

You don't have to read all the emails (smile). That's why I put information in the subject line so you can choose which one to open. If you don't care about Princess Kate Middleton, the commoner, who married the prince with royal blood, then you can choose not to read it. A donor gave us English tea with their royal pictures on the package. Their marriage is all the rave in the U.S. news. People are making money off that marriage!

Hopefully, you will have time to look at and peruse the emails. There has to be some natural way to improve your situation in Peru? Your mother is very challenged emotionally by all this talk of illness. What I see going on from a distance (between you and your mother) is Mary-Martha is a responsible adult, and mom needs to chill and let her "baby" live her life and make mistakes - if that is what is going to happen. But remember, this is my opinion, and I felt comfortable giving it! However, all the monks expressed concern and pray for their "baby sister." They have known you since you were a baby, and to them, you will never grow up. I know you as a woman, and so my perspective is very different. I suspect everything will be fine for both you and your mother. And each of us can learn from our circumstances. I place updates on the bulletin board as you send them. Of course, I blackout all the counterfeit prescription drug sales information!

Surprise- I enter the Novitiate on May 31, 2011, the Feast of the Visitation of Mary. It's a Solemnity! I am thinking of changing my name to Br. Antony-Maria. Antony for "Antony of Egypt," a precursor to modern monasticism. They call him the father of monasticism and "Maria" for Our Lady of Guadeloupe. After I read about her apparition in Mexico in the 16th century, it deeply affected my understanding of Christianity and Catholicism. But that's all a secret! Please take it to your grave, or at least until it is official! And by the time you get this letter, it will be (smile!)

Photo: My mother Effie and I, attending a volunteer outing while she visited Methuselah in 2011. The picture was later used in a birthday card in 2014.

My family visited. I included a few pictures in this letter. I would have emailed it, but you would never see them because of your modem problem. All went well. We visited downtown Charles City. Kim (my sister) wanted to see the Slave Museum in Charles City. This one goal leads us all over the place for hours until someone finally gave us accurate directions. I ate meat. I drank a case of Diet Pepsi and didn't sleep for three days in a row. I had wine and a cigar too! My mom was happy to see me and find out that her son didn't join some strange cult in South Carolina and became some kind of a brainwashed catholic zombie. It would be best if you remembered my family is not Roman Catholic. These practices are all foreign to them.

Photo: My sister Kim and her husband James in downtown (historic) Charles City, SC during the visit to Methuselah Abbey in the year 2011.

My sister and I had our usual loud and offensive arguments about religion and how one should live. You might like her because she is very active like you. She is always traveling somewhere. Her husband James (also known as J.C.) told me he was almost locked up in South America because Kim tried to bring some plant back in her suitcase. The police drug dogs thought it was drugs, and they pulled them aside, and he got frisked and questioned. He is still happy he is married to her, but he is now much more thoughtful about my sister's ways! I do love her, though. I suspect, were it not for my sister, my mother would never have visited. At her age, she simply is not going to travel by herself. And for some reason, my dad refused to come with them. I had fun and calmed down within hours after their arrival. They met quite a few people, including the Abbot, Pam, and a few brothers. The Abbot had breakfast with us on Sunday at Saint Peter's. They met Pam during the library tour. I left a few mysterious gifts for all the people in formation (smile).

On a fresh note: Fr. Bartholomew has Visa problems (from Asia). The monastery worked with an immigration lawyer to get him an extension to stay here. Still, he must change a specific immigration code to remain in the U.S. Otherwise, he will have to leave, which would ruin his Postulancy. An experienced lawyer in specific religious situations is helping. We are a little worried, but we asked God to please handle this. We don't know why they sent him here under such limited circumstances. I figured they wanted him to have a way out if he changed his mind. They didn't want him to leave. He is sharp and would make a fine addition to our somewhat crumbling monastic dynasty.

On an even fresher note: Everybody (observers, guests, etc.) is leaving. Miguel decided the contemplative life is not for him. He wants to be an active religious and become a priest. Velasquez (who went to St Joseph's in Philadelphia and came here from Charlotte!) says he needs more time for prayer, and this is too active an atmosphere (he thinks it involves too much running around.) I always agree with that comment. He wants to come back for the summer. The people here have taught me that this is the nature of monastic life. By the way, I am from Philadelphia and came here from Charlotte too! Titus left for good, then called back a month later and said it was a mistake to leave. But the Abbot is making him go through a few things before accepting him back. Br. Thomas will visit his father for a week because his dad's dementia is getting much worse. He wants some final moments with his father before the illness disables him too much. We have had two long-term guests leave since Easter. It is empty around here now! But all in all, we are surviving. We have some theology classes coming up this summer that should be interesting. And we are supposed to have a new group of guests come in the June-July time frame.

Vivian, the horticulturalist, is leaving us for good on May 24. I will go to her potluck dinner and make a card for her. She is always nice. There is no political theater with her; she's a no-nonsense type of person. She seems very efficient and organized! I cannot say the same for some of us monks! So while I look forward to this expression of "love," I don't know who we will turn to with technical mushroom questions. We should be okay in general, but who knows! That Ursula and now Vivian is gone; all my sources for chocolate are disappearing! Ursula used to let me get a snickers bar from time to time from the store. Sue and Angel are still here. They are always nice to the brothers! Sue is having surgery and will be out for a while. So she will be another person gone, at least for a period!

Br. James should be back from Canada soon (Mid-June), which will be a terrific boost of help for us. We are all tired of so many people coming and going. But this is the life of having a family of 20 people.

By the way, I hope you are doing well in every way. I am not ordinarily so open by mail, but you are in South America. What's a person to do? I don't have a lot to say this time except take care of yourself.

Sincerely,

Br. Antony-Maria, O.C.S.O. – Novice

May 22, 2011

Kimberly Marie and James Carmichael
1234 North Seventh Street
Philadelphia, Pennsylvania 12345

Br. Antony-Maria Odom
Our Lady of Methuselah Abbey
1234 Methuselah Abbey Road
Monk City, SC 29333

Dearest Kim Marie and James,

I write this letter with complete gratitude in mind. I wish to thank you for taking the time from your busy schedule to visit me down here at Methuselah. I appreciate all the personal effort and resources to fly here to say Hello! One cannot put a value on such demonstrations of love. I am also happy you all got home safely.

It was genuinely nice to see you, Kim (and Mom). J.C. (not that I expected the worse), but I enjoyed you being here too! Happy mom attended one of the prayers and a Mass.

I pray for you all to heal from all your many auto collisions. I hope all worked out well with P.C.A. I love you all, and it was difficult to see you leave. But I went back to my room and ate chocolate cake and drank soda for four hours or so and felt much better as a result! Yes, munching on Bar-B-Q pork ribs would have been much better, but I ask myself, after all, you have been through, why should I hold a grudge? I will not hold it against you! Just gratitude. Yep, all the dreams of savory B.B.Q. are behind me now!

It is good that I still have some time to get myself straight. That is to say, I am glad Judgment Day was not yesterday. I am still here getting up a 2:20 a.m. every morning. Please tell Laiene and Maurice that I said hello! And maybe next time they will be able to visit too! Please tell T.J. and Tori I have been trying to call and say hello! They never respond!

Love your brother,

Keith – Anthony-Maria

P.S. I will be robed in white by May 31. It will be on The Feast of the Visitation of Our Lady.

Regular visitors to the monastery often become your friends. If they are not personal friends with you, they are close to the monastic lifestyle and thinking. But sometimes, they are not just friends of the monastery but are personally involved in your monastic journey. You might connect with them through religious interests that you both have in common. They come to you for conversation. Sometimes they offer prayer for you and offer you gifts. Some of the most valued gifts were a first-class relic of Saint Pio, a leather-bound diary of Saint Faustina, and an old version of the Miraculous Medal. The Abbot let me keep them.

June 21, 2011

Dear Mary,

I hope all is well with you and your family. I also hope addressing you as Mary is appropriate? Anything else seems awkward at this point. I thank you for your note. Yes, please take our prayer and intentions with you on your journey. I prayed for Our Lady of Methuselah Abbey every day for six months. And I also prayed two novenas for the help of Saint Maria Faustina. I stopped two days ago and received your note. Based on your message, I should continue the daily prayer. I certainly appreciate your commitment.

I send these photos because I know you will appreciate them. We have an older color printer, so the quality is not quite what it could be. I am no longer Rodney, as you can see. I have entered the Novitiate.

I enjoyed seeing you at Lent and look forward to your future visit. Your presence is powerful. In 2008 I dedicated myself to Mary during Lent for the first time using that same book you used. Subsequently, I started doing so in October. Maybe I should change back to Lent? I will switch back to dedicating myself during Lent.

Please and always feel free to communicate with me anything you deem necessary; I regard you as a kind, generous, open, and beautiful person and truly appreciate your presence. Also, feel free not to respond to this note; I am not trying to burden you.

Sincerely,

Br. Anthony-Maria
(Antony of Egypt-Our Lady of Guadalupe)

Deron is my first cousin on my mother's side of our family. He is approximately my younger sister's age and was turning 40. Some consider that a special age. So I wished him a special birthday.

June 22, 2011

Dear Deron,

I heard about the passing of your grandmother. I pray for you and your wife during this time of grief. I sent a letter to Michelle and Aunt Hilda. Please tell your wife I said hello. I know she knew your grandmother well.

Mrs. Barnes was always very nice to me. When I came to your house for dinner during one of the holidays, I was surprised that she remembered me! 97 years old is a very long time for a person to live!

The Trappist monks of Our Lady of Methuselah have offered up prayers for your family and hers. I guess now is not a good time to say HAPPY 40th BIRTHDAY? But I'll do it anyway...

Love (your cousin Keith),

Br. Anthony-Maria Odom

July 22, 2011

Dear Mary-Martha,

I live in a monastery, correct? And, of course, monks rarely ever change anything. Monks rarely, if ever, throw anything away. So someone places an item on a desk in a room. It might sit in that same spot for years or even decades before being moved again. But everywhere I go in the monastery, I see the need to change something! So living in a monastery is so appropriate for me, who came here looking for routine. I saw the need to adopt a different way of being, and monastic living is my adopted form. Anyway, I am adjusting as best I can. I suspect it will take a very long time to adjust to this way of life. It is a lifestyle that focuses on spiritual methods and not earthly ones. So from my perspective, the lifestyle seems inefficient and wasteful. In other words, this lifestyle is not focused on material productivity. The focus is on what you are thinking and doing with each moment. "Do not rush, do not walk so swiftly, settle down and experience being alive this moment." I need to be more in tune with the Spirit than responding to the urges of my desires. Let me give you an illustration from my mind:

What if I know there is a better way to grow mushrooms, and I know for a fact that this new method would save the monastery money. What should I do? Should I implement my unique approach and save us money and tell the boss later? Or should I discuss it with all the relevant people, gather all the significant opinions, tiptoe around all the people who object to this new idea, and risk waiting months only for it to be pushed aside and probably forgotten. Or should I relegate the concept to the future? They say, "don't worry about that now, we'll deal with that new method later when we get some extra time." The monastic way would have my desire take second place to obedience. Obedience requires me to act with permission, regardless of what's at stake (except human life or some emergency of that nature). My new idea is forgotten. Ideas about productivity are secondary to monastic practices.

Another illustration:

Br. Ezekiel might have a small gadget in the copy room. It has been sitting in the same position on the counter in the copy room for the two years I have been here. I could use that gadget, and I know no one else needs it. But out of respect for the owner, I ask can I use that gadget; it would help us immensely with the mushrooms! Someone answers no! They say, "That is Br. Ezekiel's Gadget." And I say, "but it has been sitting there for two years and it doesn't work the way it is needed anyway?" So I say, "Br. Ezekiel can I use that gadget in the copy room?" He answers, "No, we may need that later for sunbathing at the South Pole! You never know when we may go to the South Pole!" The answer he gives makes a point. However, it demonstrates how monastic thinking is different from typical everyday practical methods of managing life's issues. In other words, just let it be; you cannot have everything you claim to need.

In any case, love it or leave it; this is monastic life. As a new person, I need to focus on saying "no" internally to all the little things I am inspired to do, and in time this is supposed to bring about a new "me." I will have new thinking, new behavior, and be a person who is less self and materially oriented.

By the way, how are you, Mary-Martha? Did I mention to you that I am okay? I hope all is well with you and your classes. I hope your peanuts are fine also. I am jealous! I like gardening or growing food myself. I had a small garden when I was in Philadelphia. I raised two kinds of tomatoes, lettuce, a small amount of corn that the birds ate before I could get to them. I grew squash, mixed greens, and some other stuff I cannot remember. My brother, who worked for the city, brought me some horse manure. Everything exploded with growth.

The mushrooms here are doing well. But it is hot, so we encounter a little trouble with the internal building temperatures affecting the production levels. It's nothing Br. Thomas (who's has a new name) cannot handle! We started growing a new type of mushroom called Shiitake. We buy the spawn from a company in Pennsylvania. They develop the mycelium (early stage of mushroom growth) in a wood-chip mixture. Then they ship them as refrigerated bricks for others to finish growing and sell. We soak the bricks in water overnight and put them in the growing rooms. They fruit in about nine days (this is our first try, so as I write, who knows?)

Someone else has taken over our monastic website. We have much more information and faster updates now. The local Charles City Archdiocese newspaper used a picture of me from the monastic ceremony. (I sent the one in my last letter.) They have a great shot of me kneeling in front of the Abbot, showing the top of my head. I look like Darth Vader giving my oath to the evil Sith Lord. Guess what! I ate the last of your mom's Snickers Bars gift from Christmas. They didn't last as long as I would have liked. Well, I did share with the other monks. It would be wrong for me not to. But now the coffers are all but empty! That's okay. I'll be fasting soon, and it is better not to have it around. I need to develop a "new" perception of meals, eating, and food. Ultimately my goal is to be free to take it or leave it. Not to be a slave to so many delicious foods (pizza, burgers, lasagna, etc.)

Titus is back from Maine. Hopefully, he will stay this time. He is a Postulant now. We have two novices and two Postulants. I understand that this is very unusual for a Trappist monastery. God hears your prayers! I tried to explain to the monks that this is why some change is necessary! So we can continue to improve and increase. But all they want to talk about is the new sports cars we will buy if we don't spend so much money having all these extra people around (smile). Did you know Br. Gabriel left? He has since come back to the States from Africa, and (I hear) he is supposed to be at Holy Spirit Abbey in Atlanta. Pray for him too!

We have the volunteer/employee picnic, and we are inviting Yogi the Bear. His agent said he is not religious, and our picnic baskets are not to his liking. So we don't expect him to attend. Boo-Boo, the sidekick, might be able to make it! What's that? Have you never heard of Yogi the Bear? That was a cartoon that is a little before your time. In any case, in addition to Boo-Boo, a hundred or so other people are sure to be there. We should have meat on that day! Btw (by the way), your mom reached 1000 hours as a volunteer here and is getting the Big Prize from the monastery- a 6-speed, 350 Horsepower, Yellow, Chevrolet Corvette Convertible, stick shift. Not the entire car this time! Just the stick shift!

I made your mother a dozen homemade greeting cards like the sample I sent you. The cards have different pictures from the CD-ROM I conveniently borrowed from you. She said I could keep the images, so I made some for my mom first, then I made some for you, but you can't get them or use them, so I gave them to your mom. She might be too embarrassed to use them since our color printer was manufactured by: Prehistoric-Brontosaurus Incorporated and scrapes a white line through the printing. It ruins everything I print. But, hopefully, it is the thought that counts!

You already know about Pam and Ted (or maybe you don't). They are gone for the entire summer. They are babysitting all summer. But Pam says her daughter is dating a nice man looking for the same thing as her daughter. So pray for them too!

I hope you like the paper that I wrote. It was 30 years in the making. I asked Fr. Luke, Br. Vineyard, and Fr. David to look it over. I made a few more changes. Yes! I started thinking about the subject of this paper when I was a teenager of about fourteen years old, and only here at the monastery did it all come together. I am a grown man, and I was crying tears of relief. When I completed it as part of a class assignment, it felt as if an enormous weight was lifted from my being. Do you know what it is like to be free from such a self-appointed task that takes 30 years to complete? No wonder people think I am strange! Or at least my sister Kim certainly does.

Also, as I write, Br. Dominic is in the hospital, but we expect him to recover fully. Also, we have another new community member. A retired Bishop from Florida lives here now. He comes to the prayers seven times a day, but instead of mushroom work, he is writing books.

Not much else going on here. So I guess this is it for now! Good-bye!

Br. Anthony-Maria (Rodney)

August 15, 2011

Dear Mary-Martha (Happy Belated Feast of the Assumption!),

It has come to our attention that you have an undeclared income of $U.S. 70,000,000.00 from an unknown account in Peru, South America. Based on an Internal Revenue Service investigation, you have not paid the taxes due on $U.S. 69,999,910.00 of that undeclared amount of $U.S. 70,000,000.00. Our calculations indicate you owe the U.S. Government $U.S. 34,999,999.50 plus interest. Credit Cards must be pre-approved by telephone before any transaction for amounts over $U.S. 1,000,000.00. Please contact us at your earliest possible convenience to arrange payment. Have a nice day. Mary-Martha, do you see what happens when you accept millions of dollars from some strange account in Nigeria? I know you wanted to help some wealthy general's son? But these situations do not ever go well! [*Popular email scams of that time were people claiming to sell authentic alternatives to pills for male impotence. And helping a wealthy Nigerian, usually a socially elite person, by holding millions of dollars in your bank account until they can get out of the country to claim it.*]

Anyway, how are you? Just for your information, I am cheating! I am typing this letter while listening to some old Dr. Dre on Youtube. I am just awful! You never know what I might be up to in this monastery! I have a different personality in every pocket! One day, I am wandering into the library for books on Mary, the next day, I listen to **Summertime** by Will Smith. After that, I might move onto the chapel for meditation. In some ways, all this errant behavior is a distraction from my struggle to do what I am supposed to do.

I talked about the Shiitake Mushrooms we started growing when I last wrote. We sold our first 132 pounds! Next week the Abbot, Br. Theo (Thomas changed his name), and Br. Mark are going up to Philadelphia to investigate more details on the Mushrooms and learn more about the people who sell them. No, I won't go. It's okay. I might be tempted not to come back, and then they would have to report me missing. I might make a run for it! The truth is you must be tame to stay in this life, and until that happens, I am at risk of being a "runner." Never have I paid so much attention to something as the people's homes across the river. At night I sit and stare at the quiet of the houses as the lights go on and off in their living rooms and wonder what it would like to be back in Philadelphia. I hear the people's dogs barking and feel a little homesick! I listen to the trains going by at night and remember my rides on Amtrak going home to Charlotte or Philadelphia.

Let me tell you about something you might find interesting. It is a bit X-rated so prepare yourself. I had not left the monastery in about six months, and I went out to get my driver's license. I let mine expire before I came to Methuselah because I didn't think I needed it anymore. When I went to the Department of Motor Vehicles, I found that I had to take two exams, the written or computer test and the physical or driving test with an actual car. The driver's test, as you know, is under the watchful eye of an inspector. But I also found that no matter what, I needed to have possession of my official Pennsylvania Drivers Record from the state; otherwise, I would have to wait six months to take the driving part of the exam. To the state of South Carolina, this record was proof that I already passed the permit test in the State of Pennsylvania. So we left the monastery (Fr. Thomas and I) to go to Walmart and run other errands before going back to the monastery.

Since I had not been out of the monastery for some time, Fr. Thomas took me to the Subway Restaurant for pizza. (Yes, pizza at the Subway sandwich restaurant, and it was rather tasty.) On the way back, we stopped at a local ice cream place. This store receives our local deliveries when our monastery orders are too small for the truck to drive the entire trip to Monk City. We entered the store, and what do I see? two young ladies dressed in swimwear (bikinis), eating hamburgers! I looked at Fr. Thomas and said, this is not funny! And he laughed. Here I am in an ice cream store, and women are sitting around practically naked? That sort of thing affects me both physically and psychologically. We sat there talking to the store owner (a lovely lady, by the way), and these young ladies casually walked around the store like it was the beach, filling sodas and getting ketchup and the like. I could not believe what I was encountering. It seemed surreal. Back at the monastery, I told everybody about this. Maybe you'd have to be a guy to understand? Even having been celibate for 10 years now, my hormones are potent under certain circumstances. Hormone-driven behavior is a little embarrassing! And from that point forward, I was "super" self-conscience of my body movements. These people have every right to do what they were doing. Still, it is a reminder to me of the fact that monastic life is not to be taken lightly. It is stressful in ways that you don't realize until you encounter a similar situation. Monastic life is genuinely a demanding swim upstream and, to me, a significant personal sacrifice. Being in a monastery and away from the world is far less distracting and easier to manage mentally. I am being honest about the unique circumstances occurring here.

But I have found that people of my generation are a little behind yours in acceptable behavior. In other words, we (men of my age) often make younger women angry when we think our opinions out loud. I never realized that more than when I was in K.G.S.B. at the University of Pittsburgh (the business school). Some of the younger women in my class seemed angry. Conversing with some of them was a nervous act because you didn't want to offend them with inappropriate speech. But what is natural for me could turn out to be offensive to them.

Meanwhile, back at the ranch, we are jammed-packed with guests. We have five Monastic Guests and two Observers. Most of the people are friendly. One guy is on retreat before starting the Seminary to be a priest. Being a priest is a huge responsibility. What I read about being a priest is that you don't know how big a responsibility it is until you get to heaven! Another guy is here from a Zen Buddhist monastery. He converted to Catholicism recently. He is hard to talk to because he won't let you finish your sentences before cutting you off. He speaks as if he knows what you are about to say, and he tries to finish your sentences. He is a business person and doesn't have "time to waste" waiting for you to talk when he already knows what you are about to say. If he comes here, he'd better get used to letting people finish their sentences. I am talking to Fr. David about the idea of becoming a priest. But that is a SECRET because I am not sure if they will even let me or if I am sure if that is my call. I am discerning. One of my concerns is that I am something of a maverick. And not an easy or willing follower. I am an odd fellow. How many people do you know would work on a philosophical idea for 30 years? And I only recognized that I was seeking a solution to this problematic issue until after it was satisfactorily resolved. I can only surmise that it was deeply subconscious. I suspect conformity is an essential part of the priesthood. Anyway, enough about that because it would mean going to Seminary for three years, which would mean I would need to be in Solemn vows! And those vows are at least another four more years out. And, of course, the monastery would need to spare me at such a late age. And at 50, only God could make that happen.

And speaking of old, my relative was sick recently and was in the Intensive Care Unit for seven days with a nasty infection. They had to use an antibiotic drip to her body for three days. The doctors don't know where she caught it. She found she could not stand up one day, didn't want to eat, her blood pressure dropped low, and she had a strange bump on her bottom. They took her into surgery, cut her bottom open, and found the infection. She is back at work now, but that scared my people, who already lost my older brother Tim in 2008 when he was 45 years old. It is genuinely an appropriate situation that I am so good-looking! I spend all my time looking in the mirror and never do anything to have health problems! Also, I recently found out my cousin Michelle had an intense asthma attack and was hospitalized for four days. My family does not tell me anything until well after it happens! I always find out what happened long after the emergency occurs. Still, I pray for them constantly.

The Squirrels Attack! Br. Joseph feeds the squirrels. He gives them used, almost empty jars of peanut butter. That, of course, brings the raccoons, crows, and other creatures. That is not a problem. The problem is that the squirrels see other monks and think we are him. We humans all look alike to them! And then they start following us around, expecting food. We have a blind squirrel here. And it is excruciating to ignore him when he starts following you. But I am sorry, I have no peanut butter and won't ever have any. How heartbreaking is it to have a blind squirrel following you needing food? So you have to threaten them in French or something! Because they, apparently, don't understand English! Miguel fears all of them. He will run! Especially when he sees a raccoon. It's bizarre, I'm from the city and know nothing about these creatures, but I am getting used to snakes, raccoons, and more. He grew up in rural Mexico and ran scared at the sight of any of them!

I saw your mom on August 17, and she told me you cut all your hair off because it was falling out. I hope you take pictures! I must see this! The photos of the young South American girls you showed us were a sweet bunch! Your mom is excited about visiting you in September (or is it October now?)

Well, we are collecting donations for our new retreat house. And we are building a Columbarium. It will also be helpful for income. We already have several burial sites on the monastic grounds. We are making quite a few changes. The only problem with monastic life is that you make changes, and two weeks later, monks have reverted to the way they used to be! Monks do not like change. And we need constant reinforcement to implement any change. In other words, we must be reminded constantly of the new rules, or we won't change. It is challenging to live with 70 and 80 year-olds because they have all the power and influence, and they see little or no reason to change anything. Br. Vineyard asked about you. The monks pray for you all the time!

Sincerely,

Br. Anthony-Maria.

Welcome to Monastic Life! – Who Am I?

Who Am I?

Like any other part of a person's life, monastic life fills you with surprises when one is paying attention. One situation that surprised me was the psychological testing required to enter formally. Once I reached a specific part of the enlistment process, I was required to sit and be evaluated by a psychologist. I have been interrogated to screen for background checks while in the military. Still, I was rarely required to be personally profiled for anything by a psychologist, at least not while knowing about it.

I remember sitting for two or three oral sessions with the psychologist. I was also required to take tests on paper. The testing took place over several days and was hundreds of questions. Once mailed in and evaluated, my final session took place. Based on the results, I was considered chiefly normal.

The psychologist said he was concerned about one section because I barely answered enough questions. I am not a trained psychologist. And if my mind could not substantiate an answer, the logical solution to me was to choose 'I do not know.' Some of the questions I did not see how to answer. For example, who remembers how many times they had sexual relations with a romantic partner? So I answered with a guess off the top of my head. But truthfully, I had no idea what the answer might be!

But psychology is a massive part of the monastic setting. People have no idea what might be waiting for them as they dive deeper and deeper into themselves. The discoveries can be fascinating. But, on the other hand, it can be pretty dangerous as well. It depends on who you are. It depends on the life you experienced. I have heard stories of people committing suicide.

When I was commissioned in the United States Navy, my Commanding Officer (CO) strongly recommended all the new Junior Officers make specific choices to help their early careers. Before leaving the Reserve Unit for active duty, I was informed that of the dozens of newly commissioned officers, I was the only one who ignored the CO's professional recommendations. Instead, I chose what seemed logical to me at the time. When I found out I was the only one of all the new graduates, I was stupefied. What kind of new officer was I that I did not realize that what the CO recommended was important? I now saw myself in a different light.

It was not until many years later that I realized something else. Years earlier, well before graduation, I was medically disqualified for potential assignment to nuclear submarines. That semester my grades suffered, and I did not do well. At the time, I had no idea how critical this situation was to my attitude. The rejection changed my outlook for being in the U.S. Navy. When graduation came, I was improperly influenced by a "poor attitude" about my Naval career. In other words, it didn't matter what the CO recommended; all that mattered to my "poor attitude" was what I wanted. And I wanted to be stationed in California! And so I was.

Some situations in your past might help or hinder your prospects as a monk. And unfortunately, you don't know what they are until you encounter them in the monastery and need to face them while trying to live out your monastic duties. With some monks, it is evident, with others - not so much! All we know is one day, these monks simply decide to leave. They decide monastic life is not for them.

September 20, 2011

Dear Mary-Martha,

I just wanted to write and let you know how much I benefit from writing to someone far off. Thinking about what I want to write gives me more focus on what to talk about here in the monastery and what to tell my family when I write them. The past month before this mailing date has been fruitful for us monks. You keep thanking me for cooperating with Jesus! It just amazes me that Jesus has such an interest in any of us. Please be good for Jesus in whatever you choose. Personal training from the Lord is a Grace of Graces! I think Jesus said something like, "it is because she cut all her hair off that I keep paying attention to her!" Mary-Martha—try not to be in such a demanding hurry to know your life's goal or implement some agenda. Trust God to lead you where God wants you to Go. Meditate on it, yes, but allow yourself to be shown even amid your discomfort. Trust me, I know, I am Mr. Planner himself! My past 10 years have been this enormous struggle to let go of needing to know what is next. And I had no idea what was going to happen next and ended up here. Before I left Philadelphia, I never thought I would end up in Charlotte. I never heard of Methuselah Abbey or any abbey whatsoever. My idea of monastic life was from some books I read from the fourth and sixteenth centuries. However, I read the Seven Story Mountain and books on the life of Fr. Pio (Saint Pio). **"Jesus, I trust in You!"** I don't think it is something you have to think about in terms of meaning. I feel reasonably sure it is something that you practice, and it happens to you when you direct your energy to do what Scripture and the Church require. I had a terrific conversation about you with your mom in the library last week prior. I wish I could be a bug listening on the floor when you have conversations with other Peace Corp people. I have a hard time seeing people not talking to someone with your personality. But you only mentioned that to me once, and you never really brought it up again. Anyhow she was just a little worried about her daughter as moms tend to do. I told her that in my biased opinion that you were struggling with yourself to be equal to the people you serve, especially by going out into the backcountry and living in the same way as they. As outsiders in a situation like yours, we liked to think we are equal to those we help, but we don't always act like it. The others (your coworkers) probably see simply being there in their presence as a statement of being equal to the ones they serve. But being equal is a mindset. Is separate but equal even possible? Mother Teresa was "equal" to the people she assisted. A fish and a bird cannot be made equal. One will probably end up dead. But in your colleagues' defense, we all must start somewhere on this journey. So I would not be too critical of these folks. It sounds like the helper and the helped are titles not fixed to any group in that situation.

I once told you I was jealous of your farming. Well, now I am even more jealous. As you write about how you farm together and walk the distances carrying the wood and fruits of your labor, it occurs to me that you have the basis for proper meditation. And you get survival skills at the same time. Nowadays, most food comes from commercial farms. We hardly grow anything ourselves. I felt such a connection with something special when I had my little garden in Philadelphia. Knowing that I was producing some of my food made me feel empowered. Just for your information, I already have five banana leaf mats from Peru! What am I supposed to do with another one? I would think you could be a little more original with your gifts (smile)! Try not to feel too bad; try harder next time you decide to send someone a handmade mat from a Peruvian Village in South America.

I have my South Carolina driver's license now, but I have not driven on the roads yet. I did the written and road test all in one day after I provided them with a Pennsylvania Drivers Record. Fr. Luke had his 97th birthday (September 13), and he was wondering where his mat was for his birthday present? I will give him one of mine and put your name on it so he will stop throwing computers around the administration building. He's furious, going around sneering at people! I told him to "grow up man? We can't all get a special gift!" This year's birthday was exceptional for me, and not just because I received a mat from Peru along with imported coffee! I received a surprise birthday cake out at the mushroom barn from Rev. Jim, the volunteer, and Lynne, his wife. I received cards from people I didn't expect or knew it was my birthday. I also received Nutter cookies from Ursula, along with her usual excitement and hugs. I had many comments from the brothers, and everyone said happy birthday. But it was the sincerity with which they wished it that made it matter to me. It warmed my heart. I usually spend my birthday alone, not necessarily unhappy but without company. Alas, no one asked for an autograph. Ever since I lost my crown, people avoid the subject. In my opinion, I am still the Best-Looking Monk 2008, 2009, and 2010. (So I must be emotionally resilient and deal with the grief of having only minor fame.) Anyway, my parents sent me some chemicals and work gloves for my birthday. My sister sent me a secret surprise, so it made up for her somewhat bland form of enthusiasm about monastic life and religion in general.

The Abbot is in Rome for the General Cistercian Chapter Meeting. He will be there right about when you get this letter. He heads to Columbia for our Sister's House visit; then he comes back here. We have a benefactor/donor's concert in October. Before that, we have a retreat at the end of September. Fr. Jude from Brooklyn will be the leader. I like him because he is funny. It will last for a week. Then eventually, we go to Charlotte for Sister Jeanne- Margaret's invitation, where we eat meat and visit with the Benedictines at Education Abbey. She is a Canon Lawyer with quite a reputation. She tells me Bishop Curlin is always asking about me. He retired from the Charlotte Archdiocese a few years back. I met him once, and sometimes I send him a card on the holidays. Did you know he did the funeral for the priest who did the actual exorcism (the one imitated in the movie "The Exorcist")? The actual exorcism was on a teenage male. And his head didn't spin around 360 degrees like in the film. Bishop Curlin was also a counselor to Mother Teresa of Calcutta (Saint Teresa) when a parish priest in Washington D.C.

As a matter of privacy, I want to remind you to send very private comments to my yahoo address, not the Methuselah email address. I am not asking you to defy any rules; I am just warning you that you get what you ask for if you don't take my advice! We will all be changing to Gmail eventually because the Abbot wants to save money, but until then, you don't have any privacy with the .org email here.

The paper that I wrote and sent to you is a true story. My life unfolded after I came to Methuselah based on experiences almost 10 years ago. I didn't give a copy to anyone outside the Abbey, so please treat it with care. I now sense why an Abbot must have special qualifications to lead a monastery. You must be able to gather very intimate insights into much of the human spiritual and mental journey. And then make decisions with that information to direct people. At this level of interaction, we monks are individuals in the extreme! There is no such thing as unusual anymore. People's strange quirks are openly experienced and accepted here. And the longer I live here, the more complex my reality becomes. So little of what I used to take as actual remains accurate. Thank God for the early monks of the desert and the caves. St Antony's life is a fantastic example for everyone who chooses to make this journey.

This understanding is why I am a little confused about YouTube™ in the monastery. Sometimes I listen to Oldies (music), which brings back memories. And when those memories come back, I am mentally transported in time and re-experience my life. I meditate on that, and I learn lessons I missed from back then. I grow because of YouTube, and it seems to me I am not damaged by "worldliness," at least not in this stage of my journey. But maybe I don't see the harm yet, and when I do, it will probably be too late? Save me, Mary-Martha, from my corrupt, worldly-seeking self. I only wish to do what is right with the time I have left in this life. And I can only hope for God's Mercy in this process. What else do I have? As incredible as she might sound, Rihanna won't be able to help me! I listened to a Def Leppard song from when I was 18 years old. The album was Pyromania. The song was Photograph, and it sent me way back to the beach in San Diego, California. All my struggles, difficulties, and decisions came back. I could feel the heat from the sun on my skin; I could see the blue 10-speed bike that I used to ride. All the early U. S. Navy stuff I used to do was there in my mind. Getting up early every morning, books, books, and more books, inspections, physical fitness. Even the beer at the local Enlisted Men's Club and my aspirations to go to college. My first day at Old Dominion University was on the floor of the campus Christian Club building. I had the dates confused. I arrived a day before the dorms opened. I was lugging a giant overstuffed sailor's sea-bag all over campus because I was just off active duty. The campus police helped me out. It can be scary how short life seems to be when you look back on it this way. But as you live it, especially early on, it looks like you have forever, and time doesn't matter so much.

On a less serious note, I am still trying to get used to wearing a long robe. (It's like a dress.) With September comes cooler weather and my legs are chilly-cold. And now I guess they need to invent pantyhose for monks (smile?) I am just so used to wearing slacks that this robe-thingy is still kind of new for me—anyway - time to sign off. By the time you get this, your mom and dad will be there. Tell them I said hello!

Love,

Br. Anthony-Maria

Welcome to Monastic Life! - What Time Is It Anyway?

What time Is It anyway?

We spent the better part of 10 minutes cracking jokes about the weekly monastic meeting that was now over - thank goodness! He was a monastic guest from Queens - Manhattan, New York, and a programmer. He was a long-term guest, and we worked together stuffing mushroom columns six days a week. We had a certain repour. And we both thought it was incredible that a group of monks could spend 20 minutes discussing the color of the napkins for use in the next monastic social event. We both thought that something must be wrong with this way of thinking.

And then there was the chaos amid chaos. We have complex social events calling for days of preparation and see no reason to plan for any of them. Because I spent many years designing a software application and had experience in the military, I was familiar with the idea of thinking ahead and preparing for the worst-case scenario. With so much to prepare, the notion of waiting till the day of an event and running around trying to get ready is not how I would ever think to do anything.

When you go throughout the monastery, you find many, many systems, items, and equipment that have been around for 30 or 40 years. Structures that no one has used for decades but have never been removed. Structures stand sixty years later as monuments to what the past was like for earlier monks. Some of the older monks can tell you the story of why a box is where it is and how it holds certain parts for equipment that no longer exists. They may never use those parts again but, they don't move them either.

The issue of time tends to disappear in this life. Or indeed, under certain circumstances, it becomes less and less of a factor. And if you are a planner, you will have to adjust to this new way of thinking. While walking in the area behind the monastery, I stumbled upon a hermitage. Many decades earlier, one of the monks lived in the forest hills. It was small; the bed springs were still there. The wooden furniture was still there, even if it was in disrepair. The window screens are made of steel, not modern plastic or aluminum. Through the window, one could see the propane fuel tank. It was still connected as if needed for providing heat today. One could almost feel the presence of the hermit staring at you from inside as you tried to imagine his silence in the hills decades ago.

The place was a monastery, but it was also a museum. It seems proper for a monk's spiritual development. And one had to learn to appreciate the mentality of those who move slow, think slow, and are in the habit of making decisions in a meditative and prayerful way. It only appears ridiculous to the observer whose mind is always in the habit of looking ahead, producing efficiently, and trying to save time to get more done. To the one focused on prayer and keeping God in mind for everything, this timelessness is a natural outcome of the lifestyle.

Father Peter. By Br. Anthony-Maria

I had some unique "spiritual" experiences while in the presence of Fr. Peter. Once I entered the church ahead of the evening prayer, Fr. Peter was already in his choir seat. [As you enter the church, visitor seating starts and faces the main church area. As you enter further, there are rows of monastic seating on the left and the right, and these seats face each other across the center of the church area.] Fr. Peter sat opposite my side in the rear row of his side, close to the church wall. When I entered, he was meditating. He did not look up at me when I entered. Nor did I expect him to. Most people in that state are mentally separate from the world around them. I went to my choir seat to await the ringing of the

Photo: Front entrance (inside) to the Methuselah Church. Visitor seating on the left and right of church entrance.

Vespers five-minute bell for prayer. And as I sat there, I saw what looked like a person in a white robe standing next to Fr. Peter. It was the faint hint of a person, but it was a human form standing there. I went to ring the five-minute bell. As Vespers started, I stopped paying attention to that situation. Some months later, while having a private conversation with Fr. Peter and Fr. Bartholomew, I told him I saw Jesus standing next to him in choir one day. Then I corrected myself and told him that I didn't know who that was, but I saw someone next to him before prayer, and eventually, that one disappeared.

Another time about a week before Fr. Peter passed away, he was fragile and sickly. He needed help with everything from eating to bathing. I visited him several times as it was clear he was dying. But I noticed his facial expressions clearly indicated that he objected to my presence. He had a look of fear on his face. So I stopped visiting. Fr. Bartholomew came to me one day and told me that Fr. Peter asked for me. So I told Fr. Bartholomew that his behavior indicated that my presence was disturbing. Fr. Bartholomew, too,

Photo: Methuselah Abbey Church, Front Entrance, 2014

noticed the facial expressions and agreed with me. Then one day, I went to his room while he was sleeping, kneeled by the foot of his bed, and started praying the Holy Rosary, offering it for him. I was facing the door of the room. And somewhere between mysteries two and three, his body popped up bending at the waist as if forcibly. He went from being feeble to sitting up with no need for help. He scanned the room, turning his neck slowly from the doorway toward me at the foot. He was looking for something. When his view arrived at me praying, he starred for a moment, and then his body fell back on the bed as if helpless. I didn't look at him when he did this. I didn't say anything to him; I kept praying the Rosary until finished, and I left his room. To this day, I still wonder what was going on with that situation.

A final time several days before Fr. Peter passed away, we all gathered in the Senior Wing of the monastery with guests to say goodbye to him. We each took the time to walk up and say our final words. And I told him to look forward to the Big Golden Double Burger in the sky (our little private joke!) And instead of smiling, when I backed away, he looked at me with fear. I never understood why he had such fear from what I said. When the Abbot saw this, he became visibly angry at me. After several years, I made this educated discovery. What Fr. Peter saw was not me. What he saw were the invisible ones who were following me. These things or creatures seem to be almost human in form. But they appear most often as two-dimensional. And they don't seem to have a fixed shape but seem to morph continuously into different exaggerated forms while maintaining their overall structure. They appear translucent and take on the color of what is physically behind them, but you can see a clear outline of a two and sometimes three-dimensional figure. I should say, I can see only two dimensions of the beings, it is also clear that there is a different profile that indicates a third dimensional view. I saw them once before. They were following two visitors of the monastery. And I was astounded at what I saw. When they noticed that I noticed them, they turned to look at me. They seem to respond to me with a sort of warped, changing smile - their "heads" bobbing to and fro.

What finally confirmed my experience was the nurse's toddler. At the time, this little boy could see what no one else could. Before this incident, he never paid me any mind whatsoever. But now, every time he saw me, he would point at me and say, "look mommy, look at that!" and his mother would look. She seems to realize he saw something, but she never indicated an understanding of her son's excitement. At the time, neither did I. But over time, I realized what was going on near me. This presence is also what Fr. Peter saw when I came into his room and certainly explained his look of fear and why he seemed not to want me around.

I would go way out on a limb and say that we can search the galaxy for intelligent alien life or search right here among us. This phenomenon that I observed is some kind that does not physically appear but is nonetheless detectable by the human experience in an intelligent way. They seem to respond to individuals in an observable way (i.e., they turned to "look" at me when they noticed that I could see them). If these things really "exist," it would seem that we are in somewhat separated realities with limited interaction. But, they are, in fact, somehow on Earth with us.

Br. Vineyard was traveling far away for an extended time, and we corresponded a little while he was gone taking care of business. We had a tradition of exchanging a few jokes regularly, as reflected in this letter.

November 01, 2011

Dear Br. Vineyard,

I just wanted to tell you that I had the most memorable of summers because of you. But things cannot end this way. We must never meet this way again.

Update: We received the postcard Br. Vineyard. Anyway, we all laughed at how lucky you were to find a place named after the 'Best Looking Monk' 2008, 2009, 2010, and now 2011! I put it up on the information board, and then I pranced around in full colors. I was the first to communicate with you!

Update: A retreatant was here. She was a regular visitor. It was a woman I can only describe as a blond probably. Probably middle-aged. In any case, she asked about you. I don't know her name, but she knows her way around Methuselah. She knows Dorothy. Don't worry; I made sure she didn't cause any trouble. I always take care of troublemakers (smile).

Also, Bishop Antonio is back. He is recovering in Goose Creek at a place named South Rehab. When we visited him with Fr. Thomas, he seemed very joyful. Dorothy was there when we arrived. After we left, we stopped at Jersey Mike's, and I had a Philadelphia Cheese Steak. Embarrassingly, I had loose bowels for the next 24 hours. I won't be going there again.

Peter is supposed to be coming back. Things didn't quite work out for him, I guess? He will be moving into room 9 or 10 of the senior wing. We are having a reunion of sorts. Kelvin (dropping by), Rusty (on retreat), and Dustin. (He has another few weeks to stay as an Observer.)

The humidity has been low. Humidifiers are fine [Br. Vineyard is assigned to empty all the humidifiers at the monastery.] There is no need for you to come back to the U.S. for that, so go ahead and get sleep. No need for you to stay by the phone either. Though Br. Mark did have me changing light bulbs. After so many assignments, I must learn to appreciate you more! Br, Ezekiel is wiping tables after meals along with Rev. Kelvin (a regular retreatant).

Eli has been playing the organ for a month. However, he has already been here a few weeks. Rev. Kelvin came the same day as Eli. They will be gone by the time you return. Don't worry if they cause any trouble; I'll get my people to handle it. They are both doing duty with Br. Mary. So far, so good in the senior wing. They are also managing the fruitcake wrapping this year. I am now seeing that the Monastic Guests do a lot of work around here. The Abbot is due back tomorrow. By the way, Happy All Saint's Day! We have prayed for you each day during Mass. So you owe us when you return. Just remember to bring a stash of cheeseburgers. Make it from any version of cow you choose. I'm not picky.

The Jones's are back from Peru, South America, with tons of pictures and a renewed appreciation for "Western culture." Mary-Martha knows you are away. I told her, you are always asking about her, and I was getting jealous. As you know, aside from her mother, I am supposed to be her only critical U.S. contact. She is winding down from her two-year tour in the Peace Corp with expected plans to go to graduate school.

Sincerely,

Br. Anthony-Maria Odom

November 16, 2011

Dearest Mary-Martha,

How r u? I am fine. Your family (to my knowledge) is fine also. I don't know much about your brother. Your mom mentions him from time to time. I had an interesting conversation with your mommy when she first came home. We hugged four times. She is her usual self. I told her to have confidence in Mary-Martha. I said she could handle it! I am impressed with the relationship you have with your mother.

I was thinking, what can I send Mary-Martha for Christmas that won't cost anything and will pique her interest? I was thinking of one of the donated books or magazines. So I will choose one and hope you like it. I hope it will not arrive too late. By the way, about that coffee you sent me. I feel bad because you sent it to me, but it is not enough for all the brothers, and I don't have a single-person coffee maker. And even if I did, I drink so little coffee that it will never be consumed. So I will give it to my sister Kim instead of Ralph even though he asked for it. She appreciates quality coffee, and it will make her feel better. It occurred to me that I should tell you by letter in case you get angry about me giving it away. I hope you don't feel that I don't appreciate the thought.

Also, I like the gifts you give me, but I can't use some of them. The Hat? **RAVE REVIEWS**. I wear it all the time. People compliment me so much. One lady told me that I should keep a good eye on that headgear; it might just disappear on you! Who would think a hat could be so popular? The mat--well, for one thing, one of the strings broke, and I am fixing it now. I don't do yoga anymore, so I will hold on to it for sentimental reasons until I figure out what to do with it. Maybe it will make a nice wall piece. You know, decoration for my room? I wish there were some way my sister could sell those hats you gave me. She wants to do something for extra money, and I can tell importing those hats and selling them on eBay would go over quite well. We could even modify them to add some value.

What is going on here? Italy will determine the economy for the entire world! So watch Italian news for what life will be like if you decide to come back. They have two trillion bucks in government bonds, and they are threatening default! The presidential race is heating up. The Republicans have no real front-runner at this point. And Barack Obama, I hate to say, is going into campaign mode. He and Nancy Pelosi (The first female House Leader) did a lot in their first two years, but the economy has been awful since the G.W. Bush years. We are supposed to be winding down two wars.

I have heard a lot of news about Peru. Keep both eyes open. I say trust the Peace Corp, but also use your mind too! Only you can make yourself duck if items start flying. I have been in foreign places when hostilities were about to break out, and a person does have to keep watch for a change in the behavior of the public. That behavior might be a clue about the social circumstance. If you watch and see a difference in the "mass behavior" of people around you, you may ask yourself why? But this is just a precaution, and everything could very well be acceptable.

There is so much to report. My family? Goodness! My sister fell 12 steps, fractured her shoulder, foot, and ankle. She had to stop working and is in a sling and cast. Her husband is in a sling from a previous car accident. She did ask me what I wanted for Christmas! I recently wrote her a short note apologizing for something that happened between us in the past. Little did I know this came as she was recovering from her fall. I asked everyone to pray for her for free this time (don't expect any double cheeseburger!) She wrote me a note telling me how much she loved me and that she thinks of me all the time! Wow. And to think I thought I was just good-looking!

Br. Vineyard is still away (till mid-December), Bishop Antonio is back from physical rehab with one less leg, and Fr. Peter may need back surgery. Fr. Mark had a stint put in one of his heart arteries, and now the pain in his chest is gone. We had the Benefactor Concert, and I helped with parking. I directed the cars into the parking lot area (I can be more beneficial at other times!) We started the Christmas Festival. We expect about six thousand

Photo: Br. Anthony wearing his banana leaf hat and using the golf cart for parking duty during the Benefactor Conference, approximately 2012

people this year. Dorothy (a monastic volunteer and benefactor) arranged to drive visitors to the store where the Christmas Festival starts. The guests can then park further into one of the fields, and we chauffeur them to the start area for the Christmas Festival with golf carts. This new method eliminates having so many cars parked around the monastery store. Br. James's brother (up in NYC) is getting married. He is a Jazz musician. His entire family is musical, including his father and stepmother.

We made some significant changes in the monk's daily schedule that have made life much better. We have changed Lauds from 5:30 a.m. to 6:30 a.m. and still have Mass at 7:30 a.m.. We offer breakfast between 5:30 a.m. to 7:30 a.m. to everyone, including guests. These changes give us an uninterrupted period from 4:30 a.m. to 6:30 a.m. for private reading and personal prayer. Also, we added something called a 'Desert Day,' which means we take a day for nothing but SILENCE once a month. We usually have community prayer seven times a day. But on a Desert Day, we have Mass at 7:30 a.m. and one short Benediction at 7 p.m. before we go to bed. So far, we have tried it once, and it is FANTASTICO! EXCELLENTE! So Powerful. Never in my life have I appreciated silence in this way. I thank God for that day!

Okay- I read through your journal (book one). At first, I thought, "she doesn't really have much to say!" I thought to myself, "this one is pretty boring." But as I read more, it got better and better. You have some excellent ideas, and I can see you are a "take the bull by the horns" kind of person.

Well, Merry Christmas in case you don't get my card and book on time.

Love and Prayers for You,

Br. Anthony-Maria

2012

Hello

Reasonably certain that they knew what I meant,
When I said Hello.
It was, I thought, apparent.

But, all along, I was mistaken.
And incorrect to assume.
For such a word could not explain itself.

In the deep dive, that was my thinking,
My collective state of mind said, "No!"
They haven't any idea at all - when I say Hello.

Uttering more, no mere greeting between people.
So convoluted than even I could not know.
My circumstance of imparting a word - Hello.

Offering me freely.
My many personal pieces of self.
As a public psychological dance between us.

And pouring mental activities of all sorts and
       kinds.
Inspired by preparations-initiated years ago.
Somehow charmed by you today.

Continued,

My hello is barely spoken.
The hearing a tiny, minute, small part.
A tip atop a rising elevation.

Streaming as instance, prior to your presence.
Meandering through my being, an encrypted path.
Communication corresponding to my entire me.

Chapter Introduction

The people come and then leave. Some visit for days, while others stay for months. We had a visitor come for over a year. We need the help, and they agree to live in the monastic setting according to the "Rule of Benedict." You encounter them day after day. You see how they eat at meals, whether they prefer pepper and salt on their food. You notice the type of cheese they choose for dinner.

You cannot help but notice their habits—behaviors like spending time alone or choosing to talk with others. During work and other interactive activities, you see their value system. I had to teach a guest how to sweep a floor. He did not know how to do so and became visibly upset when I asked him to do better.

You overhear or converse about their complaints, their likes, and dislikes. They talk about what they expected in monastic life and what they found different. Sometimes you cannot help but judge the people. Why did they come to the monastery if they preferred a non-monastic way of life? You wonder, "if they are engaged to be married, why are they seriously thinking of committing to monastic life?"

Some of the people are wealthy or have access to wealth. Some are poor and have access to nothing but their thoughts. Some love their family, but surprisingly, many do not. Some are recovering from a life-demolishing event, and others need to break from running too hard. I met a deacon, who lost his family to death, and he was experiencing cancer. He was seriously thinking of entering monastic life.

The people come and make friends with you and the other monks. Some seek spiritual advice from the brothers, especially the monks who are also priests. Some fall in love, not with you specifically, but with some fantastic idea of you. And at other times, you fall for your unique perspective of them, not caring that it is only a snapshot of their lives. When most people leave, they have nothing but fantastic things to say about their monastic stay. They know it is only a partial picture of what they saw while here. But they don't openly voice their criticisms. And you know they have at least a few. Very few visitors stay for good. They go back to whatever brought them here in the first place.

When my family visited for the first time, they had enlightening experiences and learned much about Roman Catholicism, the city of Charles City, and forest life with so many creatures. My mother came checking on what I had "gotten myself into" down there in a South Carolina forest. My father eventually visited out of guilt. In all honesty, I think my father was suspicious of Roman Catholicism and Monasteries. He was raised with a different form of Christian worship. But when he heard of my receiving the Best Looking Monk award, he wanted to congratulate me in person! The Abbot permitted me to lead my family around the various workplaces, forest sites, and monastic buildings during their visit. They stayed at the guest house near the monastery entrance (Saint Peters) and met many people who worked and volunteered at the monastery. While they cooked at the monastic guest house, they also tried and enjoyed the monastery meals. My mother attended Mass (and she was so nervous - brave!) Entertaining guests and teaching about monastic life is an essential duty that comes with being here.

January 20, 2012

Dearest Mary,

I was so sorry to hear of your illness. And to think I was not thoughtful enough to have the brothers pray for you. But - wait - I did! Still, they would never have known if it were not for Pam of the pair "Pam and Ted." We hear you lost a lot of weight and were in bed miserable. I thought of this when I read about your struggles. My heart goes out to everyone out there in your condition. But you will be a much stronger person if you do as I tell you —balance on your head and spin like a top. Then eat two raw frog legs and shout as loud as you can for five hours non-stop. If, after all that and you are not arrested, read this: *God Prepares His troops for His service:*

"When you are sick, when you suffer from something, don't say, 'Oh, why has this happened to me and not to somebody else.' No, say instead: 'Lord, I thank you for the gift you are giving me.' For sufferings are really great gifts from God. They are sources of great graces for you and for others. When you are sick, many of you only pray and repeat, 'Heal me, heal me.' No, dear children, this is not correct because your hearts are not open; you shut your hearts through your sickness. You cannot be open to the will of God nor to the graces He wants to give you. Pray this way: 'Lord, Thy will be done in me.' Then only can God communicate His graces to you, according to your real needs that He knows better than you. It can be healing, new strength, new joy, new peace - only open your hearts." Our Lady – according to http://www.medjugorje.org [7]

Before your mom left for South America, I told her: Mrs. Jones - you best take your baby some stuff to strengthen her immune system. If you can't get her doctor to prescribe something for viruses or bacteria, maybe use herbs. But she said the "Peace Corp provides everything; I don't need to bring her anything else." And I'm not particularly eager to rub it in, but I told her so. The Peace Corps cannot provide everything because they don't have the budget for everything. You may not avoid disease, but you make everything a little better with a more robust immune system.

What can I say about what is new around here? Br. James is leaving (after seven years as a monk). He said he is tired of them, implying that he is not into 'the life' enough to stay here. They say he is into writing poetry. He does get up early every morning to write. He insists on it. He has been away from the monastery for a long time, and in some ways, I think it may have weakened him. But that's just my opinion. They are not explicit about his future, but he feels uncomfortable because he is eligible for permanent vows, and it seems no one is supporting him. On the flip side, Br. James has a new tattoo. The Abbot approved it. It's not a design one would expect from a 30-year-old guy. It's a family symbol or crest. We will probably be down to nine monks in about five years unless things change soon.

What else? Did you want to know about my mushroom exploits? We have invented so many tools to help with mushroom production. We created:

1. A carrying device for the mushroom columns. We used to carry each sixty-pound column by hand to the truck before driving them over to the hanging trailers. Now we take five columns at a time with a device we designed for rolling them. I call it the Saint Thomas. Now, we only move three hundred pounds twice! And then we carry 10 columns a few feet onto the truck. The new setup is better for the smaller, less rugged people assigned to stuff columns.

2. We invented a device for stuffing the column bags with the mushroom substrate. I call it the Saint Peter. It holds the plastic column bag open while I load the substrate inside. Imagine how difficult it would be for one person to keep a bag open and stuff a handful of the substrate simultaneously? Now we shove with both hands and fill the column faster.

three. We invented a device for lifting 450-pound bales. I call it the Super-Bale Lifter. It is simply amazing. It used to take us four people to lift bales. Now it's me and the Super Bale Lifter with a chain hoist.

4. Len (a volunteer) and I experimented. We discovered that we could store our fresh mushrooms two and a half times longer by using the same

container we are already using to ship our micro-greens to the supermarket. The micro-green container is 50% recycled polystyrene. According to Len, this plastic allows the proper carbon dioxide and oxygen exchange, preserving the mushroom from decay. With increased shelf-life, no more nasty mushrooms en el supermercado! But, because we have so many of the current cardboard containers (pre-printed), we will not use the idea. Maybe, when they are gone?

5. One current invention is in the works. It is a bran dispenser. We need something to preserve the wheat bran from insects, keep it dry and dispense without significant opening and closing of the storage device. That invention is 85% complete. It is just a matter of time until finished.

6. We (Len and I) also designed a gadget to help us stuff the columns while standing instead of being on our knees. Everybody who visits fears the mushroom column stuffing job because of the pain of being on our knees. Even though we have knee pads, it is still painful, especially with all the bending that goes with it. Some of our guests are older, and some are not used to physical labor. Unfortunately, this will take some time to realize as it costs several thousand to build, and on "monk time," it could be a while before the funds are available. However, one of our observers, Deacon Joe, offered to pay for half of it. So it may get done sooner than we think? *Br. Anthony-Maria: SUPER-GENIUS (I'll get that road-runner yet!)*

I hope you received the Christmas card for your Church mother. Did you have to read it to her? Speaking of cards, I sent your mom a birthday card. She thought it was amusing. I used one of your Peru photos of the ladies sitting on the ground. And I gave her a picture of red roses for the inside of the card. She liked it, or so she said? March is coming fast. I probably won't send another gift box-- the Abbot might be concerned about my intentions if I keep sending stuff. But I will send you a card. I am the new "Card Monk." I more or less created the job. I give all the employees homemade cards for their birthdays. They usually like them. Also, I make cards for significant anniversaries of employees, benefactors, and volunteers. Ted Fiddie, the facility manager, said that he did not think that the brothers really liked him too much until he read the birthday card they gave him.

I read your letter about your dad's comments several times. And I have concluded that it benefits you to go through this part of your life. We must all break free of needing our parent's approval to follow God freely. Jesus said he came to divide families! So (I think) you will be stronger as a result. Besides, your dad meant well. Do you see how difficult it is to get along with just one person in a friendship? Imagine millions trying to get along? South Americans will improve their lives in due time. Besides, if you read the news, we north-westerners have many problems due to our way of life. Here in our country we live every day with the threat of total nuclear annihilation. With our current state of "industrial animation" we live with the constant threat of technical failure or collapse. Imagine going back to struggling with no GPS. I know what it was like to have to use map books. Does global warming ring a bell? Will it mean the destruction of civilization in a few centuries? Do we have that much to brag about in the larger scheme of things?

I only know one way of life. However, time will tell if global mass production and unmanaged global mass consumption and its related complications are suitable ways of life to sustain our planet. And do not get me started with the new, ultra-complex, super-fast technologies we are introducing in society. We have a history of introducing powerful, new things to the planet. And they do not always go well! It seems to me we are really rolling the dice on literally everything with things like artificial intelligence, genetic engineering, and nano technologies. We simply have no idea of the overall consequences. And with the speed and depth in which these technologies operate, it will be too late to talk about what we "should have done." Fortunately, my opinion is irrelevant; time will be our witness!

As for the hat idea for my sister, it seems that unless you can locate a reliable source for information and international transactions on your end, it will be challenging to use those "hat maker people" as a reliable supplier. I feel pretty sure these would sell on eBay and certainly in a shop. And perhaps a person could add a few amenities and make the hats even more attractive.

Fr. Peter is coming home from the hospital. He's been there a month. He was losing his ability to walk and use his arms due to spinal compression of the nerves. The double cheeseburgers we gave him were not enough. I am happy about his return. He told us he was in so much pain that he thought he was dying. He will continue rehab here at the monastery. The monks have been visiting him at the hospital every week.

Bad news: Bishop Antonio, who lost his leg to cancer, now has cancer-related spots in other parts of his body. He is going to try an experimental treatment. We hope against a very aggressive disease. They tried to save his foot by treating it, and they suspect the condition had time to spread to other parts of the body like the lungs and lymph glands.

Maybe you will see a new Retreat house and our new Columbarium by the time you get back. Br. Vineyard has been sick for a few days. His strength comes and goes.

Well, I must go now.

With love,
Br. Anthony-Maria

February 20, 2012

Dear Mary-Martha,

How are the birds of South America? I hope all is well with them. When I read your emails, I can see a picture in my mind of this scene of birds. I suppose that perspective comes from exposure to too much nature television? In any case, I hope all is well with you, your health, and your students. I got a prayer request from a friend in Mexico. Her daughter is the only Latina teacher in the Arizona school where she works and one of two who speak a different language. She prays that the principal "who is Satan" in disguise to please leave her daughter alone and for the substitute teacher trying to steal her job to just "lay off." Social issues, employment, and the like are enough to make a person enter a monastery (smile). If you are an "enlightenment-oriented" person, you need a sort of incubator to grow assertive in practicing the faith.

Thank God for the quiet life. It is tough being here too, but the monks here really focus on God in our activity. People don't slow down enough to see what's going on around them in our culture. And the stress associated with that way of life is a killer. Many of us are simply blind to what is going on; we believe nothing we hear and part of what we see! If for some reason, I were to leave Methuselah, I am determined to live a hermit's life.

There is the story of the Saint who lived as a hermit. And when he was off in his little hut up on a mountaintop above a small town, a beautiful woman knocked at the door and came in to see him, and she told him she was in love with him. She wanted to be with him forever. He was so scared of that situation, he wrestled her out the window of his hut and told her never to return. It is supposed to be a true story! Unfortunately, that is what I feel happened with Br. James. He wanted so badly to be in love that he left the monastery to find his beautiful brunette. Like most of us, he had a whole lot of other issues too. Those who decide thought he should leave to resolve his internal conflicts about what he should be doing with his life. I told Br. James - you are 31 years old, not 91. And you are going to have feelings and thoughts of this nature. But he came at an early age (22 years old), and he had the ideas about romance with him when he arrived. The way I see it, there is nothing wrong with love and romance under the proper circumstances. But once you discover a vocation for God and then leave it behind, you risk losing it forever. It is a gift that is so rich and deeply meaningful that it should not be defined with mere words. I hope I am never distracted long enough to lose what I have.

I don't belittle marriage because marriage to the right person is just as powerful. But I didn't grow in that direction for undeniable reasons. I still get carried away with the idea of beauty and, of course, double cheeseburgers and the like, but so far, not long enough to forget my gift.

By the way, I saw your mom twice since she returned from her parent's house up north. (I guess.) She seemed happy. I think your dad must be home because she doesn't email much. I told the Abbot of your interest in a week at Methuselah and mentioned that I would like to spend some time talking with you. He seemed surprised at first; then I think he remembered I write to you monthly. Maybe he will let you come out to the work area for a visit to see our Mushroom operations too! In the case I never mentioned, they finally started clearing the grounds for the new retreat house. This new house is supposed to be excellent. But I don't think it will be operational when you get back, so prepare for the old rooms. They're okay too!

I have accumulated an enormous amount of chocolate - between Christmas, New Year's up to Valentine's Day, including Fr. Frank's visit. (He always gifts us chocolate bars.) My family went nuts with gifts! They sent me three packages, all after New Year's, and I had already started my fasting from sweets. Now - because I am fasting from sweets for six months, and so far, it has been six weeks. I've broken my fast only once, and Ursula's Butter cookies are tempting me. Still, she is delightful for offering these items. In any case, it's all just sitting there (Hershey Bars, Snickers Bars, cookies, and more) because I won't touch it for six months (fingers crossed for July 1st.) This situation is appropriate for me. We are reforming my urges to have sugary satisfaction in my life in place of God. And thanks to prayer, it is working. And it certainly has nothing to do with my discipline! God loves me! He helps me! I am becoming a new person.

The effort is perfect timing because I have Type 2 Diabetes. So I need to lay off the sweets. But more importantly, I need to lower my body fat percentage if I ever want to reduce or eliminate the drugs I take for the disease. I will begin work on my horrible addiction to double cheeseburgers soon after my sweets fast, hopefully before the end of the year. Maybe you can come up with a rap and a dance that will bring on the fasting gods for your friend here in the U.S.? Or perhaps you could pray for me? That might be easier. I have an internal plan for myself (I don't remember creating one), yet somehow, I am proceeding according to it.

Anyway, here at Methuselah, we are proceeding with our plans to "look at how we do things" at the monastery. Given the nature of monastic life and our literal fear of change, it is prolonged. Changes we started last year this time we just finished a year later, and that was just the start of our list (less than 25% complete). Somehow the Abbot said we had finished the list. Well, this upset the brothers. It was akin to pulling teeth with no anesthesia - to make the few changes we did make. And then for him to say we are done upset many. Trust me -that is rare in this place. We eventually calmed the mob down and put the torches out. Then we came again with our same list of observed / agreed-upon community issues. With Br. James' leaving, everyone is pushing for an overhaul of the discernment process. So that is the next major conference on the list. Sister Lynne is here in April. She will be guiding us through this process. She is good at staying on topic and cutting through the clutter of so many different viewpoints.

Well, my brother-in-law, James, is healing and back to teaching at his martial arts school. My sister is still going through some things concerning her health. She keeps having car accidents. She is 48. But at least she is going back to work regularly. I thank you for your prayers. We are all still reeling from my Uncle Noah's death. My Uncle finally passed away from his lung cancer/kidney failure. He was subject to Agent Orange like so many of his fellow soldiers. I must have cried for three days while thinking about it. I didn't go to the funeral, but my mom sent me the program. He and I were not that close, but I knew what he meant to my family. I had a lot of respect for him. He was an honorable person, a Viet Nam era veteran with significant stress issues, an African American growing up in the era of civil rights unrest. (The era of Jim Crow and he went to his grave with trauma from all these experiences.) He was a brilliant man, but (many things being relative) he suffered quite a bit in his Sixty something short years. In some ways, I am glad his death came quicker. In general, I think he was very misunderstood. It is a weird feeling to have a relative you never felt that close to pass on, and then, in them doing so, you find yourself mourning as if you know them intimately. My heart is awakening to things I never knew possible.

In my conversation with Fr. Peter (we call him Fr. Pete, he is about 80 years old), I learned I have had a unique experience of God. You see, with Fr. Pete, when you talk to him, you talk about one thing, and he asks you some weird questions, and you are off on some unrelated subject. So in conversation with him, I go with the flow of the conversation. But all this week, I have been experiencing tremendous darkness. I felt essentially like a different person. My entire being was in pain like somebody scrubbed my insides with a scouring pad. My thoughts were cloudy, and everything was uncertain. My whole outlook on life was dark and miserable (I was asking, "why bother to do anything at all?", "who care's anyway?") I was disoriented even though I had a strict routine. My mind was so unfocused that I was not at all present in any activities. I felt like those zombies look in horror films.

As soon as my feet hit the floor in the morning, I started asking Mary to pray for me. Hail Mary...full of Grace. It's 2:50 a.m., and I wander into the darkness from my room toward the church. six months ago, I would have needed coffee, but not anymore. Now I don't need the stimulation. Maybe I have come to accept more of the discomfort associated with the early morning rises? I pray until it is time to ring the 3 a.m. bell that wakes everyone. Then I go to my seat in choir. I pray, "Holy Spirit have Mercy on me this morning as I read this Holy Scripture. Please feed me with everlasting life!" I open my bible and start "prayerful reading." I ring the bell for Vigils at 3:20 a.m., and then after, we have a half-hour period of personal meditation. Then I pray the Rosary, eat breakfast, check my email, and pray another decade of the Rosary. I go back to the church and begin reading a book.

I am currently reading a book on the Old Testament concerning the birth of the state of Israel, including the Hebrew people, or Chosen people, also called Abiru people. They have so many names! This book helps me to understand Old Testament psychology. Then too, I don't particularly appreciate that the author explains God away. He attempts to explain extraordinary events with logical, rational, acceptable modern explanations. For example, he writes: Manna was a regular part of desert life, the Reed sea (not the Red Sea) turned back on itself once a year anyway, and flocks of birds were often blown off course, ending up in the desert. The author was not very religious and seemed only interested in debunking with facts, something that was probably never fact-based in the first place. Anyway, Lauds starts at 6:30 a.m., and then Mass at 7:30 a.m.. Between those periods, I am either praying the Rosary or saying Hail Mary full of Grace over and over. This version of dedication to prayer is tremendous work, and it takes great discipline and persistence, but it is also very fruitful spiritually. I have come to realize how by myself, I am helpless. And if I don't learn to focus on God all the time, it is over for me here, no matter the conditions. I might as well pack my bags. Psychologically, I am spring-loaded to leave.

I think the proper interpretation of this "God experience" is this: The close presence of God is such that I am cleansed or healed. And my human response to this experience of being sanctified is the truth of who I am or as God sees me. I think my human response has a mental and a physical aspect. My dedication to prayer is what keeps me from crawling under a rock to hide from myself as I see who I am. Here at Methuselah, some call it a night of the soul. And I am told, it can go on for years.

We had another brother pass away. Br. Mary was 92. Shortly after World War two, he came into the order and was the last founder of Methuselah. During the war, he was an Intelligence Officer stationed in India. Before he died, I asked him to pray for my family. And he thanked me for asking him? He saw it as a privilege. His death was sudden in that he just said he didn't feel well, and a few hours later, he passed on. His little great grand-nieces and nephews were crying during his funeral, and I was exploding with joy. I could not control my happiness. Br. Mary is in heaven! Is this feeling the nature of such joy? Sadness is not even a factor. The same thing happened with one of my church members from Charlotte. When he died, I found out and was praying for him. During Mass, after the preacher finished, I screamed out -Amen! The brothers just stared at me. I just looked around with embarrassment. I have no idea why that came out. But I do know he was urging me to offer prayer for him at Mass. After that outburst, I thought to myself that that was Mr. so and so. He was saying goodbye.

On another subject, we had over 7000 people at our Christmas Festival this December. It is mainly in the library conference room. We had over 1000 more attendees than last year. Volunteers run the Christmas Festival, but the donations come to us. Nativity scenes come from all over the world made of every sort of material. People even make Nativity scenes from eggshells! It is very intricate work!

Anyway, it is time to end this letter. I will try to make you a special Birthday Card!

Merry Christmas,

Br. Anthony-Maria

Brother Monk <small>by Br. Rodney K. Odom</small>

Br. Monk was from Chile (Republic of Chile). When I arrived at Methuselah, he was a Novice. Initially, I saw him as a nice person willing to give helpful advice and guidance. But then he started pointing out to me that there was to be no eating between meals. But, he did it while unwrapping chocolate candy and eating it in front of me. And I was somewhat baffled by his explicitly hypocritical behavior.

One day while praying in the Chapel, he interrupted my meditation. The Chapel was a non-speaking area, and I simply did not understand why he thought it was okay to talk to someone praying - he felt the need to talk to me while I was praying.

Then he started disturbing me to pray for him. These interruptions continued for some time. And I was both confused and annoyed. I began to bring up my annoyances in conversations with Fr. Thomas during my weekly meetings. But Fr. Thomas seemed to have little or no reaction to my complaints about Br. Monk.

Photo: A copy of the prayer card Br. Monk gave me before he left to return home to Chile.

I heard rumors he was from a wealthy family. He did not look sixty, but when he told me his age, I saw him as different than I used to. Then one day, in the kitchen area, while wrapping the Christmas fruitcakes we sell in the store, I saw him in discussions with Br. Mark. It was a rather heated discussion about him disappearing when assigned to work. A heated discussion for Br. Mark was extremely rare. I was slowly learning about Br. Monk but had not yet drawn any "final conclusions" about him.

He was leaving the monastery. Br. Monk's final days at the Abbey surprised me. And it changed my entire view of how to deal with any of the Brothers. He came to me outside the Chapel and asked me to pray for him. And before he left for good, he gave me a prayer card for Saint Martin de Porres. It was something he held dear, and he asked me to pray for him.

It was not till I saw him in tears about leaving together with the turmoil of his struggles that I realized he was just like me. He was an older person stuck in warped behavior patterns, desperately trying to break free. Now he was leaving and had to find a new route to freedom. This monastery was no longer available.

For the remainder of my time at Methuselah on the celebration of Saint Martin de Porres, I offered prayer at Mass for Br. Monk. And in my own heart, I could still see and feel his suffering and struggles. My complaints may have added to his burden, and had I known better, I would have hesitated to say anything to anyone about his behavior. It was clear that I had to learn and understand to relate to the people around me much better than I had.

Welcome to Monastic Life! – Enter The Non-Believer

Enter the Non-Believer

Methusalah monastery is a beautiful place cared for by an army of non-monastic volunteers. The plants and trees, streams, lakes, wandering paths, and historical elements all come to life each spring and have been doing so for hundreds of years. This picturesque view started even before the monastery existed. Some visitors are firm believers in nature and are not at all religious. Other times you have people here who want to explore. They come in cars to participate in weddings and take pictures, or they want to learn about the monk's mushroom business. It is a unique experience when you have been living your life as if God is real, and then you encounter a person or group of people who have nothing to do with God whatsoever. They do not explicitly say so, but some people wonder why you are "wasting your life" in a monastery when you could be out doing "some real good in the world." And some of those are Roman Catholic. To them, there is no connection between a monastery and God whatsoever.

Once, we had a monastic guest who came from New York City. He was visiting the monastery for a week or two. He was just interested in exploring the possibility of monastic life. He was single. He was male, and he was catholic. In New York, he was a doorman for a large apartment building in Manhattan. He told me fascinating stories as we worked stuffing mushroom columns (I discovered that while working, some monastic guests need to talk to someone, even if we are not supposed to! Mercy dictates we converse.) I was most fascinated by his stories about people's wealth. He said that the men that lived where he worked routinely spent seven or eight thousand dollars on one suit of clothing. And he said this was normal for them. Such personal spending habits are not a part of my experience. But what caught my ear was when he told me that people were fascinated that he was Roman Catholic and that he "actually believed in God."

He said that sometimes people would ask him questions about his understanding of God and religion. He indicated that some of the people living there see him as a rather unique individual, and they brag to their friends about him believing in God. Hearing this was a compelling wake-up call for me to the full spectrum of people in the world. And it was quietly devastating to me that some folks have no value for or see any use for such things as religion or belief in God. Some are even offended by the idea.

For my part, I told him that he was a light for those people. And I found it intriguing that so many non-believers surround him, and yet there he stood like an island contemplating monastic life. God can be wherever he chooses. But I have never had more proof of God in my life since turning to God the way I did in monastic life. And it is through the evidence that God offers that keep me turning toward him all the time, less I lose focus and wander off somewhere dangerous. I also found it somewhat confusing that so many people, even visiting Methuselah, were so nice and generous but had no interest in God at all. And this despite our presence here in the monastery. What do we represent to them? I did not have the means to interpret the situation in my heart and mind. I was utterly baffled.

March 20, 2012

How are you, Mary-Martha?

I hope all is well? I know you are winding down your stay in Peru. I pray you to be safe and take good care while doing so. Ursula said, "I wish that girl would stop all this traveling! She scares me." Then she signed your birthday card. I talked to your mom, who seems very interested in traveling with you wherever you go! Rome? But now that you say you will not travel, Why make all this commotion? In any case, this is life back here. We are reaching the heart of the Republican nomination process. The economy seems to be turning up. And the foreign wars are supposed to be coming to an end. What's else is good with us? Well, we have an early spring. The birds and other creatures are out and about in the dark hours of the morning. Yesterday I scared a raccoon, and he ran halfway up a tree! I didn't know raccoons climbed trees! Today, I encountered a 6-foot black garden snake at the entrance to the church. It was as the guests of the afternoon tour entered. To save everyone from the vicious garden snake, I wrestled it in front of them. I had all my "monk stuff" on so they could see we monks are fearless! But it didn't impress anyone; they just took out their cameras and started taking pictures of the snake. It was nice to know that I, being a city boy, have learned a thing or two in the last two and a half years about snakes. I now deal with them without resorting to violence.

I worked on the mushrooms with a priest from the Bronx, NY. - Fr. Michael. He is leaving as I write this letter. Before he goes, he is throwing us a pizza party! And you know it is tough for anyone to beat that departing gift! He is a pretty cool guy. He was born in East Asia but has lived here since he was a preteen. Socially, he is very sophisticated. English is his second language but he moves easily about the place. Now, he is thinking of seeking a monastic life. It seems to happen at about that same time of life for many of us. I decided when I was 30ish to pursue this type of lifestyle but didn't act until my late 30's. Now at 46, I am slowly converting my heart to Jesus in this way. I freely admit I still live in fear of this monastic life. Total commitment to such circumstances can cause apprehension. And another one of the things that concern me is my elderly parents. As Sr. Jeanne-Margaret says, you don't convert just because you take a vow; it's a slow process that takes place over time. And I know for a fact that the harder I seek God, the more eagerly God responds to me. Sometimes I don't feel worthy of such consolations. But God knows best! And given my memory and personal biases, I quickly and easily forget how crummy a person I can be and go right back to my arrogant, self-righteous demeanor—still praying all the more! This behavior of mine should be one of the definitions for the word: stupidity!

Pam's family is visiting this week. Her daughter and her new fiancé are here also. Pam is so happy when her daughter is here, and she gets so excited! There is such a difference in her behavior. She is like your mom when she talks about you, "her beauty-queen daughter." Such a transformation takes place.

Did I tell you my mom and dad celebrate their 50th anniversary this year? June 30. Fr. Thomas says I might be able to fly home for a day and visit for the celebration. The Abbot has approved, and I will be there for two days. I look forward to doing so because, as silly as this sounds, I can pick up papers that I left at my parent's house by mistake, and I can also update my Facebook account, upload some pictures, and say goodbye to some people who were mad at me for leaving. I look forward to seeing my family too! We don't currently have access to Facebook here at the Abbey. When dealing with extreme lifestyle changes, you need support to change and the flexibility to fail when required. And introducing more significant "temptations to fail" when they already surround you in every way is not helpful. With access to Facebook, I might look back too much to activities outside the monastery. But still, it is a primary way people communicate nowadays. They certainly don't respond to email anymore! But, understand something, my family is not Catholic, and they don't know what it means to go into a monastery to respond to God. Many Catholics don't seem to know it either! Deep down, it is difficult for me to live this life and know that they are without me physically. But God finds a way to make it worth it. Even amid the most vicious mental struggles I have ever encountered in my life. And then there are people like you! Who would ever think I would be socializing with you over in Peru for this extended period because I decided to go into a monastery? I look forward to your return to understand who you are and not exchange a mere letter as comfort food.

We just finished a course in Canon Law. And I must admit I learned much about Religious life. We are entirely connected to Rome for much of everything. Did you know that if a Trappist in solemn vows decides to leave Religious life, he must get approval from the Pope (via the Abbot General!) But in most matters, it is either Rome or the local Bishop or both.

Well, I hope my last letter was not too much for you? It had some rather radical topics, and I figured you could handle it! I know your mom could (at least academically). Maybe you ought to keep it to yourself if you think she would not take it well. Happy Easter! Stay safe.

I pray for Mary-Martha!

Br. Anthony-Maria, OCSO

April 4, 2012

Hello Dear Family,

I hope all is well. I heard about Tarya [my cousin] and her pregnancy (due in May?) Also, I heard Lansana [another cousin] would be a daddy in June? Would you please send the pictures if you remember? I shed many tears for Uncle Bro. (Noah William). We offered a prayer for him. All is fine here. We are well into Holy Week or, as the Abbot calls it, The Feast of Feasts!

There is good news and expected news. The good news is that we broke ground on the new Saint John of the Cross-retreat house. When complete, it is supposed to be a very high-quality structure. We will demolish some of the older buildings and reassign one of them. We think the new house will be 16 rooms (replacing all the other buildings). It will be more efficient and less costly to operate. The material used will be of higher quality and include some modern considerations that guests ask about all the time. It will be closer to the church and monastic enclosure. That will mean less privacy for the monks. But it will be more convenient for our more elderly visitors to get to the church. It will also be better for those who don't like being so far into the forest. We also broke ground on the Columbarium. We already have the remains of several people who await burial. This structure is already about halfway complete.

The expected news: we had another brother die. Br. Mary was 92. Shortly after World War II, he came into the order and was the last founder of Methuselah. The Abbot called him the 'energizer bunny' because he would get sick, and then when we expected he would pass on, he would recover from his illness. In the monastery, a person becomes more "useful," so to speak, as they grow older. One reason is that tradition is essential, but record-keeping is not done in detail. Practices and historical events are handed on verbally. The other, of course, is spiritual evolution. Many people evolve spiritually over time. And they become spiritual leaders as a result. For example, I don't know Latin. But Br. Joseph knows Latin. So I asked him to translate the Our Father and the Prayer to Saint Michael the Archangel to Latin so I could pray it in Latin. And he did.

When he asked me why I told him I read about doing so in a book. Very few people coming into the monastery nowadays know Latin well enough to translate it from English.

I have decided that if for some reason I were ever to leave Methuselah, I am determined to live a hermit-like life. I don't expect that to happen, but I think about the drawbacks and experiences that might force me to leave as I approach simple vows. So far, I can think of only a few critical items. The monks are like people who own a nuclear power plant but have all their training growing corn. Everything we seem to do seems like a random shot into the darkness. Most of the monks here have no special training to help us accomplish our new business goals. The selling of eggs came along and developed over a long period. It was during a time when the monks could compete with the world around them with pretty much labor and some technical expertise. Modern times call for much more technical specificity over shorter time periods. It is a sudden mismatch of conditions for their conversion to a new business. And it is also at a time when there are fewer monks. It is true we have access to people who have expertise, but they are not fully invested in the monastic outcome as a monk might. The truth is, we are not supposed to be so dependent on donations and non-monastics for our lifestyle. Yet, we are.

Also, unlike in the past, where the monks didn't need significant outside help, now (at least to me), it seems we need (outside volunteers) to help us do practically everything! Another issue is that the monastery is a collection of "complex operations" under the Abbot's responsibility. We are many different businesses with only a few qualified people to run them properly. While we plan work, it doesn't appear to support any strategic goals. And yet, we expect processes to work out with no problems. Since I have been here, we have exited the egg business. We have tried growing many different types of mushrooms. We have thrown up ideas about two or three other business possibilities, and we have invested significant resources into all of them. To me, this is why we have so many 'sudden unexpected emergencies.' Unfortunately, it is my way of thinking that causes me trouble here. I think in terms of efficiency. I act in terms of looking ahead for possible complex issues. I think in terms of planning with detail and proper training of personnel. This process is what is required to participate in our local economy properly. I was a surface warfare officer in the U. S. Navy. I had no choice but to look far out ahead of the ship to ensure all was okay. We could not go into a practice missile shoot without review and planning presented to the captain.

The other area of monastic life that I object to is busyness. Some level of busyness is in all human existence. But here, busyness is an issue because it tends to drain you and cause you to lose focus. And I think it will wear away my determination to stay. Unfortunately, I feel that this is what happened with Br. James, who is now Jude (after being here for so many years). I think he became vulnerable. He had a busy schedule after returning to the monastery. He was going back and forth to training twice a week. And he was possessed by thoughts of being in love. In retrospect, he may not have gotten the support he needed to stay focused on being here. I once told Br. James, you are 30-one years old, not 91, and of course, you will have strong feelings or romantic thoughts. All your friends outside the monastery are living the ideas you fantasize. He said the Abbot began asking him questions about his need to write and his other thoughts, and all this questioning made him feel he was still not accepted here at Methuselah. He expressed some animosity regarding how he was treated. He could not hide it. I felt terrible for him because, in him, I saw myself when I was 30. The way I see it, there is nothing wrong with love and romance under the proper circumstances. But once you discover a "vocation" for God as a monk and then leave it behind, you risk losing it forever. It is a gift that is so deeply meaningful it seems impossible to relate or define it to other people who have not experienced that call. People write books about it. I hope I am never distracted long enough to lose mine. I don't talk down about marriage because marriage to the right person (whatever that means) can be just as powerful an expression of Holiness in one's life as a consecrated life. For me, I simply didn't evolve in that direction. I simply don't miss what I never had. If I left anytime soon, I simply could not imagine going back to life as it was before I started my journey here.

Besides, since I started my journey here, I have lived in a strange world of premonitions, weird visions, and violent attacks. Yeah, it is just like in the movies but without the green slime. Where could I go but the monastery?

Unless I had a hunch of the winning Super-Lottery numbers, I simply would not fit in anywhere else. The longer I stay isolated, the more clearly I see myself and who I am. I don't know how to continue to evolve properly except as a hermit or monk. I seem to need my entire being focused in this place to proceed down that path. And life outside this way is riddled with demands on my focus and concentration. Living this way outside the monastery would be like walking blindly across a busy street or lifting barbell weights with one leg and one arm. With the street crossing situation, I would eventually end up run over. I would not get very far. And with the weightlifting situation, I would probably end falling over. How would that be useful?

Anyway, since Br. James departed, I have made some projections about Methuselah's future and presented my ideas to Fr. Thomas and the Abbot. They had the usual frustrated facial expressions. I projected the number of monks in Methuselah's community in 5, 10, and 15 years. And because of the high average age of the monks (early 70's), all things being equal, we will go from roughly 10 people each with 30 to 60 years of monastic history down to one person with 25 years of history within the fifteen years. Everyone else will each have less than fifteen years of history. And most monks will have less than five years of experience. Of course, this calculation assumes no one joins from another community. I get the 'usual frustrated facial expressions' from people I talk to about these subjects because I still think like a business or military person. I use my educational background to describe issues from that perspective. And since I don't usually use the "monastic or priestly language" that many monks use, I suspect that makes me somewhat of a foreigner around here.

There is a monastic way of doing things, which is the only acceptable way for many monks. Strategic direction and topics of this concern are not "monastic." I developed some elegant charts and graphs to help analyze our mushroom business, and the only person who responds to its conclusions is the Abbot. The rest of the monks think it is a "really neat thing" that I can do with the computer, but they don't see any usefulness in the numbers. When we meet to get people's opinions on matters, some of the monks say they have no idea why we have a meeting to gather anyone's opinion because the Abbot is the one who should be making all decisions. Fr. Peter says starting over with new people will give "you guys" a chance to do "major reform." I agree with him (to the extent I am qualified to speak) the Trappists need major reform as an organization. Are Trappists properly meshed in society? How can they be so while still achieving the organization's goals of leading monks to perfection in God?

We are not out in mosquito-infested forests, separate from society anymore. We are in the heart of the local community, dependent on donations and influenced by the same. We are nowhere near able to deal with the shrinkage going in monasteries. I think they should consider the effectiveness of screening techniques considering the older people showing up to enter. If I am 50, I might become an excellent monk, but perhaps it will take a little longer for me to change. Nowadays, younger people have more choices, may not know themselves as well. They have far more time to make choices. As a result, they may hop from place to place, seeking answers. Older people tend to have more wisdom, depth, and decisiveness about life and thus are probably more apt to follow through after planning to transition to monastic life. And like it or not, the achievement of one encourages the accomplishment of more. So if I take a vow, others see and follow. If no one takes a vow, there is no one to follow. One person leaving disrupts a flow of people arriving.

Of course, God may not be taking all my great ideas into account, so we will see what happens. As one liturgy instructor told us (he is a Benedictine Monk with a Ph.D.), they need to combine many of these monasteries and save us all the trouble of trying to run them with so few people. But he thought that some of the monks were far too old to make such drastic changes. In western society, monasteries have aging members and fewer younger people. Even here, I'm the youngest at 46. How can they expect to bring people from high school who will stay? I suspect that as far as Monasteries are concerned, 40 is the new eighteen! What eighteen-year-old would be able to remain given the gender, age, culture, ethnicity, and every other kind of social surprise they would end up causing just by being present. Once, I put a copy of University of Pittsburgh's Black History magazine out (I get one every year.) That simple act just about caused a riot (a speechless one – I could feel the discomfort.) Also, consider that younger people do not do labor! We, as Americans, are not into labor anymore. Consider that the Roman Catholic Church is no longer just a western society church. It is now fully socially integrated into South America, Asia, and Africa. In those areas of the world, "Christianity" is growing in leaps and bounds. So are the monasteries.

Anyway, here at Methuselah, we are proceeding with our plans to "improve things" through our group meetings. Given the nature of monastic life and our literal resistance to change, sessions are prolonged. The changes we started last year this time we just finished a year later, and that was just the start of the list of goals we developed together. (A list that is less than 25 percent complete.) Somehow during one of the meetings, the Abbot said we finished the list of goals. Well, this upset the brothers. Here we were struggling to finish about 25 percent and implement the few changes we agreed to make, and he was claiming we had finished altogether. We eventually calmed down the rowdy mob of monks and put their torches out. Then we came again with our same list of observed / agreed-upon issues. With Br. James, having just left the monastery for good, everyone is pushing for the overhaul of the monastic discernment program. (This is the process by which new people proceed before entering monastic life.) This program is the next major conference on the list. We scheduled Dr. Lynne in April. She will be guiding us through this process. She is excellent at staying on topic and cutting through the clutter of so many different viewpoints.

I finally think I have figured out why Trappist monks seem to have an odd perspective on life. I believe that Trappist Monks spend so much time in introspection that their minds have developed a new/different operating mode. The new mode is like living life with a magnifying glass covering each eye. And it is this magnified way of seeing life that explains our behavior. What most people would see as a minor issue somehow gets raised to the brothers as an all-out emergency. This evolved way of observing life is probably why we use 20 minutes to decide whether a napkin should be folded to the left or the right! You would be amazed at how much time we can spend on what the average person would see as a trivial matter. Each person's opinion amounts to a close and detailed perspective of whatever topic comes up. We all sit around in silence, and each person speaks their opinion on the subject at hand. After many years of thinking this way, it is challenging to change to another. When people from outside the monastery come around and observe our life from the "normal perspective," it must seem odd. But it does seem necessary. For instance, sometimes, a person may only express their feelings accurately after 20 conversations on a subject.

We invited some guests to a meeting one night, and I caught by a glance the facial expression of one lady as we sat there quietly expressing ourselves. You could tell she could not believe what she was hearing (she seemed to be thinking, "I cannot believe I am stuck in this room listening to this?")

I recently found out that the Abbot could pretty much ignore any decision the community votes on. If he sees it as detrimental to the community, he can do nothing. We (the newer people) thought the Abbot didn't remember anything we decided, but instead, he was simply not acting. In any case, communication is quite poor. You find out you are not supposed "to move that pole" until after the roof caves in on everyone. You might ask before you move the pole: Does anyone know anything about this pole? And they might simply stare at you, or they might give you the history of the building. Then you being the hard worker (trying to take the initiative), decide to clear the pole out the way, and in comes the ceiling! But before you can blink your eyes, everyone's coming over explaining to you why the pole is there and why you really should not have moved it.

Now that we just finished a course in Canon Law, I must admit I learned much about Religious life. We are tied directly to Rome for much of everything and very little (it seems) to the local Bishop. Each Trappist Monastery is very "legally" independent. Did you know that if a Trappist is in solemn vows and decides to leave Religious life, he must get approval from the Pope (via the Abbot General in Rome!) You can go, but technically you are still under the obedience of the Abbot. We have a brother doing that now, and he was a priest. He was a monk for 25 years and, at 51, decided he wanted to leave. So he spent three years away from the monastery and is now applying to leave the priesthood and monastic vows. Sister Jeanne is one of his Canon lawyers.

I think I have a deeper understanding of why the monks are so sensitive about what people express to outsiders. If you could see some of the "just plain weird" personal behaviors of people here, you realize outsiders would have no idea how to judge these situations with Charity in mind. A person's behavior can go from one extreme to another daily. For instance, I have gone to great lengths to get and conceal even an extra slice of cake, and never in my life would I think a piece of cake would ever matter so much. It is just plain shameful what a person's invisible addictions will drive them to do. It is not until you cannot have something that you discover that you have to have it, and it seems you would make a deal with anyone to get it.

30 or more years ago, it was 90% monks doing everything. But now the monastery is 90% run by non-monks. And the non-monks have such sympathy for you. The women like to mother you. Sometimes you might mysteriously find a cheeseburger at your workplace! You may not know where it came from, but you enjoy it in secret. Or was it a hidden monastic test? And it is always so interesting to see an 85-year-old man being mothered and enjoying every bit of it! I guess we as people are never too old for these things, are we?

By the way, for those who think that the Trappists are a bunch of heartless people who believe that people should not enjoy life's basic amenities, please think again. I recently found out that when a monk's family member is sick and cannot support themselves, a monk can leave the monastery and help with the care of the said family member. However, you are still required to live a proper lifestyle. You can't decide to go out and become a competitor on "Dancing with the Stars" [a show in which couples compete through dancing] without the Abbot's permission.

As you can see, the Abbot has significant authority given the independence of a Trappist monastery. He is sort of like a Bishop of an Archdiocese. So he needs to be a person of advanced spiritual evolution. Let's face it, someone with that much authority can do a lot of damage to any organization. You may wonder if the person is mentally ill or even spiritually possessed. Probably you'd end up with a lot of grayer hair. But more than likely, you would find out with some certainty whether you are still at the monastery because of Jesus or because you satisfy your own desires!

Farewell until later, love,

Br. Anthony Maria

May 23, 2012

Dear Mary,

Happy Easter!

It is still Easter and I just wanted to comment on the Easter card I received from you. What can I say? It flows. And it seems to do so naturally. My first impression of your writing was that I was impressed with how you express traditional ideas in a non-traditional way if that conveys adequately? In other words, I clearly understood what you were saying even though it was a non-traditional version of the English language expressing it. Fine poetry does that, I guess.

I thank you for the card, and I will keep it. We are not supposed to accumulate many personal items, but this, to me, is special! Your mind is very creative and communicates ideas well with words. I hope that makes sense too! (Thinking: I wonder if she practices writing or does it just stream naturally. I could relate to just about everything she wrote.)

Anyway, I hope you had a Happy Mother's Day, and God bless you and your family. It is always fruitful to hear from you.

Sincerely,

Br. Anthony-Maria

Welcome to Monastic Life! – My Personal Prayer

My Personal Prayer

I found the definition of Tabernacle to be (According to the Hebrew Bible): (Hebrew: מִשְׁכָּן, *mishkān*, meaning "residence" or "dwelling place"), also known as the **Tent of the Congregation** (Hebrew: אֹהֶל 'מוֹעֵד *ōhel mō'ēḏ*, also **Tent of Meeting**, etc), was the portable earthly dwelling place of Yahweh (the God of Israel) used by the Israelites from the Exodus until the conquest of Canaan. [4] Roman Catholics similarly keep God. And sometimes in the chapel, while in prayer, I used to wonder whether God cared if the doors to our Tabernacle were open or closed. I asked myself if the Tabernacle's wooden doors block God's influence?

And this is how my personal prayer with God developed, in a dark church, in a chair facing the front chapel wall. I was in the presence of the Tabernacle, enclosing the Holy Eucharist. I frequently sat there for hours, sometimes meditating, sometimes just sitting quietly, and still wondering about wooden doors. In faith, we accept that water falls downward because gravity directs it. Through devotion (and trust), I developed my personal prayer with God in the monastery. Len, a regular monastic guest, joked with me when I would go running for the chapel at three o'clock every day. He would say, will it make a difference if you get there a few minutes later? But in my mind, Jesus told Saint Faustina to pray this prayer every day at three o'clock p.m., not 3:01 p.m.. And I wanted to "follow the rules" to the best of my ability! But this debate, too, is developing personal prayer. I needed to learn from the people around me as I gained confidence in my relationship with God. In my mind, I did not know if God would find lateness by one minute acceptable.

When we had a day with no work, I made a habit of finding an empty room to meditate on the Holy Rosary of the Blessed Virgin Mary. It was a weird habit, but it flowed naturally from the being I was at the time. Sometimes I would turn the lights off and walk around the room in circles reciting the Holy Rosary and contemplating my knowledge of the scripture. I was genuinely amazed by the associations that came from my little mind. I assumed it was the work of the Holy Spirit within me. But this was also me developing personal prayer. The Rosary changed from a prayer where I followed rote memory about biblical events to a deeper understanding of what those events mean in a holy, Christian, and eternal way.

Much of my personal prayer flows from having the confidence to follow divine inspiration. It comes from knowledge and confidence that Mary is guiding me to Christ. It comes from faith in obedience to small things that often have a greater purpose. Once before I was Roman Catholic, I sent an email to a church website. I was wondering what the "Stations of the Cross" was. I was curious about it. Someone from the website answered my email: The "Stations of the Cross" are the "stations of the cross." This response frustrated me because, after waiting for quite some time, it provided no new information. But this thoughtless answer also left me curious about the "Stations of the Cross" and why they were so mysterious that no one could satisfactorily answer my question. As I became more Catholic, I learned that the Cross's Stations are critical events along the route Jesus took to his crucifixion. I also learned that parishioners usually pray the stations on Good Friday. But what I did not realize is that the Stations of the Cross are prayed any time. I learned that particular freedom in the monastery. So on feast days, I would offer prayer for my family. I created a prayer by praying the Stations of the Cross, and between each station, I offered the Divine Mercy Chaplet for my family and friends. I was creative. I gained confidence in my prayer life and simultaneously learned to be Roman Catholic!

What I found most difficult in my personal prayer with God was letting go of "official procedures" and genuinely offering myself "as I am" during my prayer. That required more obedience to inspiration. I had to stop doing Google searches on proper procedures and do more reading about saints, respond to more guidance from Mary, and have more conversations with God.

They came to Capernaum. There the men who were collecting the tax for the temple came to Peter. They asked him, `Does not your teacher pay the tax for the temple?'

Peter said, `Yes, he does.'

When he came into the house, Jesus spoke to him about it first. He said, `Simon, what do you think? From whom do kings on earth take taxes? Do they take them from their own people or from other people?'

Peter said, `From other people.' Jesus said, `Then the sons do not pay a tax.

But we must not make them think something wrong about us. So go to the sea. Throw a fish-hook into the water. Take the first fish you catch. Open its mouth and you will see a piece of money. Take it and pay them the tax for you and me.' **Matthew 17: 25-28.** [14]

In reading that verse from the Gospel of Matthew, it occurred to me that it might have many meanings and implications. But what spoke to me recently was that sometimes God does not always tell you to do things that make sense to you. Sometimes his actions and directions have eternal meaning that might not make a whole lot of sense to someone who lives a mere 100 years. It might also have heavenly meaning versus the physical purpose that I usually accept. Obedience seems helpful here. I have heard the word obedience to my detriment far too many times. I must focus my mind and follow through on inspirations as best I can. From these small acts, much can follow.

July 31, 2012

Dear Mom and Dad,

This is a short one. I just wanted to let you know how much I appreciated being home. I enjoyed being near you and hearing your voices. It was rather satisfying to talk to Barbara face-to-face.

I enjoyed the DVD movies dad had in the basement. It was like old times! I enjoyed the beer and the wine. Cooking pork spareribs on a grill seemed strangely out of this world-incredible! I simply had a fantastic time. We all know I am in a monastery and not used to going all over the place. Monastic life settles one's mentality to a state of abnormal calm and peacefulness. But it was a busy weekend for everyone, so I had to adjust to the circumstances.

I put your pictures out in the senior wing for all to see. One person asked about my parents' African clothes for the Anniversary. Everyone was impressed with the awards from so many important people. I got a lot of questions about it. With all these government connections, somebody wanted to know if I could get the IRS off their backs (smile!) I said the congratulatory letters were to Mr. and Mrs. Odom, not me (smile). I am nobody important.

As I write this letter, I am preparing to drive to the Veteran's Medical Clinic at the Joint Base - Goose Creek, S.C. for a six-month physical. I have come to look forward to that since I don't leave the monastery much. Hopefully, this means a double-burger and soda for lunch.

Things are back to normal for me at the monastery. I continue to go through changes. Sometimes, I see events before they happen, sometimes, hearing conversations about me when I am sleeping and the whole bit. Sometimes it is evident that these things are happening. I don't suppose the monks know what to think of me? Is he psychic, or is he on some sort of drugs? Hell, I don't know what to think of me? If I am on drugs, no one told me about it! Here is an example: The volunteer nurse was leaving to move to Colorado. No one was supposed to know. I dreamed I had a conversation with someone who told me. So I made her a farewell card for everyone to sign. Then everyone started whispering, "how did he know she was leaving?" I said someone told me. Everyone who did know denied having a conversation with me. And, of course, for a short while after that, people start avoiding me. They think I'm reading all their secrets or something like that. The good part is the people here don't seem to remember anything beyond two weeks. So if you can make it two weeks after an incident, you can pretty much go on as usual. It occurs to me that this is why some politicians can offer the same promises every election without fulfilling any of them and still get reelected. Large numbers of people don't remember anything beyond a specific period. When the promises come again, it is as if it is for the first time.

My life here is very different now. And I am different now. It may not seem that way when I was home, but it is true. Anyway, tell Dad I told everyone he was going to visit soon. So he must spend at least three days here. This way, we can hang out in Charles City together and take in all the scenery! Plus, he needs to see the monastery- it is beautiful, and there are not as many insects as he might seem to think.

Love you all,

Br. Anthony-Maria -Keith

P.S. I pray for each of you sometimes several times a day. And, I am handsome too!

This is a circumstance in which a family asked me to pray for certain intentions and because I had a kinship with them, I did not hesitate to do so. In this circumstance I simple offered prayer from one of the books the Roman Catholic Church and its many organizations have prewritten for this situation. Their prayer was answered.

October 06, 2012

Dear Mary,

A quick note: My Prayers will be with you and your family, and I will pray for each one by name. I offer a novena for you, your schooling, and your travels. It is good to stay in touch.

Since you have a family and are in school full time, maybe you might find email more convenient: anthonymaria3@gmail.com. And since you are married, only if you feel comfortable with this form of exchange.

I am authentically happy for you. And wish you strength and Holy "fruit" in your journey.

Sincerely,

Br. Anthony-Maria

Welcome to Monastic Life! – Where Is God?

Where Is God?

*The word **Mystical** means an experience with a spiritual meaning or reality that is neither apparent to the senses nor obvious to the intelligence.* [5] Based on my Religious life experience, people do not openly speak of personal mystical experiences. Most people are quiet about them. So at least in church life, we often try to limit our talk of such experiences to those celebrated by the church. If we could get people to remember, and where to open our society for everyone to communicate their unusual life experiences, our ideas of life would become a total mess. All the commonly accepted rules that we live by would be change. Not all experiences would be legitimate, but many would be. Then perhaps we could pull up the wheat and throw out the chaff for burning. We would probably then live in and accept a more profound truth about how we exist.

There are social pressures to keep unusual experiences to one's self. I am no expert on the human mind or the theology of genuine religious, mystical experiences, but I have come to realize that reality is far more complex than we would rather accept. Life is far more "mystical" than we wish to claim openly. In what people call the "real world," life is about living to be adored, loved, and modeled. To be famous or known by others in a unique way is our community implied goal. This social construct is what we call healthy esteem. When a person lives a life in this way, at death, we eulogize these as values to appreciate. But I have concluded that a person selling the most refrigerators in their company's history or running the most yards in a football game, for instance, is not in and of itself sufficient or even required for life with God. While these activities might be a path to a relationship, they don't necessarily lead to one.

The difficulty with mystical experiences is that they often involve you personally and no one else. And many people feel life experiences are not legitimate unless all the people have the same experience. Such acceptable mystical experiences seem legitimate over time in the church and only when accompanied by a related change in reality. So when Saint Francis of Assisi hears the voice of God command him, "to repair my house, which as you see has fallen into ruin." And then following that experience, his life is ordered toward God, his actions point to God and there is the great history that comes about related to the life of Francis as he went about his work; we say it is a genuine religious, mystical experience of God. The proof is plain as daylight is to the eyes. Francis is a great saint because he heard God, listened to God, followed God's immediate direction, and God worked greatness through him.

My little test for a justified mystical experience is wondering how it came about with no one else causing it. How it might defy the physical rules I usually follow. And how much it might correlate with my understanding of Christian scripture. Once while at Mass, a priest, in his homily, publicly denounced the church's verbal prayers. He offered that effective prayer was practice without words. He was suggesting that we, as monks need to evolve. I served the Altar that day and stood near this particular priest with the bread and wine for consecration. I was greatly offended by his homily. So I quietly asked Mary, our Mother, to tell this priest to stop publicly denouncing the prayers God gives us. The prayer of the Hail Mary could not be more holy or less holy. It is a matter of who is praying it! And as we stood there at the Altar, this priest looked at me with great embarrassment. He knew his thinking was incorrect. And somehow, he heard me talking to Mary.

Later while I stood alone in the Refectory (where we eat), I looked up at the crucifix over the Abbot's table. A voice came from the direction of the icon. It spoke as if Jesus himself had spoken: this priest tests my patience. To me, this meant Jesus was in sympathy with my being greatly offended by that homily on personal prayer. Do I go telling people of such "mystical" occurrences? No, I don't.

Photo: Crucifix from the 13th century, over the Abbot's seat in the monastery Refectory.

In another instance, I was outside in the walking areas along the road to the monastery, and I encountered a frequent guest of the monastery—a husband and wife couple. I spoke and gave her a warm hug. I was attracted to her. And as I was hugging her, I saw the apparition of a demon of some sort over her shoulder, and he threatened, "don't tempt me!" I kept hugging her, but I came to realize that more than the husband was watching us. I suspect it is already too late when that happens: some sort of evil is afoot, and I had better be careful.

In another situation, I was in the Flower Room adjacent to the church sanctuary one evening before Vespers, and I was physically wrestling with something not physically present. If it tried to get me to turn left, I would resist, and if it tried to get me to turn right, I would resist again. And this wrestling match went on as one of the brothers opened the door and caught a glimpse of me struggling with "nothing." His eyes opened wide, and he stood there for a brief moment astounded. And then he just as quickly closed the door and walked away. He never brought up what he saw, and neither did I. For some reason, we do not talk about it. But I knew, and he knew what we both encountered. If I understand what I heard correctly, an Exorcist told the Abbot that Mary was allowing these attacks for my "good." He showed the Abbot some proof of what was going on and as far as I know that was it. <u>I am especially grateful for priests who do this kind of work.</u> They do not seem to get enough credit for dealing with such a great mystery.

From the Desk of:
The New Apple 'MAC' OS X
Elizabeth Lawson Library
Our Lady of Methuselah Abbey

October 27, 2012

Dear Family,

What a way to start a letter! The Abbot bought two iMac desktop computers using macOS, and they are like a computer dream come true: camera built-in, 500 GB Hard Drive, built-in applications for almost everything you could ever need! Since high school, I have not used an Apple (Apple II plus), and my goodness, how things have changed! Even though I only know about software, I have obtained the reputation as the 'tech' monk. We run MS Server 2003™ and Windows XP™ from the turn of the last century (smile). Honestly, most of the problems people have here would be so fundamental to someone outside the monastery that it makes me look like some sort of whiz-kid. Also, I know how to research and solve technical problems because I have used the internet for research for so long that it is second nature for me to do so. Some people here put all technology into the same category: video cameras, computers, servers, printers, DVD players, etc. So if it is not working, get the tech guy to look at it.

On another note, a priest from up north passed away, and he left the monastery some funds in his will. So the monastery decided to use the money to replace all the ancient vehicles. We bought a used hybrid (gas/electric) car, and it is also key-less. The monks said, "let him drive it." I freely admit it made me a little nervous since I was going to the Veteran's hospital for the first time. It was a nice car, but gas mileage seemed not much better than any other purely gas engine car. Fr. Peter says God knows what he is doing "my being here is no mistake." To me, technology is too technical to use without training or at least some type of manual. When I'm president of these here monasteries, all monks will be required to be adequately trained for their jobs, and each one will have a free cheese sandwich in every pot!

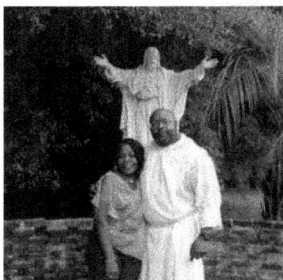

Photo: (Stacy Le Gras and me) My cousin Stacy visiting Georgia from California decided to ride up to the monastery with my Dad and cousin Jeffrey to see me. Jeffrey took the photo.

What can I say about what has happened since my last letter? Everyone was delighted with dad's visit. The Abbot was away delivering something to some organization. It ended up taking all afternoon. We had a perfect time touring, and it was great seeing Stacy and Jeff (my cousins from California and Georgia). I posted some pictures on Facebook. Yes, we have access to Facebook (FB) now. It is incredible to me how many people commented on 6 photos. Dad left delicious gifts. I put some stuff in the kitchen freezer for later. I emailed pictures to Stacy and Jeffrey. It seems that the people at the monastery think any woman who comes to visit is "secret-relationship" suspicious. So I had to explain to different people that she was my cousin about eight times. They all have lots of questions when the person leaves. They mainly want to know if your parents found the place acceptable. I said that they did.

Since you have left, we have built more stuff for our monastic duties. I now have a small cart for hauling firewood. The table carrier we made is for moving furniture and the like. At first, some of the brothers looked at the cart strangely because everyone carried things by hand. Now people are comfortable seeing it. Some older monks still look at it weirdly because it is different. Fr. Peter was impressed! He commented, Joseph (Jesus' Step-Father) was a carpenter! So was Jesus! So he asked me to build him a rolling file holder for his room. I did so, and he used it for a few days. Then pushed it outside his room to his patio. I guess it was not helpful in the way he hoped. In any case, all this building started when a guest named Jim from Florida (dad, everyone else all met Jim too!) donated a bag of used wheels. It is incredible what a small odd donation from someone makes possible. Some of the newer monks call me Br. McGuiver because I'm constantly inventing something. You have to have seen the show to know about "McGuiver." Older monks have no idea what that means.

Communication is still a learning process for me. Is it possible that I might have dyslexia? It is incredible how I can say something, and someone can comment with words that have nothing to do with what I have said. I have figured out that we as monks communicate in roughly three or four ways or categories: Literal, Symbolic, Spiritual, and Other. Then there are mixtures of each. The monks here seem to almost always communicate in a non-literal way. Maybe they assume that I do the same? I have spent most of my adult life and a good deal of my youth imitating and communicating to machines and the like.

Photo: (l to r, Jeffrey Lewis, My Dad, Anthony Odom, and Me) They came up from Statesboro, GA. My cousin Jeff was kind enough to drive my father and cousin Stacy for the visit! Stacy took the photo.

Also, I often use the Scientific Method for discovery. My thinking and language are very factual and literal-oriented. So I suspect that this is why there is such poor communication between me and others. Though I must admit, I am better at understanding scripture now. The Roman Catholic church is very cerebral in its way of understanding scripture. And they bring together thousands of years of history to interpret it all. We take many classes here to understand what we believe. It is paying off. The literal interpretation of the Bible is entirely unreasonable to me at this point. Once you see how the various books came about and the method of recording history used by people three or four thousand years ago, it makes no sense to have a strictly literal interpretation of the Bible.

However, I often think that I want to use our method for discerning scripture to analyze a book like <u>The Great Gatsby</u> and see if it too points to God in the same way scripture does? The classes teach that the books of the Christian Bible all point to God in their teachings. Maybe everything we write points to God in some way? In other words, does the catholic method of interpretation indeed reveal the holiness of the Bible, or does every book reveal the same holiness? I also question scriptural teaching so complicated that few people can understand it? To me, it seems some theologians make God very, very difficult! As human beings, we have to look for the deeper meaning, but maybe this is not the primary reason

Jesus came. Perhaps we should focus more on imitating his life than analyzing and theorizing? These are just thoughts on my part. I am not saying that we should get rid of all complicated theological teaching. And let's face it, the world we live in has reached complexity like never before. We might have to apply these teachings helpfully. Thus, our explanations for Christian life may have to follow that complexity?

When I came to Philadelphia for your 50th Anniversary, they gave me "spending cash." I used all of it. When we went to Belfast, they gave us money for spending, and at one of the gas stations, I bought an MP3 player (great for downloading free education classes). When I go to VA appointments, I take cash "just in case." When I get back, my hand is full of receipts (smile) for Rainy who handles all the bookkeeping and accounting stuff. I guess some habits do not go away. Anyway, after all that, I vowed to spend like a real monk. The monastery provides for a monk's needs, and unless it's an emergency, there is no need to spend money. In other words, I am not supposed to using the "spending cash" that they give me. It is supposed to be for an emergency!

Fr. Luke had his 98th birthday. We opened our monastic dining area to retreatants and guests. Usually, the doors between the monastic eating area and the guest area are closed. We had ice cream and two different types of cake. Fr. Luke was born in 1914. He is the only person I know who remembers everything he did in detail, even 70 years ago. He started as a Franciscan Friar, became a priest, and in 1969 or so a Trappist monk. He has a Ph.D., a J.D. (law), and is a Canon lawyer. He used to be Abbot at Methuselah but retired at age 75 years old. He is always complimenting everyone. He says I am a super genius. He told me that the root word for Maria (as in Anthony-Maria) in Latin means 'Oceans' and that it's no coincidence that I chose that name and am also a navy man. He wanted to know my SAT scores, and I said I didn't do all that well on the SATs (Scholastic Aptitude Test). My math score was okay, but that's it. He seemed perplexed or disappointed. But he looks constantly amazed with me. We share articles on science. He is always reading about astronomy and nuclear physics. Though he compliments me when I write my name correctly, so maybe some of his behavior is a little tainted. He probably should not have retired at 75. I am told that retired Abbots go off somewhere to let the new Abbot take over and get established. The current Abbot is up for re-election at the end of October. Only monks in solemn vows can vote on the Abbot. New people simply watch and learn. If they choose to, the brothers can elect someone from another Trappist monastery to be our Abbot. That person must first accept the invitation. Abbot Kline, who died of cancer in 2006, came from Monk Abbey to be Abbot here. The Abbot's responsibility is primarily for the spiritual well-being of the monks. It is not the operation of monastic facilities. Paying the bills and building upkeep are responsibilities that can be assigned to others. But not the souls in his care. For these, he answers to God. That is a substantial responsibility! The Abbot will have to answer for all those brought to him who are lost.

Br. Theo took Simple Vows. His dad has dementia. He went home for a week to see him in October because they feared that his father wouldn't remember him anymore. But minus his father, his entire family showed up (mostly from Arkansas) for his vows in July. Br. Theo has three children. His ex-wife is remarried. All his grandchildren, family, and friends showed up for his vows. I said to myself, "there is no way I will invite all those people so far a distance for Simple Vows." Vows are essential, but far too many people leave before Permanent Vows. I imagine inviting that many people for permanent vows. I am eligible for my Simple Vows at the end of May 2013--God willing.

In my novena (nine days of prayer for a particular intention) to the Blessed Virgin Mary, I asked her to help me follow her closely. Around the 4th of the 5th day of my prayers, I found myself promising Jesus I would follow him wherever he went. And I promised this without fear or hesitation, which is odd for me. But the next day, as I thought about my promise, I told Jesus, you know how I am Jesus? If this is going to happen, you must do most of the work. I'm just not that reliable, and I give up too quickly. Fr. Bartholomew had visitors from East Asia. He was happy to see them. They were nice to everyone and seemed to be very devout Catholics. They came to every Office!

I began collecting pecans. Hopefully, they will turn out well this year. There are fewer than last year. But they are delicious! On another subject,

I figured out why so many female visitors seem to pay me so much attention. I thought it was my stunning good looks, but sadly it was not. It turns out it is my voice. When we visited the Sisters of Mercy of the Americas in Belfast, N.C., the first thing one of the Sisters told me after Mass was that I had the most beautiful baritone voice she had ever heard! They went crazy over my voice...no joke. But you must figure they are not used to having men around to sing at Mass. It is incredible how having a female voice in our monastery choir changes my mentality when I hear it. Here at the Abbey, people stare at you like they are in love with you? So now, when I come into the church for Office, I look at the ground. It is the proper monastic practice to keep your mind on Christ and off people staring at you. If I don't, I will start to "socialize" with my eyes. Body language is compelling. Most people seem to know not to communicate with you verbally. Eye contact is different. After one compliment from a regular visitor, I told the lady, "I'll try not to let that compliment go to my head..." She seemed to feel remorse after that because she knew what I meant by that comment. It is just too easy to blow up a person's self-image with so many compliments. The false self-image seems to grow silently and invisibly. Then, one day, you are floating off the ground because your "head is too big! "Yes, yes, I think my third cousin on my father's side is related to Nat King Cole! It probably runs in the family." "Yes, it is true, my father is a singer too, though he is not as attractive as I am!" One day you are offended because no one complimented you. One day you find out you 'sound okay,' but you don't have much training in singing and all the hype people were giving came from the wrong source! Live what is True! Blessed are the humble, for they will inherit everything!

Most people don't know that I took a stress test (at the VA hospital) due to chest pains. My heart couldn't be better. And the Abbey got a free detailed heart examination of their perspective vowed monk. So what is causing the chest pains? The doctor gave me some anti-acid pills, but I don't think I have that problem because my diet is bordering on perfect for a guy who is now 47 years old and who used to wolf down pizzas, cheesesteaks, and burgers. I think it is anxiety. And I think I have had it for a good part of my life, but it is only under these conditions am I allowing myself to realize it. I am approaching a significant life decision soon, and I am still "not trusting in God" enough to let go of my fears of it.

I could blame the Abbey and its perspective future or the non-logical behavior of the people I observe here that make me nervous, oh so nervous. But I will be praying on it, and things will work themselves out somehow.

For Deacon Todd: I talked to a man named Frank of Saint Gabriel Catholic Church in Charlotte, North Carolina. He says he knew of your mother from Winston-Salem. And he knew Fr. Martin (the pastor of Our Lady of Consolation after Fr. Jude moved on) and a whole slew of other people. I got the impression he was here to rest. He missed quite a few Offices. But he took a few moments, during clean-up after lunch, to tell me he was from Charlotte. I see from the church bulletin you are listed as Deacon for Our Lady of Consolation? Congratulations? Though, I thought you retired?

Dialogue:
Fr. Thomas: Br. Anthony-Maria, you seem to trust issues?
Br. Anthony-Maria: Well, let us see?

- I thought I was coming here to live for the rest of my life and had a lot of trouble contacting the Abbey to talk to someone for information or guidance. I was trying to decide about leaving my job and giving away everything I own. I was disconnecting from everyone I knew to come here and live for the rest of my life. And I was getting little or no response from the Abbey!
- The Abbot was on sabbatical for three months due to surgery, injuries, and other issues when I arrived.
- After I arrived and was here for several months, I was told that I was here for a five-month trial period. At this point, I am asking myself: who quits their job for a five-month trial period? I came thinking I would never be leaving! Why would I trust people who behave in this manner?
- The Prior was stressed to the breaking point as "acting Abbot" since he had limited authority to make many decisions, yet activities needed to continue as normal.
- The novice master is the Prior, the Abbot's Secretary, the Spanish translator, the "acting Abbot," and the list goes on.
- I surmised that someone told the Abbey that I was a criminal or a person with fake identification. This information seems to have spread to many, if not all, the brothers and many volunteers. After the volunteers got to know me, at least three of them told me, "these people have said some bad things about you" or "they lied about you!" Why not do a formal criminal background check?
- The one other new guy who was here with me left to go back to Maine. He said the lifestyle is too busy. It got busier. But I'm sure he had other reasons too.
- The Abbot returned and decided he wanted to observe me himself for two additional months after previously saying it was okay to become a Postulant.
- We grow mushrooms for a living; we know very little about mushrooms and have no plans for learning except through trial and error. What people do business this way?

- I have had my room searched, work area searched, mail read, email read, and somehow, they know what we talk about at work. The workers and volunteers are like informal intelligence collectors. Anything you say to them or near them might just get reported back to the "elders." And all this is part of my "formation?"
- No one ever sees anything wrong with the monastery. Even though we are shrinking fast, losing members to attrition and death, and have had reform meetings since 2006. Advice from our last visitation (Abbot of Monk Abbey) was that our lives here are out of balance (especially with us in Formation). I receive this "trust comment" as probably a cross-cultural observation. In other words, I do not think as he does.
- I am African American, grew up in a primarily African American family and neighborhood. I am in a monastery occupied by mainly elderly White American male monks whose world view is from several decades ago (and who seem suspicious of every little thing a person does). I asked for this, did I not?
- I grew up in a big city—of millions of people. Anonymity is what many city folks like about the city. I like the occasional exploratory walk. Here at Methuselah, I cannot go out for a walk in the forest without starting a conspiracy. What's he doing out there? Smell his breathe, check his room. He won't stay around long if he leaves the monastery like this.
- I'm free to skip breakfast or supper, but I get my room searched for food when I do.

One day I told the Novice Master I am not the only one with trust issues! Methuselah is overflowing with trust issues. Truthfully, for them, all this sharing of people's personal information and searching of guest's rooms for rule violations is normal behavior. But for someone new, it is an extreme culture shock! Outside of this monastery, people do not get riled up over a missing muffin. I should also add that I am a big guy. And anyone paying attention would have noticed my eating habits when I first started visiting Methuselah. Thus, I would think mercy would be in order and not law enforcement.

The monastery is not supposed to be a legal enforcement system but a school of charity. I do not think that we should allow new people to do whatever they please. But direct, mature communication would be more helpful. Unfortunately, the monks seem to thrive off supposition and conspiracy and not investigative facts. Does no one ask why you are away from work early? They assume you are up to something. And this even though you are out in the open and not trying to hide anything. The monks don't seem confrontational. I guess they don't like to ruffle anyone's feathers. So they are very indirect. It takes quite a bit before they will come right out and ask, "what the heck are you up too?" But, to me, this indirect way of dealing with people's issues forces the development of some terrible communication habits!

What is challenging to get used to is the reaction to having food in your room. It is against the Rule of Benedict to eat outside prescribed times. I freely admit that adjusting to this is taking some time. But in the meantime, the reaction to not following this rule seems bordering on loony. I used to sneak a muffin to my room from time to time. Is it essential to harass a person to the brink of insanity because the rule says no eating between meals? Especially since most of the time, their conspiracy thinking proves false. There are just not that many opportunities to sneak burgers into the forest without people knowing! By the way, I am overcoming my addiction to sweets through fasting and prayer. So now I hardly ever sneak a treat to my room. Do you think anybody notices that? No! Once you get the reputation, you take it to your grave. You become the monk who sneaks food.

Other Updates
The new Shiitake mushroom house is 75 percent complete. The retreat house is not finished until May or June. Bishop Antonio passed away. His entire family came here to the United States to his funeral. He even had a niece come from Australia. He was a good guy. I pray for him. He was the first bishop of his archdiocese. He organized the entire archdiocese from the beginning. But he endured horribly before death from aggressive cancer. He lost his whole leg in fighting cancer-- it had already spread everywhere. Now I have his rocking chair in my room. He gave it to me. [I didn't read about the scandal associated with the bishop until after his

death. And all I can say is that the articles published about him don't seem to match the person I met.]

Jungle Fever:

The squirrels near the monastery disappeared for a few days. I wondered why? So I watched the area for a few more days and saw no squirrels. I became worried. I kept wondering, "where are the squirrels and what does their disappearance mean?" Then one day, on my way back from work, I saw a large owl taking off with a squirrel in his claws. I told Br. Joseph who often feeds the squirrels with leftover peanut butter jars. I never saw anything like that before. For some reason, the idea of squirrels being hunted surprised me. It turns out the squirrels are reasonably intelligent. They figured out that the owl was feeding in this area, and they hid for a while. But now they are all back, playing as if nothing ever happened. However, I did see one squirrel with a large scar, so maybe he got away from the owl that day I was watching.

Once Br. Theo saw a squirrel, he decided to follow it. It looked back at him and started walking away. It continued to look back at him from time to time while walking away. But instead of running up a tree to get away out of fear, it began to run in circles. It turns out the squirrel was looking for fun and games! After that incident, I noticed they have a sort of follow-the-leader game that they play with each other, and I guess the squirrel figured it was game time with Br. Theo!

Fr. Bartholomew was watering one of his plants and found a snake in his flowerpot. And when he came and told me, I went to look. I wondered how it got inside the screen door of our patio? Even though it is screened-in, somehow, snakes and insects find an entrance. We concluded the snake was poisonous because of the shape of the head and what looked like venom sacks behind the head. It was a small snake. So I asked him to hand me his walking stick. And then I went nuts smashing the snake with it. He said, "okay! Okay! It's dead!" I said, "it's still moving!" Then I obtained a pair of scissors and cut off its head. Then he said, "You think it's going to grow another head? Stop already!" two days later, I found one at the chicken house. I picked it up and threw it out into the forest. This one was not a threat, nor was it poisonous. I was learning my lesson. I was learning to share. While there are times when we should kill snakes, I should not if I do not have to.

One day I was followed by a grasshopper? I know, it sounds crazy. But it kept spring toward me, moving in my direction. I tried walking in a different direction. But it turned and came jumping after me again. I became a little confused by this strange event. Why is a grasshopper following me? So I decided to walk off the concrete onto the grass, and only then did it stop following me. I have no idea what that was all about. Why would a grasshopper want to follow me?

One night after Compline, there was a party boat behind the monastery on the Jordan River. We heard loud party music blasting for another hour as we went to bed. It was just strange to hear something like that right before bed. The county says it is public property, and anyone can do what they want if legal. Blasting loud music into the night is not illegal (even if we are going to sleep at 7:30 p.m.!)

When the hunters are out, we hear automatic shotguns all day long. They have permits to hunt during the various seasons. They hunt mostly turkey, deer, and duck. However, when hunting season starts, the forest sounds like a movie war scene. And that noise is going on even while we are in the church for the Offices and Mass. Once I was walking in the woods, a truckload of hunters came past with dogs. They screamed to me to clear out because they were about to let the dogs run. The dogs help with hunting. I figured that maybe they were after a coyote I saw earlier. Earlier that afternoon, I walked down the road outside the monastery when I saw it. And when it saw me, it turned and went into the forest. All the large creatures I have encountered here in the forest have proven non-confrontational except for the alligators. The alligators don't seem to move out of anybody's way.

Spirituality

I threatened to leave! Okay, that sounds worse than it was, but I was serious. I came into the Catholic Church because of Mary. I was praying the Rosary before I became catholic. The *Rosary of the Blessed Virgin Mary* is a prayer or meditation on the stages of Christ's life. So when the

Novice Master started complaining about my verbal prayers (he says we are supposed to be Contemplatives - our prayers are in our work and silence), I eventually pushed back. He said I should not focus on formula prayers. Still, the Abbot permits me to pray The Divine Mercy Chaplet every day at three p.m. in the chapel. I told him this, but he still would not let up because he saw things differently? So I stopped praying the chaplet in the chapel and started praying it at work. But he continued to pressure me concerning verbal prayers. Then he started in on me praying the Rosary. You must understand his perspective; I wake up at 2:30 a.m. saying Hail Mary full of Grace. And pretty much don't stop until work at 9:30 a.m.. When he insisted that I stop praying the Rosary prayer altogether, I sent him an email saying I could not stop and that he was forcing a situation that does not need to be. Then he said, "stop praying the Rosary during the hours of lectio" (4 a.m. to 6 a.m.). He claimed he never said stop altogether. So I stopped praying during Lectio hours. Eventually, he went to the Abbot and explained that I used the Rosary as a crutch to avoid contemplation. And he told me that, in time, the Abbot was going to demand that I stop praying the Rosary so much. Then he never spoke to me about it again. And during this time, I was sleeping on this issue of disobedience and praying day after day because I didn't like the idea of being disobedient. But I eventually felt it was immoral to ask me not to pray the Rosary, so I felt justified in refusing to stop. Heck, this monastery is Mary's school of charity. All Trappist monasteries throughout the world are under her protection and guidance. Many books I have read indicate that the Rosary is Mary's prayer, the prayer of Angels, and the most potent prayer given to men. I am sure some people might dispute that last idea, but still, it's in the books I read. So after meditating on it and still finding myself unable to stop praying the Rosary, I simply kept praying it. I said I'd live with the consequences. The problem is that I knew or was aware that some brothers had a problem with me openly praying the Rosary but would not say anything directly to me. Then one day in a community meeting, Fr. Luke was talking, and suddenly he changed topic mid-sentence and said, please, whatever you do, don't take away a person's charism. It is theirs; it is given to them as a grace. We have common prayer and personal prayer. And personal prayer is just that, personal! After that, everyone was quiet. They knew he was talking about me.

From my perspective, the issue comes down to what church we joined? They joined a church that prayed the Rosary in 'secret' (long ago). It was personal and not prayed publicly. I joined a church that has Rosary marches in the public streets. I don't hide my Rosary. The church has changed. So all those who quietly objected to the Abbot and the Novice Master about my prayer stopped. It is not a matter of who won; it is doing God's will. I pray the Rosary based on my personal path into the church. Also, aside from that- Saint Maria Faustina was a contemplative nun, and Christ gave the Divine Mercy Chaplet to her and told her to pray this prayer for souls. Jesus didn't say but try not to let it interfere with your other prayer time! And she prayed the chaplet all day long!

A Little More Information

I have explained many of my experiences here at the monastery and elsewhere in various letters. These experiences have led me to believe that we only think we live in a "causal reality." But the more authentic reality may very well be non-causal. I use the term 'causal' as when one uses the phrase "cause and effect." The casual reality says I swing the bat; it hits the ball, it flies out to the ballfield. The bat caused the ball to fly out into the field. That is an example of a fundamental cause and effect or causal reality. The following example demonstrates the non-casual reality: we run into the same person three days in a row when we get off a train. It piques our interest that this has occurred three days in a row. We pay attention. We tend to focus on that particular person we keep seeing, and we ask why am I seeing this person at this spot so much? With no apparent cause, we perceive a relationship with this person we are encountering. My experiences lead me to believe there is another way of perceiving the circumstance in a non-causal way. The simple, apparent reason for the encounter is that we catch the train to get to work, and we need to keep the same schedule to be at work on time. The meetings are considered a pure coincidence. I suspect another set of rules that support that casual way of thinking but is more fundamental to our sense of reality. In other words, our causal reality is a subset of a greater one. So one might view the meetings as more than coincidental, that perhaps they are happening for some more significant, hidden reason, and that reason is not apparent to you and may never be. This new perspective of reality appears to be independent of time; it relates us as beings in a way we have not figured out yet. However, it is not causal in any obvious way.

From a religious perspective, I perceive Carl Yung as almost obscene in some of his understandings and thoughts on God. But because of his position in history, I have read some of his books related to Christianity. One might just as well say the same about me! I read only half a page out of his book: <u>Memories, Dreams, and Reflections</u>, which simply confirmed what I was already thinking. He says that synchronicity is our insistence that we live in a *cause-and-effect* universe. We see synchronicity as unique when it is the more usual case when we drop our cause and effect expectations. The greater reality is not cause-and-effect. He also thinks we humans live in a subset of this greater reality. In other words, we are limited most of our days to a cause-and-effect reality. We only occasionally experience another type of reality but not enough to completely perceive it as such. He thinks that the reality of cause-and-effect is simply a superficial understanding of the more authentic reality. Events do not necessarily have to be linear (one causing the other). I take that in a slightly different way. There might very well be a force that connects you and me that determined us meeting each day at the train station, but it may well be one we don't yet understand. I like to think of the circumstance in which Jesus pays his taxes by telling his disciple to: get the first fish you catch and take the coin out of its mouth to pay the temple tax. He is using a set of rules within a cause-and-effect reality where the circumstances at hand seem to have no connection whatsoever. The reality at hand is disjointed or not logically connected. Why on earth would a fish have a coin in its mouth? How would Jesus know about it? And why would he think to look inside a fish in the water for cash in the first place? Yet, all the circumstances somehow produced money for paying the temple tax. As modern Christians, we are in the midst of a time that only accepts a physically causal reality. The past observations of our world have tried to get us to receive a spiritual one. And it relates ideas and activities by a different set of rules. The study of Quantum Mechanics in its simplest form leads one to draw similar observations. Reality is not as simple as it appears. One of my bosses in the Navy used to call me 'the professor.' Now I know why!

Well, it is time for me to sign off. If my little list up there sounds too much like I am complaining, it is because I am. I have discovered I am very much a perfectionist. Once I commented to Br. Mark about the weird rust spot on the surface of a sphere on the roof of the church steeple. In my mind, I could not understand why we were letting the church rust so. He noted to me that I seemed to notice everything. This tendency to notice everything is just another personal issue I am working on through prayer and meditation. However, what I have written about above is mostly fact and not an exaggeration. It does not mean I am packing my bags to leave; it just means I am watching others and myself very closely. I think it is the best way to follow Christ at this point in my vocation. Because of our culture, even the most caring, giving people sometimes seem arrogant and self-centered. And people say, if you notice it in others, you have first recognized it in yourself.

Love,

Br. Anthony-Maria

Every Christmas, benefactors of the monastery offered gifts to all the brothers. And it was exciting from year to year, wondering what people would give. But no matter what they gave you, one could not help but feel gratitude for this approach to giving. While the benefactors often knew the monks in the monastery for a longer time, they knew nothing of the many newer people, some of whom were not full members. So we often wrote a joint note to thank specific families for their generosity and kindness.

December 31, 2012

From the Desks of Some Novices and an Observer
Of Methuselah (and Br. Theo Too!)

Dear Mary and Joseph,

Every year since we have been here at Methuselah, the monks have received generous gifts from your family! And we always wish there was some way to express our gratitude to you. We have all decided to offer a prayer for your family.

Your gifts are unique because it makes us all feel a little closer to our loved ones elsewhere. Why? Simply because the tradition of opening a gift at Christmas makes us feel a little closer to our family, who is far off.

May God continue to Bless You.

Br. Theo (Simple Vows)
When they asked me, what was in the box, I told them Jet Skis and a Harley [motorcycle]!

Make sure you cover for me...thanks!

_____

Br Anthony-Maria

_____

Fr. Bartholomew

_____

Observer Michael

2013

Once while I was praying the Divine Mercy Chaplet given by Jesus directly to Saint Maria Faustina (a nun from 1920's Poland), I could feel my mind fill with all kinds of hysterical, bizarre, and offensive thoughts. My initial reaction was to jump up from the ground and try to understand. But as I lay there on the floor of my room trying to combat these thoughts, I could feel a hand on my back pressing me to the floor and whispering for me to keep praying. And so, I kept praying all the while wondering why I was thinking such nasty, evil thoughts.

That's another one of those experiences that stuck with me even as I write this page. I learned so much from that situation. A lesson I learned is that Jesus does hear my prayers, and in fact, he helps me pray. And no matter how insignificant I seem to think he might think of my prayers, they matter to him. So I should have faith and pray no matter what I think about the situation. A second lesson I learned was that during the craziest turmoil, I need to keep on praying. This communication with God was authentic, but it was also a lesson on praying no matter what circumstance. With my mind in the most bizarre turmoil, I was somehow able, through faith, to continue praying the words of that Divine Mercy Chaplet.

And the third lesson I learned was that I am not always responsible for the exaggerations of my mind. I may create the warped inspirations of my mind, but other influences play a severe role in their exaggeration. And this is one of my life's major struggles. It is one situation to have jealousy, but still, another to be savagely ruled by it.

Chapter Introduction

Most of us grow up experiencing death in some form. Maybe your religious background helps you to evolve what you accept about death. Before I went into the monastery, my family and friends lost my older brother Timothy Odom Sr. in 2007. Some things surprised me about my brother's death. The first is what occurred while attending his funeral. People from all his previous jobs, the military, and friends from our childhood, along with their families, attended. They all came to his funeral. For some reason, I had just never realized how many people knew my brother. He did not seem to me to have a large social circle. I mostly saw him at family events and his home in Germantown. And other than his wife, Christina, and her family, I knew few other people in his social circle. I never knew so many people knew my brother.

The other surprise was that there is very little preparation you can make emotionally to lose someone so close to you. As adults, we were not very close. But in our childhood, we were. I was like "social luggage" for my brother. Where ever Tim went, he had to take me. Whenever he played a ball game, my brother included me. And when we decided to be troublesome, he forced me away. Growing up, we shared the same bedroom. We told each other stories at night. We made plans for the next day and argued at every opportunity. His death was my first actual, truly intimate emotional exposure to death. And all I can say is that you never know how much space a person occupies in your life until you encounter them in their death. It is too overwhelming an experience to process in a usual way. Emotionally it takes you places you have not prepared for and leaves you in a state of being not ever experienced; this kind of encounter with death is a surreal encounter with life.

My experience at Methuselah was parallel. In getting to know and learn from the older monks, you do so authentically and intimately. Some monks are well along in age and on the verge of death, sometimes by a painful illness. With Roman Catholicism, there is only one death, and that is death through permanent separation from God. With us, a person does not simply disappear under the ground, decaying until they are no more. What some recognize as physical death is merely a step in an eternal process. Accepting the Roman Catholic details of death in such a personal way took some time. Still, after communing with, caring for, and learning from so many people around me experiencing death, I found myself learning to accept physical death as a transition to life eternal.

A monk's life is primarily preparation for dying. While the monk doesn't abandon life in the world completely, a monk's life focus is on their permanent relationship with God. That relationship is eternal, and thus, the focus is on life now and life after physical death. The monastic is concerned about where they will end up eternally, not just tomorrow after lunch. And this brings about a rather extreme change in psychology compared to many people in the world outside the monastery. Cosmetic preservation of the body is a lower priority. For me, seeing other people die in a close and personal way and seeing God involved in that transition gives me both confidence in this monastic way of life and hope for my own experience to come.

I can confidently say that one of the most educational and spiritually enriching experiences I have ever had in my life is at this monastery living in faith and prayer with the dying and the physically dead. These experiences added dimensions to life that have helped me recognize eternity, take it seriously, and realize its gift for me like never before.

February 07, 2013

Dear Mary,

I thank you for your note. As usual, it is good to hear from you. I can say that I am excited that you are excited about Methuselah. We are struggling relative to the 1960s when Methuselah started as a sort of overflow from another monastery. Yes, all your prayers are helpful!

As you know, we have many elderly monks, and at 47, I am currently the youngest one here. And in case you are not aware, 47 is not very young for a newer monk. We have many people interested, but not many are willing to commit right now. We are in a phase of reorganizing. But the reorganization is happening at monastic speeds, so it is slow compared to the outside world. Monks operate on a much slower timetable that is often out of sync with the outside world. Traditionally a person starts monastic life in their earlier years, and I hear all monasteries accept somewhat older monks like myself.

I always enjoy your writing, and I think I may study some of it in more detail. I probably could learn a lot from you. I am glad to hear you are traveling again. Did you call off school entirely? You should know I pray for you and your family all the time. And God answers prayers. How often do your check email? I would write more often if you do use email. I prefer email because my handwriting and spelling in personal letters are horrible.

Stay in touch. PEACE.

Br. Anthony-Maria

P.S. I have been doing much better since The Feast of John the Baptist! I thank you for your prayers in that also.

February 20, 2013

Patient Representative
Charleston VA Medical Center
109 Bee Street
Charleston, SC 29401

Dear Sir,

I am just writing a simple note of thanks for the **EXCELLENT** staff service I received at my January 17, 2013, 10:30 p.m. appointment. The information is below:

Location:
GOOSE CREEK OUTPUT CLINIC

Clinic:
GC EYE IMAGER

Clinic Phone:
843-789-6500

My visits to the Goose Creek Clinic are always positive. But, the staff member, Kim, was the most pleasant and professional person. This visit is my first experience with her, and she was most helpful in educating me on benefits I don't ever recall seeing in my benefits book. She saved me much time, frustration, and money. And she did it all, working two different nursing stations. And I just wanted to thank you and that precious woman for her help. May God Bless You All!

Thank You!

Sincerely,

Rodney K. Odom, ssn: 1234

February 28, 2013

The monastery offers the brothers classes on Church, Religious and Monastic Life. The instructors were often priests, sisters, or theologians from civilian universities. While monks in permanent vows can attend, attendance is required for those still transitioning. Below is a class assignment from one of the teachers of our courses.

From: Br. Anthony-Maria

Christian Anthropology - Professor: Sister Sarah

Reflection Paper: Naming Grace in Your Life

"...author Karl Rahner has stressed that Grace is first and foremost God's own divine life ("uncreated Grace"). Giver and Gift are one. Grace therefore refers to God's own life as God shares it with us through Jesus Christ in the Holy Spirit." [Sachs, 71] Therefore, to perceive God's life within my own experience is Grace at work!

Recognizing Grace is recognizing God in me. When seeking God within me, I seem to contrast the expectations of my behavior with my actual conduct in life as a way of recognizing Grace at work in me. We all have a personal history, and we tend not to change significantly from that historical behavior. When I find myself doing something that genuinely astonishes me, I tend to think it is Grace at work. That is not to say Grace is not at work in other less visible ways, but these dramatic behavior changes are the ones most apparent. I offer this personal example of Grace at work in my behavior as a small sample of God giving me his life as part of my own.

The experience I write about occurred over 10 years ago. I lived in Philadelphia, Pennsylvania, and was coding a software application that I would eventually sell online. But I was also driving a cab at night to pay some of my expenses. The night was cold and windy, and I picked up a fare over the radio dispatch at a homeless shelter. The people at the homeless shelter used our taxicab service regularly. The woman I picked up was a single parent of three small children, one little girl (age five), and nine-month-old twin infants. She intended to go to her friend's house in the Oak Lane section of the city. It was not far away.

As I did with most customers who got in my cab, I made trivial, small talk. And the following conversation was her "small talk": that she was asked to leave the homeless shelter because she accused a guy of sexual assault, and in this shelter, if they must call the police, all parties involved must leave the shelter for the night. The shelter administration warned her ahead of time of the consequences of calling the police. So she needed to go to her friend's house for the night. Her friend was a firefighter and was on-call and not home (at least not yet). She seemed serious about her situation, and I felt great empathy for her circumstances.

Since it was cold, I waited for her as she exited the cab to check her friend's house only to find he was still not home. We then proceeded to her mother's house to seek someplace to stay for the night. She left her mother's house rejected! Her mother told her she could not stay at her house. But her mother gave her cash to go to New York City to be with her sister for the night. As she came from her mother's house, I saw the look on her face. To me, she was in a complicated situation. It was freezing, and she had a little girl and two nine-month-old babies with no refuge after being forced from a homeless shelter for being a victim of a sexual assault. She even showed me the report she filed with the police. I was numb from the circumstances! So when she returned to the backseat of the cab, I stared at her asked her: Is there anything I can do for you? I asked this, wary because her mother rejected her too!

The next stop was the supermarket to get milk and diapers for the babies' bus trip to New York. I agreed to come back and pick her up from the store if she called me on my phone. I figured the bus station would be an excellent fare, and it would be worth my returning for her from far away. When I did return to the supermarket, the store was closed, and she was waiting outside the store with her children, groceries, and a young woman who was the store's night cashier. I got out of the cab, and I helped her pack all the grocery items and her baby's carriage into the cab. I was prepared to go to the bus station.

But as I went around the front end of the car to get in the driver's seat of the cab, the young woman who was the cashier spoke to me. She looked at me with such concern in her face, and in a soft but stern voice, she said, "do something to help her." It was the way she said it that affected me. She communicated her words to indicate I was responsible for this woman and her situation. I thought to myself, "what if she decides to accuse me of assault?" But I shook my head slowly in agreement as I walked around the front of the car. Many concerns flashed through my mind as I wondered just how involved I should get in this lady's tragic situation; after all, even her mother turned her away! As I started the cab, I turned and asked her if, given her situation, the time of the night, the babies and little girl out in the cold that perhaps she would rather stay at my apartment for the evening. Why go all the way to New York City at this point? And she said (quite calmly) okay. I drove the few miles to my house. I let them in, showed her my room, handed them some clean sheets, turned the house heat up very high because the children were in the cold all night. And I told her to eat whatever she wanted from the kitchen (there was not much to eat). Within minutes I was gone back out to earn some money for the night.

I arrived home about three o'clock a.m. (about three hours later) and immediately checked on them. They were all curled up in my bed as if they slept there regularly. She sleepily looked up at me (bothered by the brightness of hall light I left on for them), and I told her I was home. I wished them good night, and I closed the bedroom door and went to sleep on the couch. That morning, some 4 hours later, I woke and cooked breakfast for her and the little girl; she fed her children and then ate. And from there, I took them to a local mall where she could catch the bus to return to the same homeless shelter and re-enter.

This day, so many years later, I don't quite understand what to think of that night. For me, the experience was just a complete mystery. My primary interest in staying in touch with her that evening was making money from the fares. She was driving all over the place, and for me, it was easy income on a slow night. And though I felt great sympathy for her and the cute babies being out in the cold, I was earning a living, not running a homeless shelter. Yet somehow, I ended the night, letting them stay at my house and sleep in my bed. And I left them there in my home with no apparent regard for what might happen when I was gone. After all, this is Philadelphia - a central metropolitan area where terrible things can happen at any time involving just about anyone!

When I ask people what they think of this story, they say she must have been mentally ill if she was willing to stay with some strange man. Interestingly, I saw her as the stranger, and that she was the most significant risk to me and not the other way around. And others asked me if I was worried about her accusing me of sexual assault. I said yes, a little, but I didn't allow it to dominate my thinking for some reason. I just did what my sense of 'good' told me to do at the time.

As I cooked them breakfast, I thought about the parable of the Good Samaritan. And in my mind, I tried as best I could to imitate that parable. When she ate her breakfast very slow (really...really slow), I suggested that she didn't have to eat it at all if she was not hungry. But she explained that she was just an extremely slow eater. I kept thinking about what I knew from reading the Bible. Some years later, it occurred to me that it didn't matter if she was mentally ill; she was still a person walking the streets late at night in the cold with a small child and two babies and nowhere to turn. Letting her take a bus to New York for a few hours made no sense. I see it as Grace that allowed me to be attentive to her and the people around me. At least enough to try and help.

Grace opened my heart that night to overcome fear and uncertainty and let her into my home under some extraordinary circumstances. It was my need to be a Christian or a "Good Samaritan" that had me cooking breakfast and trying to do all I could for them before they went back out into the cold. Without God, what would I have done? Today I am glad God offered me such a tremendous opportunity to please Him. This evolved circumstance was God's gift of his own life as part of my life, guiding me and teaching me to do what was proper and not what was fearful.

Welcome to Monastic Life! – Which Reality Is It Anyway?

Which Reality Is It Anyway?

My physical being takes in sensory data and processes sensory data. As an individual, I am walking down the street; I notice the world around me. Using my natural sensory perception, I am, in some ways, a data source to myself. That is to say, my eyes take in the light presented, and my mind and body helps me to understand what I see. Through my interaction, I am also a data source to the community in which I reside. So when someone asks me for directions on finding the local sandwich shop, they can use my information to locate what they need even though they have never been to that shop. Based on these notions of me communicating with reality through the processing of data and transfers of this same processed information, it makes sense that how I perceive and interpret my world determines, at least in part, how I behave. My perception affects what I do. Remember that how I act (which, to me, is my response to my perception and understanding) also affects my community.

However, suppose I find other sources of information outside my known world or community to include in my being as I process the world around me. In that case, it too will affect my formation as a human being. Adding this new information source affects my current behavior and future behavior. Since I am also a source of information to my community, I affect it as well. Therefore, allowing myself to evolve properly (develop a proper perception) helps my community and me. So the Buddhists say, make of yourself a light! And through this transformation of self (or becoming a light), you improve the world around you. The Christian Scripture says:

> *You are like light in the world. A city built on a hill cannot be hidden. So also with a lamp. People do not light a lamp and put it under a basket. But they put it on the place for a lamp. Then all the people in the house can see its light. So, let your light shine to all people. Then they will see the good things you do. And they will praise your Father in heaven.* **Matthew 5: 14:16.** [14]

What does all this have to do with monastic life? Why do people go off to live in a monastery? Why do they participate in unusual spiritual ceremonies based on historical tradition and actively subject themselves to belief in "invisible powers?" For me, I think it pretty much boils down to the gift of **FAITH.** I now look at faith as a potential conduit for vast amounts of new information. And that additional information leads to a different understanding of one's internal sources. Which, in turn, lead to a different human formation of both myself and others. For example, I will not ride the bus or train without faith in the local public transportation system. And if I have no other personal transportation source, I lose the benefit of getting where I need to go in a reasonable time. Faith is critical to human existence both as an individual and community. And from a Christian standpoint, it leads to a new reality.

John was put in prison. Then Jesus went to Galilee. He told people the good news of God's kingdom. `The time has come,' he said. `The kingdom of God is here. Stop your wrong ways, turn back to God and believe the good news.' **Mark 1:14-15.** (14)

Then Jesus talked to the people in the temple. He said, `I am the Light of the world. The one who comes with me will never walk in the dark, but he will have light that gives life.'

The Pharisees said, `You are talking about yourself. What you say is not true.'

Jesus said to them, `Even if I do talk about myself, what I say is true. I know where I come from and I know where I am going. But you do not know where I came from, or where I am going. **John 8: 12-14.** (14)

In this situation, Jesus, through faith, is providing unfathomable amounts of new information – we are not required to comprehend it. Once appropriately processed, that information changes my reality and not just mine but my entire community's. Jesus is the doorway for the sheep to enter the new reality. And he is the shepherd to those sheep to guide them in through the portal. And he makes that new reality possible for all who eat his body and blood. Once, I sent this note to a friend: "Pray for my intentions when you get a chance. I am writing to fewer people and I am saying no to just about every social event here. I did that because I realized I must move gradually (toward hermit life). And it is difficult when your mind is so dependent on externals and so unaware of internals. I have to be careful not to move too quickly [toward hermit life]." In my mind, moving too fast leads me to the possibility of falling into danger due to blindness about my internal frailties. If I am blind to my internal sources and am too confident, I may do something harmful without knowing it. In my ignorance, I might even lead others astray. Again, I said, pray for me because my internal source or internal understanding influences my behavior more and more. And I am not confident I can predict the consequences.

Faith is the conduit that feeds my effort to move toward those consequences. And such information coming through faith may be subtle, as in me telling myself not to use so many offensive words. In this case, I may focus on my thoughts all day and night and struggle, through prayer, to reform my thinking processes so that I communicate to myself and others in a better way. Or internal information brought "through" faith can be far more potent as in: leave all this behind and seek God with all your heart, just let go of everything and re-root yourself in a more nutritious way of life while you still have time to make progress.

I often use the terms information and data interchangeably in this writing. The structure of one's mind is essential in interpreting reality and making proper choices with any data given. It seems to me that faith is a function of the mind. Like a gift or tool, faith carries me above so many valleys where understanding is lacking, or perception is wrong. However, faith must be used properly. For instance, I need to consider my internal biases and tendencies when I have "faith" in some process or situation. With reasonable work and help, these biases can be observed and known in my daily living. Thus, self-knowledge becomes critical to understanding reality and participating in it. One must be careful with what truths one accepts through faith because there are consequences for all involved, including the community.

Everything that is hidden will be seen. Everything that is secret will be known and come out to be seen. Everyone who has ears to hear, listen!' And Jesus said, `Take care how you listen. How much you give to others is how much will be given to you. You who obey God will get more than you give. Anyone who has some will get more. But he who does not have anything, even the little that he has will be taken away from him.' **Mark 4: 22-25.** (14)

Once, many years ago, Jesus appeared to Saint Maria Faustina. She documented this event in her diary as a contemplative nun in Poland. He appeared as a small child, and he explained to her that greatness in heaven was: in humility and love of God. Restated, truthfully living who you are and following Christ constitutes greatness in heaven. And Saint Faustina questioned how a small child could know such things. And he simply said to her: I know, I know everything! And he disappeared.

What information source was she valuing in seeing and accepting such experiences? Was it her inner sources or her external sources? What about this event indicates her way of processing reality? Where does her interaction with her community come into all this? Her external sources, lacking understanding, might have asked her to see a therapist or ignore such nonsense because she imagines bizarre stuff that no one else imagines! But she was not dependent only on those sources. She had her understanding, and she had the monastic community's guidance around her. But where would she have been if she did not have an excellent understanding of her internal sources? If her faith was not in Truth, on her own, would she have been able to withstand the blows of the world's harshness on such matters? I would probably not even know of her experiences to learn from them had it not been for the uniqueness of who she was, as created and formed by God alone. Not just any evolution makes this person possible. God knows the intricate, intimate details of forming a human being who cooperates with his Will.

March 20, 2013

Dear Perspective U.S. Naval Airman,

I hear you are going into the U.S. Navy. That is a big step! So I just thought I would offer a word of advice to (perhaps) help you out. And receive it as my perspective only, since certain items may be particular to the female persuasion. It is the military, and despite some social evolution, it is still pretty much dominated by men. Moreover, even with the "don't ask - don't tell" policy, I say still be careful about your public lifestyle choices and practices. You may suffer discrimination. I would check YOUTUBE for videos from women on active duty to help you gain insight into so many other items you need to know before joining. There is much to be gained by watching, but be careful what you discern. Remember, these videos are also a particular person's experience.

The military is different than a usual job because, in many cases, you end up living with the very people you work with 24 hours a day. People often become like family members. In the military, the people senior to you are more than just "your boss." They can be your coach, parent, confidante, trainer, or buddy. I think you get the point.

When going through Boot Camp and A-school, you should always pay particular attention to all safety and emergency procedures. Learning what to do in an emergency is very important, and you should never depend on anyone else to retain it for you. You may be thinking that advice is obvious! Well, you'll understand after you leave training and are in an emergency and no one knows what to do but you! And safety procedures really do save lives. Enough said?

Get to know the career counselor on board your ship or facility (designation used to be N.C. or Navy Counselor). They can make your stay in or out of the Navy worth your while. They often know about programs and training offered in the military about which your officer in charge may know nothing. Always let your chief and division officer know your aspirations (unless you have no plans whatsoever to reenlist). It is best not to tell them you have no plans to reenlist unless you have no choice.

People often change their minds at the last minute. You do not want your division redirecting career opportunities because they think you are not staying.

I strongly recommend that you read a book on a historical naval event. This reading will help you have a larger sense of the function of the U.S. Navy in the military. I read a book called the <u>Sinking of the U.S.S. Indianapolis</u>. But if you end up working with aircraft, you may choose something related to aircraft carrier battles. Don't go into the Navy blind. Seriously - take my advice and use it.

If you have not joined yet and need to retake the A.S.V.A.B. for a higher score, then make sure you get some books to practice the test. Take them over and over, especially in the area where you may have been weak. A higher score will get you more opportunities in the Navy, which is how it was when I first enlisted. Any questions: stay in contact with me via email: anthonymaria3@gmail.com.

I will answer anything you may be curious about, but you need to make some effort to contact me since I don't seem to be able to contact you.

I hope all is well with you, and I love you very much,

Uncle Keith, (Br. Anthony-Maria)

That is why I tell them stories. They look, but they do not see. They listen, but they do not hear or understand.

They make what Isaiah the prophet said long ago, come true. `Isaiah said: "You will listen and listen, but you will not understand. You will look and look, but you will not see.

The hearts of these people have no feeling. They do not hear well with their ears. And they have shut their eyes. They do not want to see with their eyes. They do not want to hear with their ears. They do not want to understand in their hearts. They do not want to turn to me. If they did turn, I would heal them."

`God is blessing your eyes because they see. God is blessing your ears because they hear. I tell you the truth. Many prophets and good men wanted to see what you see, but they did not see them. They wanted to hear what you hear, but they did not hear them. **Matthew 13: 13 – 17**[2]

April 03, 2013

Dear Mary,

The poem that I send you is a result of your last email. Having read it, it occurred to me that most of my family members have no idea why I am in a monastery. It seems that no matter what I explain verbally or in writing, they create another explanation that satisfies a different understanding. Even my parents are still confused about my behavior, and they think it is Post Traumatic Stress (PTSD or something of that nature). Anyway, I am sending you a copy of this poem as inspiration. Let me know what you think and if I should stop sending. I will. There will be no hard feelings in putting a halt to all.

Why am I sending them to you? Philadelphia>Pitt>Philadelphia (we met at University of Pittsburgh) Just think about it, when I came across you on Facebook, you had over five hundred friends. I think I had about 10 or 12 friends at the time. And most of those friends were family members. Let's face it - now you have even more friends! I still have very few friends. But that does not mean I do not have great taste in choosing the right people. So I contacted you. Based on your list of people, I am not the only one who thinks this way.

Also, I thought you might find the subject matter curious. And who knows, you may decide to offer some free consulting work at your local monastery as a result! Anyway, Happy Easter to you and kind thoughts for you and your family!

Sincerely,

Rodney Odom (Br. Anthony-Maria)

After visits, time as a long-term observer, and a year as a Postulant at Methuselah, I officially requested to be accepted at Our Lady of Methuselah Abbey as a Novice. According to https://www.merriam-webster.com/, a Novice is a "person admitted to probationary membership in a religious community." It also means that I have entered a new level of commitment to Religious life; I am not wearing a shirt but putting on a robe of white. It helps other people to know you are walking on a path toward God as a Trappist Monk. It is spiritual and psychological change along with physical change.

April 18, 2013

Dear Abbot,

As I draw near completion of my two years as a Novice (May 30), through the Grace of God and the prayers of Mary, the Mother of God, I request to profess Simple Vows as a member of the community here at Our Lady of Methuselah Abbey.

Having drawn support from the brothers, I make this request with my God-given free will!

Respectfully,

Br. Anthony-Maria Odom

Photo: private monastic ceremony. Seated center room as a Postulant, before taking the Novice Habit. Author unknown.

Photo: bowing, after taking the Novice Habit. Author unknown.

Welcome to Monastic Life! – The Virgin Mary's Quiet Voice

The Virgin Mary's Quiet Voice

Somewhere along the way, in the quiet of retreat (the year 2015), someone whispered in my hearing that I should pray the Hail Mary with more affection and with more thoughtfulness. I figured it was me telling me this, but on what basis did I configure such ideas? I was recommending that I be less mechanical in my relationship with the Mother of God. But, I was not sure how I should approach this situation. I am and was of the mindset that more was better. So to pray the Hail Mary six hundred times was better than to pray the Hail Mary one hundred times. But this new suggestion indicated that if I were to offer more thoughtfulness in my prayer, I would need to slow down and focus my efforts more on what I say and what I mean. And that would mean fewer Hail Mary prayers!

This change went against my sense of right and wrong. But I decided to try and see how it might turn out. So I reduced the number of times I prayed the Hail Mary to 10 repetitions and focused on being thoughtful and present with my words. I tried to feel my words in my mind and heart as I spoke them to the best of my ability.

Slowing down was much more challenging to accomplish than I thought. Not only did fewer Hail Mary's violate my moral thinking, but it also seems that in my propensity toward numerical productivity, I repeatedly "forgot the journey" and focused on the end of the trip. My mind had a pattern, and I needed to change it! The goal was a pattern of meaningful conversation, not numerical production. I persisted in my struggle. But I did not seem to make progress, and I always ended up wandering off into the mechanics of prayer. In my mind, I was still reciting the Hail Mary like a high-performance machine churning out widgets in an efficient, productive manner.

Then one day, alone, while on retreat in the forest, I was affected with a deep feeling of affection as I prayed the Hail Mary. And as I prayed, I felt it through my mind and body. All my prayers slowed down tremendously. And I recited the prayer over and over. But gently and with great love and affection in my heart. I could feel my entire being glowing with sincerity as I prayed. And I was amazed at how much this situation differed from what I thought was possible.

I think Mary was helping me to pray. As Saint Louis Marie de Montfort indicates in his writings on her, she shared a tiny part of heaven with me.[6] I now have in my mind, as an example, this loving and prayerful way of saying those words: *Hail Mary! Full of Grace, the Lord is with thee. Blessed are you among women, and blessed is the fruit of your womb, Jesus. Holy Mary, Mother of God, pray for us sinners now and at the hour of our death. Amen.* Under the proper circumstances, I can approach that example given to me in the forest. However, I am very poorly duplicating that example most of the time. But at least I have this goal in my memory, and I think I am progressing at being present with Mary when I ask her for help.

I considered myself to have a special relationship with Mary. Not because of my efforts, but because of hers. While monastic, from two o'clock a.m. until seven o'clock p.m., I often focused my attention on prayer to Mary, the Mother of God. Because my state of mind was always wrestling with distraction, I imagined my mind to be like an octopus with arms extending in so many directions, involved in so much vanity. And since I was aware of my tendency to be distracted from God, I used this prayer both as a crutch and as a means of seeking Mary's help.

One of my mother's nursing school friends lost her son. They were like our aunt and uncle when we were smaller. Their children were slightly older than my siblings.

April 26, 2013

Mary and Joseph,

I just wanted to let you know that the monks here at the monastery are praying for the eternal rest of your son. We pray for you and your family! My mom told me she visited you. And she also told me she acquired some lumps from a slip and fall at your local Walmart. According to my dad, she is recovering well. I hope you have a happy birthday!

I am about to take Simple Vows in about a month! One step closer to staying here forever!

Love your nephew,

Keith Odom (Keith is my middle name).
(Br. Anthony-Maria, O.C.S.O.)

Note One
Having been tossed and flipped.
Thrown and dragged by the
Restlessness of my emptiness.

I am finally so many barriers closer to the
God within that now I rest quietly.
Sometimes, but only sometimes.

Note Two
It is a great gift
To have in one's heart
And even in my entire being
A sense of God.

To have in some limited way
A sense of alarm in danger or corruption,
A sense of joy in goodness.

What responsibility,
Accountability comes with such
Gifts.

Note Three
We have overcome
So many times, now,

Been persistent in turning to Jesus
In the very midst of the worst depths of shame.

And it is true that it is power over slavery.
And all because I take Jesus to

The very depths of my darkness.
And use him as a weapon to seek freedom
        for myself and others.

This letter offers an excellent example of how we end up living a physical reality that has no basis in the physical world. In this letter, I describe my mental state. I was confident in my reality and did not need any proof to accept assumptions about my surroundings, yet somehow, I was utterly wrong about the events around me. In this letter, I write about dealing with low blood sugar, which created a medical situation. But before I learned my lesson, I was exposed to rumors that dictated a new reality for myself and others. Some monks realized my behavior was odd, and eventually, I spoke to the Abbot about it. I understand that a rumor spread about me that drugs were the cause of my bizarre behavior. And since I knew I was not taking any illegal drugs, there was a brief period that I thought someone might be drugging me! And thus, rumor became established as fact and influenced many people as a real circumstance. Suddenly, my medication coming through the postal service disappeared. I think the idea was that I was secretly taking a drug I was not supposed to take. But using online search methods, I established the probable facts for myself. Despite the rumors implied and accepted, I researched and found the following: According to http://www.webmd.com: Diabetes (especially low blood sugar or low insulin levels) *Symptoms can vary.* **'Some people become quiet and withdrawn, while others get nervous and upset. They may: Struggle to focus, seem groggy, like they can't wake up all the way, mumble or say things that don't make sense, not recognize you or know where they are, get worked up and upset for no reason, 'see things that aren't real.'"**[8] *Due to my plan to lose weight and deal with diabetes, I ate fewer calories, specifically, fewer carbohydrates. However, I was not monitoring my glucose levels close enough. My glucose readings were, thus, persistently low. And paying more attention to my glucose levels and eating more at the proper times solved the problem.*

May 29, 2013

Dear Mary and Joseph,

Hearing about all the events in people's lives long after they occurred is awkward. Tori is graduating and going to college, Laienne is going into the military, and then not, then going again. And then not. That is a big step no matter what she decides. Maurice almost went on to the police force and then almost transferred to Penn State. Tim Jr. is turning into a local acting sensation. It looks like life is in full swing for all of them. And I heard Kim contacted Anthony Bernard -- Jr. Too bad he didn't come up during your get-together and meet everyone. Thanks for the picture of Nina. Little "Lansana" is cute! It is hard to hear that Aunt Babe and Harry are very sick. I am still praying for them. God's will be done!

Great News! I have lost 17 pounds so far. Well, it's good news and some bad news. My diabetic A1C was going up. The Infirmarian-nurse said my pancreas probably stopped producing more and more insulin. So my body was less able to process sugars in the blood. The good news is, with the Abbot's approval, I took immediate action and cut 90% of simple carbs (rice, potato, white and specific wheat bread, etc.) from my diet. And that isn't easy to do with a Trappist diet! All we eat is cheese, peanut butter, potatoes, and pasta. I do eat some sweets on Sunday. Some Sundays, we might have all starches for a meal. Then I fill up on fruit (and get tuna later). All in all, I am dropping about 2.5 pounds of weight every three weeks. The significant issue is that I need to adjust my medication as I lose weight. Otherwise, my glucose might drop into a range that causes a low-glucose coma! My behavior becomes strange, and sometimes I don't realize it until after it sneaks up on me. Ringing the buzzer at the wrong time, thus waking us up late. Lighting inappropriate candles (constantly apologizing: so sorry, so sorry about that, I don't know what happened?) The nurse says your brain needs sugar to function, so you can imagine what happens when it doesn't get enough. I try to explain to people that I rang the buzzer! "I know I did. I remember walking up to the button and pressing it!" But all the brothers say, "Nope! We didn't hear anything." Yet my memory of it seems so natural. I must monitor my glucose carefully when I have low blood sugar from Glipizide. Glucose drops quickly, and I may get weak and disoriented, and then I overeat to compensate. The bottom line is that I had the wrong diet for a person with diabetes long ago. And I knew I did, but I never took any serious action. It simply never occurred to me the seriousness of the situation.

After these experiences, it amazes me how vulnerable we as people are to a false "reality." I remember having a vision while praying for Tim (my brother who passed away in 2007) in the Blessed Sacrament Chapel about a year and a half ago. I saw Tim laughing and talking with someone. And then he looked up at me, pointed, and smiled. How he saw me, I don't know. Several months later, I read in a book that sometimes, when you pray for someone you love and who has died, you receive the Grace of seeing them in a vision. But about six months after that, I read don't trust visions and occurrences of this nature because you don't know how they originate. The author says it could be false and misleading information. After my experience with low blood sugar, I don't know what to think. It is clear how easy it is to be misled by confidence in your thoughts. But it also reminds me just how protected I am since I have not walked off a cliff or something like that!

Let me tell you of an event that occurred three times since I have been here. I wake up. I start to get dressed and prepare for Prayer (Vigils). Then suddenly, my alarm goes off, and I get up and get dressed to prepare for Prayer. And it was during this second time waking up that I realized I had already gotten up and started getting dressed. Then I knew that what I experienced the first time was some sort of event that I must have dreamed. Why this happens, I don't know. It doesn't happen frequently enough or in a predictable way such that I can study it. But when something of this nature occurs, it makes me question the nature of reality and the reliability of the mind. I cannot help but wonder, "What is reality?" And just how dependent are we on faith in Christ? It seems to me we are truly dependent in the most intimate way.

Bad news! Br. Theo is gone. As you know, he was married for decades and had many children. He just took his first Simple Vows. But he had a severe family issue and had to leave to deal with it. The older brothers were thrown for a loop because it all happened quickly! Everything around here happens typically slow. He told us one day and was gone the next. You miss people who must leave. And now we all must fill in to make up for his missing mushroom knowledge. Now the Abbot is the only guitar player. So the Abbot hired (for Sunday) some local violinists to help with our Sunday Mass. From time to time, we chant without music. It all sounds pretty good.

The positive news is two days after Br. Theo left, Titus (55-years old from New Hampshire) came back for a fourth try. He will spend three months as an Observer, then become a Postulant, or he will leave forever as a monastic possibility. The Abbot cannot allow people to come and go because it disrupts monastic life. To give you some idea of how much he struggles, he was a Postulant with me when I first arrived. We have a Diocesan priest coming as an observer; he is about 60 years old (but he should have been here by now). We now say a daily prayer for vocations during Mass. And so we have people knocking at the door out of curiosity.

Br. Vineyard is now in a wheelchair. As I understand it, he has heart problems. You might remember him. He was the tall monk who pretty much could talk on any subject. He is young compared to the rest at only 73. He looks amusing rolling around in a wheelchair. He doesn't use his arms to move. He uses his legs. And he moves fast because he has long legs. He is a history buff. To me, he is a really nice guy who is horribly intellectual.

Br. Joseph can still split a log with his bare hands, but he will forget things at 84. He's starting to sing out of sync with others and has similar issues associated with aging. Once when he did sing out of sync, I heard a voice in my head say, "God is calling him home." I guess I should not use the phrase "voice in my head" but instead use the word "intuition" as the Abbot recommends because the first term has too much baggage. Whatever the case, I hope he doesn't go home tomorrow because he is a hard worker!

Br. Ezekiel is 84 now too. He does a lot, but he fell back off his chair while attempting to sit down and injured his back one day. Now he is using a walker! Br. Ezekiel is a guy who will not answer a question about anything even though he has read just about every book in the library. Once I sent a comment he made on an article in *Smithsonian* magazine. It was on the subject of "time." They printed his remarks, and he received many comments-responses. People were impressed with his comments. On another matter, he received free address mailing labels one day. He decided to put one on his room door. The Abbot told him to take it down because no one else had mailing labels on their door. Then he decided not only to have a mailing label but a name tag on his door. He refuses to take it down.

These Brothers work daily and come to every office nearly seven times a day. Br. Matthias is 88. He used to be in the U.S. Navy and worked for the government. He is friendly when you get to know him. But when I first came here, he was the biggest snitch (counting all the cheese slices!) Then another time, he screamed at a group of us for talking in the Commons. He said, "This area is not a talking area (he walks away!)" Back then, he was 86. He has mellowed with age. Now he jokes and laughs from time to time. His memory is going. He says he cannot remember any subjects of any conversation. At community meetings, he will tell you that he is just here but don't ask him to comment on anything because he cannot remember the subject of the conversation from moment to moment.

Fr. Peter was supposed to have spinal surgery to walk again, but they say he is too old (80 years old). It has to do with his diabetes and his ability to heal. He can stand but needs a walker to get around if standing. So he is pretty much in a wheelchair for life.

We seem to be hiring people to replace the brothers who have become unavailable. Or volunteers, when they are willing, replace monks. We have to employ some pretty stiff boundaries between us and the non-monks.

Since I've been here, I have learned some cultural differences between the people and me. When you live this close to people with different backgrounds, you soon notice differences in how you communicate and interact with each other. And you can use this difference to expand yourself or let it drive you crazy. More than likely, it will be a little of both. The one thing that I notice is "the smile." When I look at the lady in the first retreatant choir seat, a smile pops on her face. When I turn away, it disappears. When I turn back, the smile pops back on her face. To me, that is just plain weird! Some people say you should smile. Some say a proper Christian smiles! I think: I smile when I feel like smiling! When I feel joy, I explode with smiles. When I don't, I don't. When you ask me how I feel, I answer about how I feel. I don't give a positive answer unless

I think it is warranted. I use the example of John the Baptist. He was a very "rough and tumble" guy living in the desert. He didn't bend his personality to fit the world around him. Yet, he still attracted droves of people because of Holiness. Holiness is Holiness, smile or no smile, social conformity, or no social conformity. I suspect the hardest thing for me to get used to is the monks smiling in your face (not literally) as they are "checking your back pockets" in one of their search episodes.

At this point, I can certainly understand why the monks don't trust outsiders too much. Most of us have done something we are ashamed of, and perhaps it was illegal, immoral, or both. And many of us have not been caught (no, not me, silly! I'm practically angelic!) And I guess when people come here to the monastery, they simply don't tell all. But the brothers invest so much emotionally in a person that suddenly, the person must leave. Most of the sneakiness on the monk's part is for the discernment of the individual. They need to know who you are! They use the people you form close relationships with as a proxy to pry into your personal life, test you, and search for personal information. (If they suddenly ask you to lock the gates one night, it is probably to see if you will drive somewhere to get a burger). This tendency towards "slyness" seems to have morphed the monastic lifestyle into one of constant suspicion and sneakiness. "By any means necessary" seems to be the Methuselah motto. But I am not in total agreement with that philosophy. If that way were okay, then Jesus could have just lived to a ripe old age of 50, died in peace, and still drew all of us to Himself! He had to live and die a certain way, and we, like him, must live and die a certain way too! In other words, not just anything goes.

Most of the monks here (in their 70's, 80's, and 90's) joined a diverse monastery. Some guys descended from Poland, and others from other primarily European countries. But the key here is "European." You pretty much get the picture. So if you come from Asia and don't think or use the same ways or have the same values or social etiquette, it can cause a sort of "whispering emergency." I call it chatter. If you don't "act appropriately," the brothers can silently gang up on you in an attempt to fix you.

Individuals entering must stick it out until everyone can get used to each other's new or odd ways. Sometimes adaptation happens quickly, and sometimes, there is still no adaptation after 30 years. In that case, you end up with monks smiling at each other as they struggle to be better Christians. But believe it or not, it is during these internal personal struggles with each other that the ability to keep praying strengthens your relationship with Christ. And it works! Stay Focused on Jesus is what I tell myself.

Church diversity is different now. Europe is no longer the entire church. And most new Catholics come from South America or Africa. We had a visit from some Brothers from Viet Nam asking us to accept two young monks for training. They were not Trappist. After three years, they were supposed to go to a seminary and become priests. After all that, they would then go back to their home country. We voted yes! But the 'monk transfers' never happened. We voted to get a guy from Nigeria. That went away also. Now we are asked to take two brothers from Nigeria. But it must be approved by the U.S. State Department. Part of the goal of temporary transfers is to pass the Trappist monastic heritage on to the areas of the world where monasticism is exploding.

In the meantime, some monasteries in this country are turning seriously international. One monastery just elected a non-American Abbot - he is from India. I never met him. But Fr. Thomas and the Abbot have already. They speak highly of him. He must agree to be elected.

Self-Discovery
My time here at Methuselah is personally very fruitful. I see personal growth. I think the key to this growth is to be open to God's love and to know that Eternal Life is real. It means knowing how I live now actually matters concerning eternal life. This knowledge motivates me to respond to inspiration. But I do not think I do this entirely on my own. For human beings, it is easy to say "I believe" and not do so. We just do not know ourselves well enough to be truthful. Or there are times when what we think is truthful only seems so - disguised misinformation. Contemplating the love of God together with the notion of eternity, spurs me on in my struggle to change. I have learned that even this ability to believe is a direct

result of a gift from God. Somehow you have to receive the ability to do so. Therefore, Prayer for others is so important. Through Prayer for others, they receive Grace to come to know God too! And to deepen my relationship with Christ, I always ask him to "help my unbelief."

Interestingly, in the three-and-a-half years I have been here, I have found that I am not merely here for self-discovery. So many people say, I hope you "find what you are looking for" in that monastery. Implied in that statement is an acknowledgment that they have no idea why you are in a monastery or that you are only searching for something. Being here is more like going after an athletic championship for people in monastic life. Everyone here knows what they are after even though it is not an item of substance like popularity or a trophy. It is walking in faith toward what God has planned for you without needing physical proof. And the monastic atmosphere accomplishes this in a more controlled way. I may never have a label for that goal that I seek in this life (other than Jesus,) and I am okay with not knowing.

If I am to serve Jesus according to his will without hesitation, I must be free to do so. And in this monastery, I have found that I am a slave to so many invisible psychological restraints that I cannot count them all. As a result of this way of life, my mind is more fixated on what God calls me to focus on, and I am far less divided mentally in trying to do so. What are some issues I learned about myself thus far that are enslaving?

I worry...excessively.
I calculate...excessively.
I judge myself and others harshly.
I am very anxious about everything.
I routinely shun others.

I worry about what others commonly worry about, but I do so excessively. I tend to project into the future or anticipate. I also create possible "futures" and worry about them in my mind as if they have already happened. One Sunday morning, while in bed, I spent about 45 minutes worrying whether I should remove some wood from the Abbey's white van just in case someone else needed to use it. Then I fell asleep. As it turned out, no one needed the van, and all my worrying was for naught. But even if someone wanted to use the van, all they had to do was remove the wood and use it. With my mind preoccupied with worries, I cannot experience the real joys of living.

Jesus said to his disciples, `So I tell you this. Do not be troubled about what you will eat to keep alive. Do not be troubled about clothes to wear on your body. Life itself is worth more than food, and the body is worth more than clothes. `Think of the birds. They do not plant, cut, or keep any food. Yet God feeds them. You are worth much more than the birds! `Can any of you live any longer by troubling yourself about these things? If you cannot do a small thing like that, why do you trouble yourself about the other things? `Think about the flowers. See how they grow. They do not work or make cloth. I tell you, King Solomon was a great man. But he was not dressed as fine as one of these flowers. God dresses the grass in the fields so it looks nice. It is in the field one day and the next day it is burned. If God dresses the grass like that, he cares much more that you have clothes to wear. You do not believe in God very much! `Do not keep asking, "What shall we eat?" and, "What shall we drink?" Do not be troubled about that. All the people who are not Jews work for these things. Your Father in heaven knows that you need them. But work for God's kingdom. Then you will have all these things also.' `Do not fear, little family. Your Father wants to give the kingdom to you. **Luke 12: 22-33.** [14]

And I make Jesus' job of helping me more difficult by distracting myself from what's more important. There are some benefits to worrying. For instance, worrying can be a sign of a responsible person, and it indicates the person can conceive how they affect future events and other people's lives. But overall, worrying needs to be kept in proper perspective. That means I must be free from its enslavement; reduce it to being an indicator. This discussion brings me to my subsequent discovery.

I am (my mind is) constantly calculating. Even when there is no reason to figure anything, I create one. A person plans their day. But when you have serious control issues, you may find yourself calculating everything you do. Trying to be precise at everything and thus eliminate all sources of surprise is not healthy. I guess I try to make everything predictable to reduce possible stress. So for instance, when I forget to pray the Rosary soon after I get up in the morning, I may discover my mind was preoccupied with what type of spoon I would use when stirring my hot chocolate. Why am I thinking about mixing hot chocolate even before leaving my room to go to the food serving area? I may contemplate what steps to use to return to my room on the way back from work. And it is not even 3 a.m. yet! I may decide what clothing to take off first to save time undressing when I return from work.

I seem to need maximum efficiency in using my energy and time. I need it to all "run smoothly." These exercises create excessive mental stress and rob me of the joy and peace of living correctly. It probably has some horrible implications in terms of faith too! Why? Because I always try to know or calculate what will happen ahead of time, I leave no room for God. These tendencies are not useless but skill sets that should be kept in proper perspective! The bottom line is that it is probably not the best mindset to have when striving to make progress living the spiritual life.

Now I need to lay off myself. I shouldn't judge myself too harshly. I told Fr. Thomas of a mental breakthrough concerning my tendency toward harshness and how I treat myself (this is a part of monastic life - learning the intimate details of one's behavior). I discovered that I relentlessly condemn myself when I make a mistake. I never realized I was this way at all. Quiet gives me time to listen, openness helps me receive, and intelligence helps me figure it out to write this boring letter. What you hear in your mind and heart is incredible when you live this quiet life. Being a perfectionist is functional, but Mercy is supposed to be the rule here, not condemnation. So I am learning to be more gentle with myself. And all this change should extend to my treatment of others. As I grow in my relationship with God, I grow with myself, which cascades to my relationship with others.

The anxiety issue is my diagnosis, but I have so many symptoms (look it up) that I would be shocked if I were wrong. It is a reasonably common issue. It affects people to different degrees. I am more able to focus on my anxiety issues here at Methuselah. I could ignore the symptoms when I had a job outside, expenses, and other "life distractions." I was functional. But for me, there is a long list of cascading issues associated with this anxiety. Here goes: When I am highly anxious, I don't sleep more than a few hours a night. Lack of sleep makes me tired all day and less able to process daily events. Thus, it affects my relationships with people. It affects how I perceive others too!

Over-The-Counter sleep medicines work for a few hours a night. The Abbot strongly recommended against the Veteran Hospital's prescription drug, so I never used it. I have a more profound sense of rest with the Over The Counter (OTC) drugs, but it is still the same amount of time (only a few hours). The effect of the anxiety is such that it simply affects me in ways cascading through my life activities. The discomfort or pain of the mentally anxious state tends to drive me to eat. Or it seems that eating is a distraction from the state of anxiety. The nurse here says it's better to eat than to be violent. I am hardly ever physically violent. Some people are fierce when they become anxious. Then too, I am diabetic! So I shouldn't eat or consume any more than I need to! I must learn to deal with this anxiety through a means other than eating! So far, what I am doing is working. For instance, I used to get set off and anxious from a simple schedule change. And even now, I still get set off, but I have learned to know when it is starting and tolerate it better. I am healing by learning to process my life experiences better. All I can say is Thank God for the Angelic Salutation. Hail Mary, Full of Grace...Pray for me!

So I try to remember when I first started having symptoms of anxiety. I think my issues were exaggerated due to my military experiences. But I can vaguely trace some signs back a little earlier than that. Throughout my entire life, I have avoided large crowds. It is not apparent why I am avoiding the public, but there is probably a reason. I found that the tendency to avoid significant groups of people did not stop after entering the monastery. The monastery has many social events. And the monks are expected to participate. I tend to avoid the crowds associated with these events too. However, I found in the monastery that I avoid crowds more out of habit, not out of requirement. I have a latent fear created by past experiences that I never learned to process correctly. But my tendency to act out, clearly based on my past, reflects something tangible that happened in my past. At best, this past experience was irritating and, worse, mentally painful.

Anxiety here at the monastery occurs for several reasons. I am a very private person. On the other hand, the monks have developed a culture of constantly searching and snooping. To me, their personal boundaries are limited. I cannot speak for other monks, but I am aware of the searching and feel personally violated. Think about it. Trespass of privacy violates something most of us are taught is a sort of fundamental right. Mind you, the Brothers don't tell you when you arrive in the monastery that they will search your rooms, mail, and workspace when you get here; they just do it.

Another cause of anxiety is that their way of doing business is chaotic. As I wrote before, I am a planner. And I don't think they adequately consider the impact of chaos on the newer people. Some events are planned, and some are not. They probably do not see their way as chaotic at all. And I, clearly, have issues with lack of planning.

Though I don't think the anxiety issue became apparent until I came here. Monastically speaking, this realization of "loss of privacy" is a positive. I equate my sense of privacy with "my personal territory." And it could be that the violations serve to destroy my sense of ownership. This release of ownership allows me to fellowship with others in the community and live humbly and openly to obtain true freedom to follow Christ. And as far as privacy is concerned, God knows all about me. I can't have secrets from Jesus (who is all that matters,) so why should I live and act like I can have so much privacy anyway? Faith in God means to trust in God too! As difficult as it might be for me, trusting in the Eternal Outcome is my goal. We are in communion with the Body of Christ in ways we do not quite understand. We give and take with the living, those passed in friendship with Jesus, and other heavenly beings. I have to learn to live that truth.

Having said that, I think genuinely intimate "private matters" should stay behind the monastery walls unless we place them in a book or film to benefit others. I thank God for these insights and discoveries. In addition to having fewer addictions to food, sweets, news, and other sensual issues that have incredible power over me, I can obtain freedom from the need for privacy through God's Grace! Somehow, I have acquired this great habit of saying "thank you Jesus," even when I have tied my shoes well! Sometimes I find myself saying thank you to Jesus all day long. If I remember a person's name, have a refreshing drink, lose another pound of weight, have a good night's rest, finish a fantastic day's work, smash my finger with a hammer, bump into a tree limb, stub my toe, I say thank you, Jesus! Sometimes I say thank you, Mary, too (I guess I would not want to forget how this relationship with Jesus develops).

Jesus loves me; even though I constantly fail him in many matters, he keeps coming back to help. I KNOW I AM WRONG when I choose to read the news online instead of praying. But Jesus doesn't say - I'm fed up with you, Anthony-Maria! He knows me better than I know me.

The Mission
A priest who was an instructor for one of our classes indicated that when in the scripture Jesus says, I give you a final commandment, "love one another," he was not giving his disciples another rule to follow. In saying this to his disciples, he was commissioning them for a new mission or new purpose. He said God explicitly "breaks" into your life to trust you for an assignment. It all started back in 2007 in a dream. I was sitting on one side of a long table. And dead U.S. Marines were on the other side of the table in a line facing me (I do not know how I knew they were dead!) They handed me papers as they approached me. Of all the strangest things, they gave me credit card applications. And my job was to evaluate for approval these applications. Since I was in the U.S. Naval Service in real life and the U.S. Marines are part of the U.S. Naval Service, I saw an immediate correlation to my circumstances. Also, upon coming to the monastery, Fr. Luke tells me that the name I chose, "Maria," as in Br. Anthony-Maria, translates from the Latin word for 'Seas.' The U.S. Marines are a part of the Naval Service they are considered seagoing soldiers.

Then recently, I had another dream: a troop of U.S. Marines took over the monastery and turned it into a barracks. Anyway, to make a strange, long dream a little shorter, I started giving tours of the monastery because the Marines could not seem to find anything they needed. A Marine

General arrived and assigned all the brothers something to do; for some reason, he did not give me an assignment. Then one day, while sitting in the novitiate classroom with nothing to do, a 4-star Marine Corp General walked into the room. He was thin and tall. The General's dress uniform was covered entirely in medals. And for a moment, I remember thinking, is it even legal to have so many medals on your uniform? It seemed exaggerated. He had so many awards that they were overlapping all over his coat. And he looked far too young to be a General. And when I saw him, I jumped to my feet and stood at attention. Then for some reason, I remembered I was no longer in the military and relaxed my stance. As I continued to stand there, he stared into my eyes as if contemplating me and my situation. And as he stared at me intently, slowly moving his head up and down, I knew his thoughts had to do with me - but what were they? I did not know.

I took notice that he radiated a powerful sense of peace. The feeling of peace emanated in waves from his being. And I remember thinking, maybe he was Jesus in disguise? I did not understand how anybody's presence could radiate such a powerful sense of peace. I think about this dream often. I believe this is related to my purpose, and my success will be through the help of Maria, the mother of Jesus. Wrapped in Mary, I will achieve my mission. Other than that, I don't know what these dreams mean.

Conspiracy Theory 101

He parked his rundown donated golf cart in the parking lot this time. Normally he would park it in the bike area to plug it up and charge its batteries. But since he moved the charger to a new location, he started getting ideas about where to park the golf cart. That is what started all the commotion. The question now is: when was he going to learn that there is no need for new ideas in the monastery unless specifically requested! And worst yet, why did he not get permission to move the battery charger first? By the second day, someone noticed he was parking the golf cart in a new spot—the news spread. And Monk suspicions began to stir, chatter and whispering grew. They began to stare and mumble. He should have known that this radical new idea about parking the golf cart would likely set them off. Why was he so determined to be different? Is he constantly stirring things up for attention or for no good reason?

Determined to be his "own person," he is trying something new. He was going to do what made sense to him. He didn't care what the others thought about it! This new spot was closer to his room, which meant less walking after work to get to his room. So that's when the investigations started. People started mysteriously showing up at his workplace after he left. People began searching his room. After all, a radical like this must be up to something, right? He must be trying to sneak something back and forth to his room, right? Why else would he park in a new spot?

It does not take much to set off an avalanche of monastic hysteria by doing something most would consider insignificant. One reason is that the slow, tedious lifestyle almost screams out for drama. Another reason is our tendency to analyze everything that goes on for some type of symbolic meaning. Contemplative monks look at life with "magnifying glasses" as they perceive the world. A small bump to others is a giant hill to us. Sometimes it is challenging to keep both perspectives in mind when interacting with the world. And the other thing is becoming more and more apparent: we tend to function and form our idea of reality based on guessing instead of actual measurable facts. We do not have quantifiable facts for so much of our reality. So we must fill in or guess. As a result, conspiracy naturally evolves. And in our world, approximations, schemes, and guesses quickly become "facts." My mind comes up with one plot after another, and it takes tremendous energy to keep control over them and verify them over time. I just realized that we all are the same way. It is not just me. If we do not know, we fill in the blank and act like we created fact, not fantasy.

Hesitation: I just wanted to update you all on my prospective Simple Vows:

My Simple Vows are canceled for now. The Abbot has six months to decide whether to advance me or not. When I started this letter, I was on my way for sure. However, the formation committee decided that I needed more study, was too independent, and didn't think like a monk. They said I still had trust issues, and (I believe) the Abbot wanted punishment for a public smirk I gave him in front of a group of people. He said that I needed to be humbler. They said a few other things, but I forgot some of them. I had many compliments too! But let's face it, rejection overrules everything. They said I am kind, sensitive, genuinely committed to seeking God, thoughtful, hardworking, dedicated to common prayer, etc. But they compared me to a cake in the oven that is not entirely baked.

As of now, I am pretty much packing my bags. You may think I am leaving because I am upset. No. That is not it. I was upset when I left the meeting between me, the Abbot, and Fr. Thomas. After all, their decision pretty much destroyed me psychologically. I was not expecting any of it. But I was willing to wait. Then after trying to sleep and thinking about it during my regular periods of insomnia, I decided they were correct. I don't trust them! Their entire way of doing business contradicts my sense of appropriate behavior. The monk formation process is counter to my value system. At eighteen, maybe I would just ignore their thinking, but at 47, I cannot. I don't want to be like Br. James. I am 47 and a half years old. I am not 32 like Br. James was when he left. I don't think I should invest three more years in finding out they cannot accept me because I am not changing fast enough to be a proper monk. From what I can see, this sort of nebulous, back-and-forth thinking with no commitment is a typical contemplative process. The other weird thing is that the Abbot now has a new policy. He has decided that he lets too many people advance to vows— people who were not quite ready. So starting with me, he was going to make people wait. He likes making me wait for some reason (as in when I was an Observer and then again in the Postulancy).

In any case, I was overworked, stressed from diabetic dieting, dealing with anxiety, etc., so hearing this was too much for me. Overnight, I let go of being here and started looking into my future for other possibilities. I told Mary (in prayer), I can't pray to stay here anymore. I simply don't want to be here anymore. Before this time, I felt obligated to stay, but now I feel free to leave. I am not getting any younger, and their decision doesn't seem to consider my age and my employment potential if I were to leave here too many years from now. But I still attempt to say to myself, "God's will be done" someway-somehow.

Another thing I noticed is that I seemed to have a unique nature, and frankly, I just don't think I should be around all these people all day long. Sure, monks are isolated from the outside, but they are still around the brothers all their waking moments. I told the Abbot my opinion and said so with very little uncertainty. I would be gone the next day if he asked me to leave. Others have made far more tremendous sacrifices to accept God's will. This situation is a perfect example of human frailty. I cannot turn and be the person they need me to be. My urge to leave was sort of spring-loaded. And their decision is all it took. Perhaps these almost 4 years have prepared me for something of a hermit's life. I will attempt to find a quiet little spot and learn to disappear. This "disappearing" is what I seek, forgetting I exist.

So the Abbot and I talked, and I will be here until July 1, 2013, and then the Abbot said he would support whatever decision I make. I have inquired about life with the Hermits of Bethlehem in N.J. But I see life as a hermit in private. I don't know the specifics of that group just yet. But I will see what they are about as I transition from here. They, too, have a screening process. And since all the organizations talk to each other, who knows where my prospects lie. The key in this situation is obedience. Self-rule is deadly! Monastic life works based on Rule under an Abbot.

Well, I hope all is well as you receive this letter! Love,

soon to be: Rodney Keith, once more...

hermit
1. a person who has withdrawn to a solitary place for a life of religious seclusion.
2. any person living in seclusion; recluse. (9)

Welcome to Monastic Life! – Which Way Is Holiest?

Which Way is Holiest?

When someone asks me how I am doing, I stop and take the time to think about the question. I will try to answer it. But in doing so, am I attempting to be honest about answering a person's question? Or am I wasting this person's time trying to answer a question they are not expecting me to answer? Which way is practicing for holiness? Not everybody is required to do what I do or as I think. Should I limit my interaction to those who wish to practice this time-consuming, detailed socializing? Or am I to adopt a more superficial, limited practice of personal communication? Once I was told, "I did not really expect an answer...I was just saying hello." But with all the "little flowers" I wish to offer God in life, should I not try to deepen my relationship with God even in these small opportunities. Should I not always reach inside and express and behave more authentically who I truly am - thus practicing what I am to be?

Which way is the holy way? When I ask: how are you? And I look into your eyes, read your facial expression, and then wait for your verbal answer. What am I demonstrating? I should practice the quick, urgent form of communication if I do not honestly care how you are. But in doing so, do I not lessen in a small way my practice of holiness. The practice of indifference is not proper. When I listen to your response and offer some words of genuine thoughtfulness, am I being more god-like? Is there an opportunity to practice holiness in life's small details or "little flowers"?

Once when I went into the abbey store, Angel, the store manager, looked at me and immediately commented that I looked like I was having a bad day. She asked me what was wrong. And while I never answered her question because it was simply a general sense of dryness that discomforted me, I responded by saying how sensitive she was in noticing with such attention. This encounter was a unique level of interaction with another person, and since it affects who I am with more depth and goodness, I ask, is this the holier way of communicating? Does this form of human interaction matter to God? Am I not more holy if I am more truthful, more factual with sharing, and allow my existence to revolve around events with more meaning? I should be living the small details of life with increasingly profound effort in this direction!

If I wake from a dream in which I experience the future. And I see that day unfolding according to my vision or dream. Do I participate in that day's experience according to my dream? Do I offer others my "special insight" according to what I have learned in my dream? Or do I ignore it all and casually act as if the dream meant nothing? Which way is more holy?

Life as a human being here-and-now is short compared to all the historical human activity. We participate and process it according to our cultural understanding of time. Moreover, animal activity has existed for thousands or even millions of years. Often, I see monastic life as exploring and observing my understanding of this reality. And using what I learn to transform into Christ. There are so many layers to reality. Just seeing life by looking back on the past creates a reality. Seeing now makes a reality. Seeing life through the eyes of another creates still another.

But I have also found that I have different levels of authenticity, creating a new version of realness. And my most profound authenticity is always what I seek to offer to all creatures, no matter what. Perhaps this is what is holiest? Even now, I still have and practice behaviors that are not authentic due to poor self-awareness. I consider this activity an indication of a false self - not the full depth of me. But I only seem to realize a false self once I transcend to a more profound perception. And when I identify such faulty behaviors within me, I sometimes feel tremendous shame that I ever behave with such a poor presence of mind.

Sometimes I imitate the world around me in my communications not because I want to but because the world around me has no time or tolerance for such struggles for authenticity. Sometimes, I lie to people to spare them my authentic opinion. This pain avoidance is an accepted social practice in some parts of our society. But, I ask, is this holy? In the deepest part of myself, where should I be reaching as I participate in life? What role should I ultimately practice? And once I know better, should I risk offending Jesus by "practicing" so many fake life practices? And I will not be able to hide any of it! I will have to answer for it all.

My existence is more than physical. And while I do not have a complete or even cursory understanding of this notion, following Christ is the more significant concern, and the rest will work itself out with God's help. Jesus was far more aggressive with authority figures than he ever seemed to individuals coming to him, and some books indicate that's why he was put to death. Indeed, his cousin, John the Baptist, was beheaded for being factual and authentic with authorities. Following Christ may require similar social modeling. And I must not forget that not everyone is offered such heights of inner-self. I should not waste mine in vain!

July 02, 2013

Dear Mary and Joseph,

Since my last letter (okay, for people who are not Roman Catholic: I am still at Methuselah), and expect to be here for the foreseeable future. For those who are Roman Catholic and like a neat story--read on.

I initially decided I would be moving to Pennsylvania, specifically Allentown. It is a small city of about one hundred thousand people, growing fast and replacing old industries. I look to an atmosphere where I won't be socializing unnecessarily, finding, or creating a hermit's life for myself. I also decided my life needed to revolve around the Eucharist, so a local Roman Catholic church would be necessary. How was I going to move with no money and no job? That never really stopped me before; I figured it should not let it stop me now!

Some people who read this won't understand what it means to be on a mission. And I see myself as being on some mission (hopefully assigned by God), and my job is to hold on tight to my "sense" of God no matter what God has in store for me. But simultaneously, I must survive the struggle (that results from who I) am amid this process of following God. I need to survive my internal battles involving change. Change that is not comfortable, sane, or attractive in its expression. Sometimes the self-acts out in silence, and other times it is very graphic and painful. I see myself on a mission to seek or work out my salvation. I sense that time is short, so I don't want to risk wasting a single moment.

The other day, I thought that if I could accomplish that mission better in another place, I will! I need to keep going after God but do it elsewhere. Thus, leaving Methuselah was natural since I no longer felt required to be here. Then too, it amazes me how many people project their hopes in God for their survival here at the monastery. They seem to think it is the only place to seek God. It's a little unnerving. One does need great determination to stay. It is a great and powerful place to seek God. But one should not evolve some fantasy about it as required for salvation. It is not—at least not for everyone. My frustrations are many. But I doubt whether I can survive the frequent, painful, and emotional value conflicts associated with living here; even as I write these words, my anxiety flares from the memories of such encounters.

Since I decided to leave Methuselah, I found the ability to pray for "God's will be done." Before then, I asked people to pray for me because I could not pray for anything but to leave this place. Then I began reading St. Faustina's Dairy one morning and read this (Jesus as he spoke to the Nun, Sister Maria Faustina):

Paragraph 1485: *Do not be afraid of your Savior O sinful soul. I make the first move to come to you, for I know that by yourself, you are unable to lift yourself to come to me. Child, do not run away from your Father; be willing to talk openly with your God of mercy who wants to speak words of pardon and lavish his graces on you. How dear your soul is to Me! I have inscribed your name upon my hand; you are engraved as a deep wound to my heart.* [13]

And then I reread it the next day. I was worried because this paragraph spoke to me deeply, and I already had plans to leave. Now I was afraid because, to me, Jesus was saying I was running from Him. So I decided to tell Jesus all my troubles. I told Jesus that my coming to the monastery was a mistake, that it was nothing like I expected, and that my life here was worse than my life outside the monastery. And yes, I was grateful for the gifts I have received since coming (and that He says He doesn't take back), but all in all, I think I am better off not being here but being on my own. So I told Jesus I was planning on leaving, but I prayed that His will be done.

Then I read her diary another day and read this (it jumped off the page to me as I read): It was clear God wanted me to stay at Methuselah. God can come at you from any direction. After a while, you kind of get used to it, and you learn to trust it. If he speaks to you in the wind, then he speaks to you in the wind. But I told Jesus that He knows I can't stay here with "these people!" But your will be done. I started praying a 27-day novena every day, "Your will be done."

By the eighteenth, on the Feast of The Sacred Heart of Jesus, after Mass, I was walking about behind the rooms where I sleep, and I heard throughout my body the following words: "You were not meant to leave here." And just like in the Gospel of Mark (as in immediately), I went to the Abbot's door and asked to stay. I told the Abbot I needed a break from this place, but I'd like to stay. He arranged for my leave to Philadelphia. I explained to him what had happened and what I had heard. Then I asked some people to pray for me because the reasons I was leaving in the first place had not changed. I did not see how I would be able to stay. But God has "allowed me to know" that I am to stay. I was weak, but now I am stronger and more dedicated to God's will than ever. God wiped my heart of resistance of every kind and made it possible to do his will instantly. His words are power and life!

To all: Thanks for everything, especially prayer! I enjoyed my short time in Philadelphia, but my relationship with God is much deeper now and even more real now that I am back at Methuselah. I am more fearless and more open.

Love,

Br Anthony-Maria

Deacon Todd was my sponsor coming into the Roman Catholic Church. He was an instructor during my R.C.I.A. classes, and he was in touch with me from time to time with encouragement. Monastic life is an intensely mental lifestyle, and one must discern what step or progress is authentic and which one is "imaginary" at each step of the way as you proceed. I discovered that the actual life I was living before coming here was a mixture of truth and fantasy, and I think that is the case with most of us. Determining the influence of the illusory *part and accepting what is true is God's job! Not everyone is helpful in discerning illusion, and not everyone is capable or able to help! This letter is my response to the material from Deacon Todd, intending to help me understand my circumstances in the monastery.*

August 01, 2013

Dear Deacon Todd,

I just wanted to take a second to thank you for your preaching. What can I say? These are the values of very different people. Somehow-someway I need to fit in here (God willing). There is a conversation for my simple vows. Fr. Thomas has reminded the Abbot of the time constraint. According to the Abbot, this entire event was supposed to be a simple delay that "meant nothing." And look what happened due to a simple delay that "meant nothing?" It is now months later. But only God knows (not us) what would result from a so-called 'simple delay' when dealing with a group of people who seem to be constantly struggling to have some "idea of what's really going on around us." To me, the entire lifestyle is in a tremendous fog such that you work at times to know what is happening around you. The monastic reality seems to me to be one of vagueness or uncertainty. I was at my breaking point here at Methuselah, and nobody knew or had any idea. I did not know either. **THIS IS WHY I KEEP INSISTING THAT COMMUNICATION IS A SERIOUS PROBLEM.** And now I know it is not just me who struggles with the idea of certainty.

I have read your letter about six times. I agree with you. For instance, I didn't realize that discovery is crucial in my relationship with God, and I looked at it as more of a path to a relationship. And most importantly,

God is supposed to be all our focus, but in the nit-picking, tit-for-tat of daily life, we all get separated from that focus. On the other hand, when recommended to turn to God in prayer at the Blessed Sacrament, I was humble enough to listen and be determined to seek God's will. Thus far, I gained much and lost little! Although in a relationship with God, all is Gain.

However, my assessment of the situation around me is not inaccurate. Br. Titus left to go back to Maine. He said it was too busy here. But he and I had serious conversations about life here at Methuselah, and just between you and me, he and I have observed life here with the same perception. The younger guys who come here to seek are often very educated. They also have a strong sense of what life here should be like from Charity's perspective. Yet they are just as confused as us guys who are 50 years old. The brothers are not awful as they might seem by my description. We just need to learn to live with a little less Holy clarification. And we are getting there. For some reason, the hardened people are constantly using force for accomplishments; these are the types of people who end up in charge in monasteries (from what I can see). In my mind, I feel I must remember to learn from this situation in my dealings with others. I tend to be challenging too!

That article you sent was very enlightening also. Since I am growing in my awareness of God in my life, it never really occurred to me that God would need to give me access to his voice and my conscience simultaneously. That He is the one enabling me to know my reaction to leaving Methuselah is a point of enlightenment. I honestly see God in a new way. We are far more dependent on God for everything, and we don't realize it. I am perceptibly changed. I will keep the letter and reread it in some months' time.

But probably more important is that I received honest feedback from someone knowledgeable and concerned. Though they try, my family's concern is limited by their knowledge and acceptance of me being here. And the monastery is biased; they do not seem to know how to deal with me. I do not think you don't deal with me the same way you deal with a 20-year-old. A "20-something" wants behave properly but are not informed enough to assess their situation appropriately. I am less able to cooperate so freely. Though I freely admit their behavioral assessments of me are accurate. I also know that the older dog does not learn new tricks quickly. In my opinion, there is not a single "neutrally involved" person here who would not offer an opinion different than "hang in there!" Thus, your letter profoundly affected me. God bless you for your preaching, sir.

Sincerely,

Br. Anthony-Maria

P.S. the blatant contradictions in my letter prove that I am Monk material! My communications are getting worse by the day!

A Monastic Guest (probably in his early twenties) visiting the monastery was in a mental state of turmoil. We chatted during work hours. And some days before his departure, I offered him this gift that a visiting guest bestowed on me. It was a miniature version of a Chapel with a small picture of the "The Divine Mercy" placed inside. I was impressed with his appreciation of the art and the idea of Divine Mercy.

August 9, 2013

Dear Mary and Joseph,

I was given this handmade 'Divine Mercy' by an artist who visited Methuselah some years ago. I think it is oak or cherry wood? He said he thought I might value it. And I thought you might also. You seem to have an attraction to the icons of The Divine Mercy. Besides, I can't keep everything friendly people give me. My room is too small! "Stay Real," my friend. Read what I copied for you about this message.

Sincerely,

Br. Anthony-Maria

The Divine Mercy Message and Devotion

The message of The Divine Mercy is simple. It is that God loves us — all of us. And, he wants us to recognize that His mercy is more significant than our sins so that we will call upon Him with trust, receive His mercy, and let it flow through us to others. Thus, all will come to share His joy.

The Divine Mercy message is one we can call to mind simply by remembering A, B, and C:

A - Ask for His Mercy. God wants us to approach Him in prayer constantly, repenting of our sins and asking Him to pour His mercy out upon us and thus upon the whole world.

B - Be merciful. God wants us to receive His mercy and let it flow through us to others. He wants us to extend love and forgiveness to others just as He does to us.

C - Completely trust in Jesus. God wants us to know that the graces of His mercy are dependent upon our trust. The more we trust in Jesus, the more we will receive.

This message and devotion to Jesus as 'The Divine Mercy' is written in the book a diary of Saint Maria Faustina Kowalska, an uneducated Polish nun who, in obedience to her spiritual director, wrote a diary of about 600 pages recording the revelations she received about God's Mercy. Even before she died in 1938, the devotion to The Divine Mercy had begun to spread through the church.

The message and devotional practices proposed in the *Diary of Saint Faustina* and outlined in the publications of the **Marians of the Immaculate Conception** are in complete accordance with the teachings of the Roman Catholic Church. All the instructions are firmly rooted in the Gospel message of our Merciful Savior-JESUS. Properly understood and implemented, they will help us grow as genuine followers of Christ. [10]

This writing is a long letter to family and friends, attempting to reconcile my sudden bizarre lifestyle with people's interpretation of my behavior. I now realized how odd I must have sounded after rereading what I wrote in the past years, especially in consideration of their behavior towards me during that time. But I was unwilling to abandon my little journey to God in order to change how others perceived me.

August 12, 2013

Dear Mary-Martha,

I am writing this little letter due to conversations I have had with people. Some have gotten all my letters, notes, and booklets, and some may have only gotten recent letters. I have been writing now since at least 2002. And based on the conversations I have had as feedback, I feel that my notes probably require some explanation. Not all the letters have been unusual, but some require reasonable explanation.

However, this writing will probably be the last attempt at an explanation. Most letters are just personal descriptions of what is going on for me here at Greenville, Charlotte, and now Methuselah. Also, please do not be offended by anything I have written this time or in any other period.

What about the letters need an explanation? The early letters discussed (what I concluded) were spiritual attacks of some sort—excruciating and emotionally draining experiences. Most of which I'm sure were difficult to believe. I have those less frequently through prayer (myself and others) and the Eucharist. But other letters indicate hearing voices, unusual "sixth" sense experiences, and the like. If you remember the letter "Answers," both Parts one and two included unique events when I still lived in Philadelphia. I realize it is wacky stuff. The biggest mistake I made was sharing this information, which is highly personal, without considering the implications of sharing it! I probably shouldn't do that anymore. But as far as the past is concerned, it is too late. One person asked me to stop sending her this stuff; she said it was too strange. I stopped.

Most material I reference as I learn more about these experiences is from Roman Catholic sources. Please don't think I am trying to convert anyone to Roman Catholicism by sending this letter. As I searched for an understanding of these bizarre events, I concluded two possible explanations: (1) I might be physically or psychologically ill, or (2) They were events that I didn't understand. Since I have been evaluated medically by doctors, including mental therapists, and could find no explanation for the experiences, I choose the latter reason: poor understanding.

When I first came to Methuselah, I shared Answers Part two with Bishop Antonio (he has since passed away). If you remember, Answers: Part two, was the story of my last few years in Philadelphia. I shared it with him because I thought, "he seems to be a humble, open and spiritually oriented person." In addition, he is a retired Bishop, has a broader scope of knowledge than the people I have met thus far, and (I thought) would be better at judging my situation as a nearby member of Methuselah. If things are not well with me, he can deal with the monastery properly. He was not officially a community member yet had been at Methuselah for 10 years. He read Answers Part two, asked me a few questions, and laughed! He said it was well written (he used to be an English teacher) and said, "well, I guess Anthony of the Desert doesn't have anything on you! My Goodness!" Then he asked me one question: "Did any of the people you encountered, following you, act in a threatening way, etc... did they ever say anything to you?" And I answered, "come to think of it, no! They never actually said anything." They watched and stared and followed but nothing else. And he shook his head, and that was it. I then let him read my poem booklet and my "Letters from the Desert Home" book (Part I). I listened to what he had to say, but it was all information I had read before. In any case, he seemed to believe what I wrote. I also understood that Jesus allows these things to happen to those he draws closer to himself. As Saint Teresa of Avila said of Jesus when her horse and carriage flipped her into a mud puddle, "Lord, if this is what you do to your friends, it is no wonder you have so few of them." And apparently Jesus answered her, "I do this and worse." These events help to convert the mind and heart to God. It aids in understanding how utterly dependent you are on him in this life and the next.

There are very few answers to situations like mine documented in any other place other than in Catholic books, tapes, and videos. In any case, over time, this choice to be here, while challenging, is fruiting quite well as I learn and understand the nature of who I am and who God is to me. The vernacular I use for understanding this relationship is Roman Catholic Spirituality.

Some of my references include but are not limited to:
(1) The Holy Bible (Christian), various translations.

(2) Contemplative Journey (Volume 1 and 2, CD-ROM)
His teachings on Centering Prayer -- a path to God rooted in the "Lost Christianity" of medieval times ... On The Contemplative Journey, Father Thomas teaches a brilliant synthesis of modern psychology and ancient spirituality, guiding listeners to the holy "still point" described in legendary Christian texts.

With The Contemplative Journey, Father Thomas ... has created a long-awaited guide to the authentic tradition of Christian contemplation. In Centering Prayer, he explains, the listener engages beyond thinking, beyond emotions, connecting with God's infinitive love. Inherently and uniquely Christians, this "divine therapy" draws on a receptive meditation technique similar to those that have attracted many contemporary seekers to the Eastern mystical practices.

The Contemplative Journey is the fruit of Father Thomas' life as a devoted monastic, theologian, psychologist, and philosopher: a sweeping masterwork that points the way to the Christian ideal of unity with the divine. [12]

(3) An Evening with an Exorcist, by Rev. Thomas J Euteneuer, Audio CD (I sent this to a few people), Out of Print.
In an Evening with an Exorcist, Fr. Thomas Euteneuer explains the anatomy of an exorcism. As a practicing exorcist, he discusses how a person may become possessed and what happens during an exorcism.

(4) Christian Mysticism *Today, William Johnston.* Harper Collins. 1984

I will be the first to fully admit that hearing voices that I don't consider my own when there is no other person to cause them is not normal. Being attacked in nightmares by a black, dark, violent, formless creature is scary. Seeing beings not physically present seems like it would be signs of severe mental illness at first. And to some extent, I am "mentally ill." I have many issues compared to what I read in books about healthy psychology. But consider the source. Many of these people who research these matters don't believe in any God whatsoever. The ones that do often believe what they choose about God and nothing more. And for some, God is only available at 11 a.m. on Sunday. And even then, mainly on Christmas and Easter.

Also, consider Jesus' actual words and what is written about him. At one point, because of his nature, Jesus knew people were trying to kill him, and when he made these accusations, the people called him crazy or possessed. They resorted to insults. It turned out they were trying to kill him, and he knew about it before they did. So he was not mentally ill two thousand years ago, nor is he today. In the past, despite all his incredible works, they still insisted on forcing Jesus into a sort of "bell-curve" version of human understanding. And to me, Jesus's presence on earth is a statement that the "Bell Curve" model of human existence is too limited and does not capture all human reality. It defines us with human limitations by human limits to understanding and nothing more!

Consider the modern version of evil? And it is undoubtedly not beings that are counter to God. The contemporary version of evil is something that causes illegitimate pain or suffering to people or other creatures. The idea of being attacked by evil, invisible spirits in the daytime while mid-conversation with other people is pretty much laughable to the so-called average person. However, when insanity is not a legitimate explanation, and you do the proper research, you find that this kind of thing happens frequently and with far more people than acknowledged. As a modern scientific society, we leave those books on the shelf, collecting dust as if they do not exist. We say the people who wrote them did not know any better.

We then behave as if we understand the whole nature of human reality. That reality is essentially the people's popular experiences distributed as a statistical or numerical curve. Anything too far from the center of the curve is an outlier. How many people would admit to experiences I write about knowing the social costs of doing so? I suspect very few people would. And my experiences are not just Roman Catholic experiences. Other religions or cultures often use a different language to describe similar experiences. In other words, I reaped what I sowed in looking beyond the superficial. I found an answer.

Since I am no expert on spiritual matters or human matters either, what I present is my best interpretation of my circumstances:

(1) Probably around 1998 or so, I probably gave up on the idea OF being Christian. I was exploring other religions and other spiritual "possibilities." I needed something else. I listened to a lot of self-help tapes and CDs. I looked intensely at various forms of Buddhism and learned about other major religions. Some of my exploration led me to so-called "New Age Spirituality." I didn't think of it as new age; I was merely exploring and learning new information. Based on documentaries I have watched and books I have read or listened to, this path is something that many people take when they decide that life as plainly presented is significantly lacking or missing something important.

(2) Somewhere along the way, I figured I picked up a spiritual "friend" who was willing to entertain me and my spiritual fascinations with the "new stuff" I was discovering. I didn't choose this being; I was engaged by it as I wandered about exploring myself and my ideas.

(3) Around 2002, having reached a bottom in my spiritual desperation, I returned to Christianity. Having contemplated various forms of Buddhism and Buddhist Mysticism, I concluded I had trouble with the idea of reincarnation. I admitted that I am a Christian, and my thoughts and values are Christian-based. I saw that all religions have their harmful elements. God needed to be the focus of my situation (if I could just stay focused!) To me, there was a God; my life needed to be the best path to the realization of God.

(4) I began exploring all my doubts about Christianity using the Philadelphia Public Library. And I started reading about a lot of Roman Catholic Saints. At the time of my reading, I considered them famous people, not famous Catholic people. Other Christian sects didn't have this history of people to read about this way.

(5) But as I was exploring and reading, I decided not only would I be Christian again, but I also discovered a need to seek God in a very unusual and extreme way. In a life of quiet, sacrifice, and prayer (I found that in The Life of Anthony of the Desert (online). I also discovered Mary (the mother of Jesus).

(6) In the main library (Philadelphia), while looking for books on Mary Magdalene, I discovered two very long rows of books all on Mary (the mother of Jesus). Having been raised Baptist and then Presbyterian, I didn't hear about Mary except at Christmas or Easter. So I wondered how so many books could be on Jesus' mother when she is barely mentioned in the New Testament? Even the Gospel of John refers to her as "the mother of Jesus."

(7) I read about six or seven books on Mary and her various apparitions and miracles throughout world history. She was appearing all over the world, including in recent years. Eventually, she became my new guide as I tried to turn back to the God I abandoned in my young adulthood. A lot of my reading was from Roman Catholicism. I never saw Catholicism as a different religion. Even growing up, I saw it as a different version of the Christianity I followed.

(8) Now Mary looks over my shoulder, guides my behavior, recommends prayer; she even taught me the Rosary (okay, I was inspired ... does that sound better?). She prayed for me. My prayers were heard. Now I'm back "in good" with Jesus, and she still comforts me. What can I say? This relationship is my experience. I would be stupid to turn her down.

But, how many people would walk around saying they heard the Blessed Virgin talking to them? Not many in their sound mind, right? So neither will I! Once I asked Mary why Jesus abandoned me to become this way? I was not consciously aware of her presence, but I asked, and she answered, "You abandoned Jesus. He did not abandon you." And then I saw in a brief moment an understanding of how my life slowly pulled further and further away from God. And I felt sudden fear at how it all happened without my knowledge. I was less the "good son"; I was more the "bad one" and became so without knowing how I obtained the status! (9) Before you freak out (those reading this), I don't have conversations with her. She only says a phrase or two when she does say something. It is usually to guide me in a decision I am making. Or steer me away from an activity I am about to participate in that I probably should not. For instance, when I first moved to Greenville, N.C., I was trying to decide if I should donate to a group called "The Marians." I was on a website. And as I was deciding, I heard and felt her pleasant approval. I was still struggling with my cynical perspective of religion being corrupt. And I did not want to waste my money on "more religious nonsense." I felt a certain softness with a sound, and a sense of joy fills my being.

And how do I know who she is? Based on my responses to her (before I knew who she was) and then again when I moved from Philadelphia to North Carolina. She once told me. Usually, I don't see her; I just hear her. When she told me, " I am the Queen of Heaven." And I thought long and hard and didn't know what to say, so I said, I don't know what that means? But I concluded she must be important.

Again, I do not usually know when she is present. I merely start talking to her as if she is. So- some part of me does know she is present. Perhaps some part that is not in my conscious awareness. Much later, after she told me her title (Queen of Heaven), I remembered I had read about her title years earlier in Philadelphia. Frankly, after all that occurred in Philly, I would have easily believed anything, including a visit from the Virgin Mary. Another time she asked me: for what I am grateful? She did not announce herself, but I knew it was her asking. And I answered why I was grateful. And she said there was so much more to be grateful for! And from that point forward, I realized that I should start to understand gratitude more and pay more attention to my thoughts on gratitude. I wanted to expand my perception to meet Mary's viewpoint.

(9) With that came the blatant spiritual attacks and other ferocious experiences about which I wrote.

(10) There have been witnesses to such attacks on occasion. Once I entered the main office at Sears in Greenville, NC, where I worked part-time, I noticed a young lady, an employee, standing, in the manager's office, behind a desk handling paper. I asked her if she had recently seen one of the department managers. I needed to ask that manager a question. I also noticed (without trying) her cleavage. She always wore clothing that exposed that part of her body. And as I turned to leave the room, something lifted me off the floor and flipped me front to back until I reached the front of the desk where she was. And whatever this was, it tried to force me to stare at this young woman's chest area. But each time it turned my head toward her; I naturally and quickly turned my head away.

It left me after three or 4 times struggling against this controlling force. What did she do? As everyone else did, she stared in amazement with eyes widened, and mouth opened. I was 240 pounds (of pure muscle, of course) and was handled like a toy doll and manipulated like a puppet. My feet barely touched the floor. I shook my head in the mystery of it and walked away. I was used to being harassed at this point. Though not so openly and aggressively as this. And I was very much used to not saying anything to anyone about it. However, most people are too amazed to ask questions when they see it. They just stare. I guess (like I was in the beginning) they are trying to process what just happened and make some sense of it.

(11) In experiencing this turn toward God through Roman Catholicism, I have discovered I have much more to me than what is "physical." But these things are for me to accept, not anyone else, and it is my relationship with God that I am verbalizing. Though ultra-personal, I feel this writing is warranted since I have already sent letters with these stories.

I don't have much else to say. I have enough sense to realize this is too much for most people to accept. But these experiences are the primary reasons for my radical changes. These experiences are definitive proof of God's love for me. Nothing happens beyond what God allows. And I am grateful for them. Please read the additional files attached to this email, and you will see the experiences I am having are not new for people. I have found many books that document and explain these experiences.

For some people, this email is utter nonsense made by a mentally ill person. For others, it is entirely believable and would be the basis for increased faith, thus separating (a little more) the wheat from the chaff as explained in scripture. I have always thought to myself that - a spaceship from Mars could land on the front lawn of some people's houses, and the only problem they would have with it would be, how do I get to work tomorrow with this thing in my way! Some situations simply do not "compute!" In scripture, Jesus always says, "if you can accept these things," then do so. He knows many cannot. Belief in any Christian practice is critical to changing one's life in God's direction. It is a basis for redirecting your energy and efforts toward that goal. Persistent changes in behavior are proof of deeper and deeper belief in those practices. Christian scripture says blessed are those who believe without seeing and touching the hole in my side.

Sincerely,

Br. Anthony-Maria (Keith)

Welcome to Monastic Life! – Personal Inspirations

Personal Inspirations

If your thinking is anything like mine, you may see odd correlations in your perception of reality. Sometimes I have great ideas that make sense but do not develop them. At other times I have ideas but don't have any sense of the idea's purpose and don't bother with them beyond the first moment of their occurrence. As I became more dedicated to my religious beliefs, my thoughts about them came forth, and I fell into the trap of: is it me inspiring me, or is God inspiring me? I did not realize frequently enough that the Spirit of God leads me once I turn toward God. And yes, gaining confidence in the Spirit is often socially painful. It takes social courage to give someone a gift buried in dirt, only to realize it symbolizes something much more significant.

> *When Jesus came to the town of Capernaum, a Roman army officer came to ask him for help. He said, `Sir, one of my servants is in bed at my house. He cannot move and has much pain.' Jesus said, `I will come and heal him.' The officer said, `Sir, I am not good enough to have you come into my house. Just say the word, and my servant will be healed. I myself am a man who takes orders, and I have soldiers who take orders from me. I say to one, "Go," and he goes. I say to another one, "Come," and he comes. I say to my servant, "Do this," and he does it.' Jesus was surprised when he heard this. He said to the people who followed him, `I tell you the truth. I have not found any Jew who believes as this man does.* **Matthew 8: 5-10** [14]

Once I accepted the idea that God can speak directly to me and everyone else, I always listened more for any inspiration. Who would want to be guilty of ignoring God? And often, these ideas come to me while doing chores. Or while I stare at the ceiling and even while solving a problem, even during prayer.

This "voice of God" often comes as a whisper so quiet that even my ears don't hear it. It is a subtle vibration of my being that somehow communicates. It comes through the mere perception of the world around me. Other times it comes through an intermediary, and I hear a voice. It might be a voice offered by an actual person, and other times there is no one present, yet I still hear. The communication may answer questions, give insight into misunderstandings, or offer guidance or direction.

But during all this listening, I must discern if I am well enough to know what this means? Am I "seeing clearly?" I must determine whether it is just my little mind communicating to me for some unknown reason. Or is it my imagination running wild with wishful thinking? I must ask, do I need help understanding this communication? Should I act or wait and see what else happens? Once while sleeping, I received directions to take specific actions. And because of my state of being, I lacked certainty. And as a result, I waited to see if it was me or God speaking to me. Then some days later, while watching television, I heard a woman's voice say, "if you do not do this, the Lord will find someone." Maybe it was Saint Faustina because it involved the subject of The Divine Mercy? At the time, I did not care about who!

I immediately went online and ordered the items needed. I jumped on the bus, went to stores to get supporting materials, and eventually put the project together. Then I sent the item to its destination. After reading Saint Faustina's Diary several times, it was not till later that I read that you must trust your inspirations in faith. And eventually, I realized that what makes no sense to me could easily make eternal sense to God; what minor little things I do now may influence something or someone in the future or even the past. Restrictions of time are not present with God. And obedience is essential.

I should add that "I" should trust in my inspirations; I do not need to tell the world about all my little inspirations. Most are for building me up for some eternal purpose that may or may not have anything to do with my knowledge at the moment. Also, telling others is merely an invitation for a lot of drama and unwarranted attention. It is probably best to limit who I talk to about such things. I am not exactly like everyone else, and everyone else is not like me. We all have different ways of responding to our reality. And there are social consequences to writing even this little story.

Deacon Todd, in Charlotte, North Carolina, received an improper date for my Simple Vows. It goes Postulant, Novice, First Vows. He was the only person I invited to my vows. The rest who attended were employees and friends of the monastery who participated in all such events anyway. It amazed me how many people were offended by no invitation. I guess I was just out of touch with their concerns?

October 11, 2013

Dear Deacon Todd,

The date for my Simple Vows here at Methuselah has changed from the previously announced: December 8, 2013, at 5 p.m., to the new date: December 9, 2013, at 6 p.m.

Photo: As a Postulant, listening to the Abbot speak prior to the Novice Habit. Author unknown.

Photo: Blessing from the Abbot after putting on the Novice Habit two years after the start of my Postulancy. Author unknown.

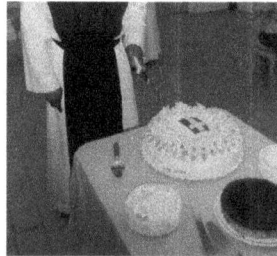

Photo: Celebrating Simple Vows is different at each Monastery. A Chocolate cake decorated with cream cheese icing generously donated by Shinskie Family was part of mine. Author unknown.

We do not celebrate a feast day on a Sunday during Advent, and the Feast of The Immaculate Conception of Mary is thus celebrated on the following day, Monday. Sorry for the confusion. Say a prayer for us.

Sincerely,

Br. Anthony-Maria

My cousin Harry was in the Veteran's Hospital in Brooklyn, New York. He was terminally ill, and my family in Philadelphia made several trips to see him during his remaining time. Thinking about his death affected me, especially knowing I would probably never see him in person again. I have no idea if he received my letter, and I could not even imagine what my Aunt Addie was going through watching her son die. My cousin Lauren, now in Statesboro, G.A. actually wrote a book as a result of this loss. It is called "Cancer: At My Backdoor" by Lauren A. Lee. It is a therapeutic self-help journal for healing. In the monastery, you often experience these intimate situations from afar.

October 20, 2013

Dear Mr. Harry Jackson,

I received a call from my sister Kim. She said they had a little family reunion up there in Brooklyn. Terry, Don, You, my mom, my dad, and Barbara. They said your mom was on the phone, and you are hanging in there (with your illness). They also said that you are cheerful and have a good attitude through all your suffering. I got an email from Stacy a little earlier, and she said you were having another operation. I'll get the inside information of what is going on at some point.

Kim (my sister) said that Don (Harry's younger brother) looks like Timmy (my older brother who passed away in 2007), no matter, I look better than both of you! Did I tell you I won 'Best Looking Monk' five years in a row? Yeah. I'm world-famous for my good looks now. I got my pictures on sale online. Sears sells my posters, and I have public relations people handling my fan club. Then I woke up...

Anyway, I just want you to know I have the Brothers praying for your Peace whatever is going on out there in the world. I told them the people from Brooklyn talk funny, but they still need prayer. My mom's sister (Aunt Babe) of Raleigh just passed away. They will be going to her funeral this Tuesday. Say a prayer for their safe trip. My mother always says my Aunt Babe was like a 2nd mother to her.

I will be taking my Simple Vows as a monk on December 9, 2013. It's a Catholic holiday called the Feast of the Immaculate Conception of Mary, and it marks her "immaculate" conception and sinless life. If you happen to be in Statesboro at that time, you are welcome to come. Kim said you might be visiting your mom (Aunt Addie). Bring some N.Y. Pizza if you can make it.

Anyway, tell all I said Hi! And don't make me have to come out there! That's right, get it together or else!

Love and Peace,

Your Cousin Keith
a.k.a. Br Anthony-Maria, O.C.S.O.

P.S. It doesn't get more REAL than this, Bro-ham ... all I can say is I am hoping for you -- no matter what!

The previous year the Abbot permitted me to mail my family some pecans from the trees out on the farm for the holidays. I scrounged the grounds around the old chicken houses where they used to fall in abundance. I ended up handing out bags of pecans to everyone working at Methuselah. But this year, there were few. When I asked the Abbot about helping the trees produce more pecans, he said that the monastery planted the trees to provide shade for the chickens, and the monastery does not have chickens anymore. The trees were left as they were, and the monastery had no plans for doing anything with them. Eventually, the trees stopped producing fruit altogether. I was disappointed :((.

December xx, 2013

Please, everyone, thank you! I thank you for both Gift Boxes! Tell Kim and J.C. thanks for everything. Aunt Addie and Aunt Hilda- thank you for the Cookies! It is so sad we have no pecans this year, and the trees have simply given up! The next time a retreatant asks me if I need something, I will say Yes! Pecan tree fertilizer! I hope everyone has an excellent holiday.

I thought Barb and mom might enjoy some of these articles I collected, and I read most of them when I had time. I created the book on the Holy Land from pictures a retreatant named Deborah Shinskie took with her iPhone while on retreat in the Holy Land. That research was a natural learning process for me. I knew Bethlehem existed, but I had no idea, so many Christian sites are researched, estimated, dug up, and preserved in the way these are in the pictures. I simply had no idea all these places existed until I researched her photographs on http://www.Wikipedia.com.

Know that I am always praying for Harry!

Love your son,

Br. Anthony-Maria (Keith)
P.S. my little poem booklet received excellent reviews.

Welcome to Monastic Life! – Live Your Dream

Live Your Dream

You do not know what you have been taught in your life until you are in a situation where your mind is allowed to roam freely. The void created by the monastic setting is a space for the mind to create fantastic stories. And you must learn to remain "conscious" and not get caught up in the fantasy. It so happens that our monastery is an open monastery, and it is a monastic setting that includes a public garden, trails, ponds, and the like. Though Trappists are known for not talking and living a socially separate lifestyle from the world, our monastery was rather social with the surrounding community. And it is that interaction with the world that makes life here most challenging for me. The Abbot once said that a monk must learn to dance in the rain, and I always thought that he meant that we must learn to be exposed to ourselves and our responses to the world around us in a healthy Christian way. But, under those circumstances, I realized the power of my "being" to fight against personal change. I observed my being act out in a rebellious way.

Once during a social setting where the monks were having a special meal, and the monastery guests were invited to socialize, we had several attractive ladies in attendance. And while I was aware of my ability to become overly visual, I was doing okay this particular day. I could feel my reaction to the women present; I did not mentally fixate on the circumstance at hand. However, I encountered one young lady who gave my body a physical reaction. As I looked at her in conversation, I felt my entire body move. And it made me stop in my tracks. I looked her up and down and realized something powerful was going on with me.

As I stood there, she noticed it also. She saw my physical response to her presence, and it made her think. Her facial expression led me to believe she was processing my behavior, and then it changed to one of discovery. She realized my response to her was one of attraction. And she smiled as if complimented. On the other hand, I realized something beyond my understanding was going on, and I quickly backed away from the woman. I had just experienced my body jump in a powerful way to the presence of this woman, and it did so with no warning. And what was I to do about it?

I was not in the monastery to "live my dream." In my mind, I was in the monastery to discover the truth of who I am by living a celibate, chaste, and separate lifestyle. But it was clear that I was having trouble "dancing in the rain." And it was another unknown part of me that I had to process amid this crowd of strangers. Who I am was laid bare for all to see! But I was determined not to let shame or embarrassment overcome me. I was determined just to let it pass and appreciate it as my new reality. One of the monks across the room noticed the incident and mumbled something about me being attracted to her. He was correct. And so was I; others did notice! From the diary of St. Faustina:

"Now I understand well that what unites our soul most closely to God is self-denial; that is, joining our will to the will of God. This is what makes the soul truly free, contributes to profound recollection of the Spirit, and makes all life's burdens light, and death sweet." (13)

If I were to live "my dream" instead of the dream I thought God preferred for me, I would have fallen in love and gotten married a long time ago. Besides, now, I had already gotten married. And frequently to women I met before and other times to women I created in my mind. Sometimes, we had children in these relationships, and other times it was her and me in endless romantic situations. This "ongoing aggressive fantasy" is the reality one might have to live while adjusting to this life. Some people survive their mind's storylines others do not.

Once, in a conversational email, I had with old friends, we caught up on our particular life circumstances. One was married, divorced, and had three children. Another was married, divorced, and had one child. I emailed them that I had been married nine hundred times, never knew divorce, and some of the marriages had children, and some did not. This mental condition is the circumstance of being laid bare to your own mind's raw power. I think this partially happens because there are no distractions to take you in another direction.

I am aware of the many interpretations one might have of my mental picture, but I struggled to live my monastic life the way it is intended: separate, celibate, and chaste. It seems I was still working to "dance in the rain," and over time, I did:

Conversations Inside A Monk

It is the sweet smell of fresh milk on her breathe.
It moves me to realize its fragrance.
My seamless response to its aroma,
An enticingly rousing experience.

It is the mysterious rising within,
As our common cordial conversation,
Sheds light on vain mental safeguards,
Manifesting many vulnerable insecurities.

And through its magical nature,
I am a fleeting arousal of undiscovered terrain,
Intoxicated by tools of polite discourse.
Dragged, clinging to the joy of shallow infatuation.

And still unfolding within.
I borrow language to color it all.
I must trade for what I see,
What I feel in this moment.

Though forever grateful for this freedom,
This experience of ethereal being,
Self, appearing and disappearing;
A subtle collection of ghost - like phenomenon.

Responding elusively in a space.
Intensely listening, a source of grace.
Transmitting unique impressions outward.
A struggle or comprehending of consciousness.

2014

Living in the Presence

It is a great gift.
To have in one's heart.
Or even in one's entire being.
An authentic sense of God.

To have in some limited way.
A sense of the holy presence.
A meekness toward the spiritual.
In the face of all things.

A sense of joy,
At the sign of goodness.
A perspective on eternity,
In the face of death.

That I continue to stand,
In the midst of my destruction,
Is a great sign of Mercy.
A remarkable and heavenly act.

Chapter Introduction

Trust is critical to the Christian. As a Christian, you are part of the Mystical Body. Jesus as Christ is head of this Mystical Body, and without trust, it isn't easy to get us all cooperating with that head. But we all come from different levels of brokenness. We all perceive reality in our way as we go about life. One person can see the world and all its corruptions and still participate as if there is nothing wrong. Others see the same corruption and refuse to be apart. Still, others see nothing wrong with anything, and if it is – so what!

Deep down, my trust issues probably stem from my interpretation of the world around me. When you tell me everyone is invited and mean it, I trust what you have to say. When you tell me everyone is invited and mean it, but certain people are turned away, I begin to learn not to trust what you have to say. When you insist that you mean what you have said but continue to turn people away, it only leaves me even more confused and filled with mixed feelings about who you are and whether you are genuinely trustworthy. Some say we earn trust. And I suppose being consistent is the basis for achieving it. Also, knowing our inconsistencies is essential for self-correction.

I suspect we all react to the world differently based on how we have formed as beings. Each of us has a sense of what we detect as trustworthy. Because of how I have developed as a person, I listen to what you say, watch what you do, and perceive how you respond to events around you. All that activity affects my tendency to cooperate with you and what you represent and produces a level of trust.

I tend to have less tolerance for situations that indicate false "facts." Once proven not true, I am suspicious of the circumstance involving the lies involved. And nor do I perceive someone who lies to me, for instance, as someone who needs to be forgiven. I see the one who violates me with lies as one who needs monitoring for "uncertainty." In my mind, forgiveness is another matter. It is one thing to forget and still, another to learn. In other words, I want to evolve from my mistakes. And to me, it is a mistake to keep believing someone who tends to lie. I subconsciously build my "little house" of reality, and I want it on solid rock!

In a conversation with the Abbot, I used an example of having apples thrown at you when you walk down a particular street. If it happens once, you might enter the street again. But if it happens twice or three times, eventually, you avoid the street. The impact of a thrown apple can be painful, and I want to learn from the painful experience and put an end to it. I think I monitored the monastic life from that perspective, and once early on, I explained that to the Abbot. At the time of the conversation, he agreed with me. In retrospect, maybe he should not have.

It so happens that certain people, groups, organizations are only capable of certain levels of accuracy in what they say. And if, for instance, the organizations say that they do not tolerate racism or sexism, they might mean what they are saying. It does not necessarily mean they are fully capable of monitoring such occurrences for corrective purposes. I grew up paying attention to exactness and eventually found that the world was not doing so.

For many people, a guess or assumption about a circumstance is the same as a fact, and in my world, it is not. Because of differences in perception, I lost levels of trust in the world in which I lived. What was a lie to me was not a lie to them. What was true to me was not true to them. This dueling perception was a constant source of conflict between me and the world around me. And I think this very perception led to distrust with the monastery and the brothers. It affected my relationships and my ability to function freely. It is much like walking on a roof that may cave-in at a specific spot. And you proceed with caution because you do not know what location is that spot. You are trying to avoid the possible pain of injury. And when you take into consideration their evolution as people of faith, you might see great reason for a social disconnect.

Religion, faith, communication, emotions, relationships, and things of this nature are not exact. And sometimes, your confidence in them leaves you lost on how to react or respond under some circumstances. But like a child learning to walk, I gained confidence enough to realize my immediate circumstantial limits. I realized my communications were no longer trustworthy. My understanding of faith was not solid. My emotions were not in many ways predictable, and I had to be okay with that. For almost six years, I allowed myself to coexist with this "cloud of unknown" until the pain of its presence was no longer tolerable. I realized I needed to end it or be lost forever.

The year 2014 was the beginning of the end for my little time as a monk. I did not know until later, but my trip to Colorado to commune with other monks in Simple Vows was undoubtedly the beginning of the end of my time as a monk. Having learned so much from my visit, I began to let go of my "dream" of what monastic life truly entailed. I realized that monasteries the world over were probably about the same in how they operated, and I was sub-consciously in conflict with that. <u>Monastic life was more about socializing than I wanted to admit. I would never reach the heights of the people I met with sixty or sixty-five years of monastic devotion.</u>

But for me, the amount of social activity was mystically more draining than I had ever realized. On this brilliant trip, I met people who wanted to dedicate themselves to God in this extraordinary way. It was there in the mountains of Colorado (that I enjoyed so much) that some part of me let go of wanting to be a part. In a very subtle way, amid the sprawl of monastic activity, I was disappointed far too much with what it all meant. And I realized I had no tolerance for it anymore. It is quite possible that I was simply not worthy of it all. Or maybe I was a being that reached a point where I could no longer operate on the same "frequency" as others around me.

My older sister, Kim, was celebrating her 50th birthday. And I wrote a letter to celebrate with her in my absence. For many people, five decades is unique!

January 15, 2014

Dear Kimberly,

You are my loving sister! And I am fond of you too (most times. - note the dry humor!) I am writing this note in celebration of your upcoming 50th anniversary of life. Unfortunately, I will not be there, and for that, I am sorry (for the most part- :()) But, you surround yourself with people who love and care for you. And they would do so much for you (if it is not too much). And so, my mind is at ease.

Dad turns 75, and Kimberly turns 50 years old? What were your parents doing when Anthony was turning 25? Just do the math, missy! Love Child. Liberian Girl!

I am happy for you! Stay safe! Tell JC not to celebrate too much. Tell Mo and Lai (my nephew and niece) to try and make it to the party (it might conflict with their bowling night and all, you know). All is well here, knowing that you have reached a Great milestone (and I thank God!)

Love,

"Rith"
Br. Anthony-Maria

PS If my letter sounds a bit wishy-washy, it is because I had waffles for breakfast! (Yes, folks, he's killing it today; the crowd goes wild!)

My older sister was turning 50 years old, and I was offering my comments for support as she adjusted to being a year older.

February 3, 2014

Dear Kim,

What a way to turn 50! Filled with worry! What is there to worry about, just look around! What is there not to worry about, just do your best to be a decent person. Keep striving and grow your faith in the infinite.

I love you even if you are not in your forties anymore. Let's face it; I'm only 18 months behind you (smile). Then I will celebrate with a cheese sandwich. My dream is finally coming true too!

Tell James that he is in my thoughts, but now that he is a known diabetic, he should stop with the carbs! I am going to send you some critical information on diabetic diets. Maybe it is not as scary as you think? And losing weight makes a huge difference. If he can earn a black belt in the Martial Arts, he can certainly change his diet to a more diabetic-safe one.

love always,

"rith" – nickname
Br. Anthony-Maria Odom

P.S. I forgot what I was going to say... sorry?

Welcome to Monastic Life! – Abbot and Abbess

Abbot and Abbess

The Abbot or Abbess of a Roman Catholic monastery carries tremendous responsibility. It is a position and not a job. It comes with significant spiritual and social influence. Thus, every Abbot can go a long way to helping or harming their monastery in every decision they make. But, most important, God.

The Abbot is the central person for information on all that goes on in the monastery. And thus, what gets reported to the Abbot often determines his decisions concerning monastic operations and individual spiritual guidance. Suppose I say, "Br. John is a really hard worker!" The Abbot takes note. But, if enough people say, "Br. John is slow and hardly does any work!" the Abbot might investigate and influence the situation.

The Abbot is the "face of God" for the monks. We are to respect him or her as if speaking to God. It is a position that most people revere. In Trappist Monasteries, the position itself is filled by the votes of the brothers in Permanent Vows. As of now, it must be a member of the priesthood.

For the first four or five years in monastic life, in addition to having to meet with my Vocations Director, I met with the Abbot once a week. For me, these meetings were stressful. I initially dreaded all of them. Social anxiety was a real issue in all this. But gradually, I got to know them as people, and it became easier with time. The meetings were tremendously helpful in understanding how I was perceived by the monastery, improving my understanding of monastic life, conveying any reasonable complaints I had, or reporting significant issues of any kind. It gives them an opportunity to evaluate me as well.

I witnessed our Abbot attempt to be fair, receive guidance, and adequately consider what was essential to the monastery. I noticed how he dealt with non-monks, financial issues, work issues, and even monastics. In all this, I always thought that this "job" required far too much complex activity for any person, given the available resources. But do not ever forget God! I thought, it was an improper position, especially given a monk's background or lack of worldly exposure. No person is perfect, but together with the Abbot's council, some pretty effective decisions are made.

As you approach key points in your time in monastic life. And especially in your decision for Permanent Vows, the **ABBOT** and those he assigns will specifically test your staying power. Events are very blatant and offensive incidences to test your resolve. Some of these issues come up because of spiritual influence and other times they are manufactured by the Abbot himself. The goal is to withstand the blows and make proper choices under stress. Being falsely accused or lied about are ones that occur frequently.

Monks are human beings and even with God's help still make mistakes in judgement. Human bias is part of the flawed human view. For example, one of the newer monks complained to me about his being blamed for something he did not do. He was upset that I did not defend him. I explained to him that I knew the situation and chose not to defend him on purpose. It was so blatantly obvious to me that it was a test of some sort. The conversation did not go over well for him. But that is life in the monastery!

Our Abbot, like most, was often traveling. And he often had to delegate decisions to the Prior. In all this time, my perspective was often too focused on his human frailties. I had to learn how this man needed to represent God on earth and still be considered a human. And that is not easy. We as people can be very picky about our needs and what is important to us. The Abbot must try and meet our needs and that of the monastery. And manage it all for a holy outcome.

There was a time I remember thinking to myself that I did not envy anyone with that position, especially during this time in monastic history. We do tend to blame ourselves. We have declining religious dedication in our population, less support for the monastic way of life, and more distraction from God as society speeds faster and faster. Abbots and Abbesses must come up with some explanation for all this shrinking monastic interest. They must make their way into the future for all Trappists, hopefully under the guidance of the Holy Spirit.

Like in other sections, the names in this section are changed to protect the innocent. Br. Joe Smith was actively seeking entry into the monastery. He was a long-term Monastic Observer, and then one day, he was a Postulant. In this writing, no one asked for my input; I felt inspired to give it. So I sat down and wrote what I observed of him and his time at the monastery and offered it to the Abbot. But soon after becoming a Postulant, he left the monastery, and he decided against entry.

February 7, 2014

To: Abbot
From: Br. Anthony-Maria

re: Smith – Some Observations

Br. Joe Smith is an honest, decent, friendly, pleasant person who is most often sincere to himself and others. And I write this to document some observations of him as he is here as an Observer and Postulant. I do it in my spare time for the benefit of the Abbey, and I have no other motivation for doing so. For some reason, I think this feedback to you might be helpful. This document is not meant for public use.

Observations of Br. Joe Smith:
§ Smiling, Pleasant, Offering himself, Helpful (Generous)
§ Limited Openness- at times
§ Angry- at times, not expressive
§ Tired- at times
§ Forgetful- often
§ Generic in personal communications
§ Not always open to advice

- In Chapters (Monastic meetings), Br. Joe Smith spoke in generalities that indicated to me that he was sincere but overly positive. For example, "Everyone here is Holy," "They're all great people," "Everyone is so nice," "Everything is perfect." But I didn't seem convinced that he believed what he was saying. Nor did he seem aware that he was probably not being sincere.

- When given specific instructions, he didn't remember 24 hours later. This memory lapse, in my opinion, created frustration for many of us who are already tired and "short on patience." He seems to sincerely have a problem remembering what he is told to do when working with us out on the farm.

- He openly listened to advice but often failed to follow it. Could it be he forgot the direction? Sometimes that was probably the case, but other times, he seemed not to trust the advice or simply ignored it.

- He communicated a presence of being happy and satisfied while simultaneously seeming to be frustrated with his circumstances. This circumstance, to me, is a conflicting presence. I didn't believe he was as happy as he expressed. He often worked hard, but his facial expression was one of being "tired and fed up."

- He sometimes seemed to behave as if he was "doing us (Methuselah) a favor" by being here at the monastery. But I felt he was receiving something in return for being here. He benefited from his presence here. I don't think he consciously expected to spend his remaining life at Methuselah, though he became a Postulant anyway.

- I believe he respects the Trappist way of life and simultaneously thinks that a more active way of life is more appropriate for serving God. To me, he thinks all Christians should be more active. He never expressed this opinion to me. He had some trust issues, which limited his ability to be completely open with us, especially authority figures. EOF.

One of the professors teaching a class at the monastery was also on staff at a university in Pennsylvania. I knew another professor who worked in the same university. She and I were classmates in the 1990s. So I offered him a note to deliver to her with a card I had made. She eventually did get the card and sometime later visited the monastery. We had fun on her visit, and she probably increased her understanding of Monastic and Religious life as well.

February 9, 2014

Dear Mary,

"Surprise! Surprise! Surprise!" (That's from the show: Gomer Pyle, U.S.M.C. (15), in case you are too young to know what that means).

Photo: Dr. Quinetta Robeson visited the monastery while in the area at my invitation. I invited her when I discovered that one of our teachers worked at the same university as she.

What a tiny world we live in today? We have Fr. Laird here at Methuselah for a class on Christian Contemplation and BEHOLD; he is a faculty member at Villanova! When I heard that, my face lit up (as much as it can light up!)

I just wanted to say hello in a unique way, so I asked him to take this card back with him, and he said he would get it to you somehow. He figured he could probably use the university mail system.

Anyway, I hope all is well with you! I hope you like the card (it's my latest creation). And my video is due out as a blockbuster in 2015, starring Denzel. A three hundred-million-dollar budget (smile). Be kind when you watch it!

Sincerely,

Br. Anthony-Maria (Rodney Odom)

When I first met my first Roman Catholic Pastor, he evaluated me as mentally ill. He did not understand why I would stand in the freezing-cold to wait for Ms. Brown to discuss Catechism. Why did I not merely come inside! At the time, as well as now, I put myself in his position and concluded I would have drawn similar conclusions about someone acting like I was. I imagine he was concerned for her safety as well – some strange guy "out of nowhere." But, I was told by people at Methuselah that he wrote me an excellent recommendation for entry to the monastery. I also learned that word-of-mouth weighs heavily in religious organizations.

March 5, 2014
Ash Wednesday

Dear Br. Anthony,

Peace and all good to you! I received the DVD you sent me, which I viewed of your journey from Charlotte to South Carolina and your vows (Simple) as a Trappist Monk. I enjoyed viewing it, and it made me pause and thank God that He put you in our lives and what a joy to see how far you have come. Thank you for sending it.

Here where I am, I am the director of the Retreat Center. I find it gratifying to see how many people want to come and spend some time with God in prayer and silence. We are blessed by various groups, not all Catholics, but from many different religions. What is nice about it is that they get a new perspective on what Catholics do, and many false notions and stories they hear are swept aside, leaving us with a better understanding of our lives and admiration of it.

On weekends I travel 60 miles to New Jersey to work in a parish by offering Masses on Saturday and Sunday. It is an excellent opportunity to be in contact with people and be blessed by enabling me to preach to them.

Ms. Dale Brown has not been well, suffering a tumor in her back. I occasionally speak with her by phone, but prayers are needed for her.

Once again, blessing, congratulations, and thank you for what you did and who you are. I am sure God is pleased. May you continue to persevere.

Fraternally,

Pastor

Welcome to Monastic Life! - Telling My Little Story

Telling My Story

Whenever we encounter God, whether emotionally positive or negative, joyful or brutal, dull or astounding, we want to tell someone about it. These encounters leave you with feelings that "scream: 'I had no idea!' ", "God is real, and people need to know!", "I am so grateful for God" or sometimes even "God does crazy things!" Fr. Timothy visited from Rome. I understand that he was part of the Trappist's representation at the Vatican. He says that his tradition on monastery visits is to sit and talk with each monk. I mentioned that I was not born catholic in his conversation with me. One of his questions was how I came about joining the Roman Catholic Church. He said he always loves to hear these stories. I felt he sincerely wanted to know my story, so I told him.

I told him, laughingly, that I joined the Roman Catholic Church, sort of like going into a building by the seventh-story window and discovering the front door to the building by coincidence or dumb luck. I think about that statement that I made to him very often because it says a lot about how I see life in general. My perception of life does not always lead me down a straight path. And because of how I perceive, I usually create a path on my way amidst the many ways present. And while, over time, I have learned much about conforming to the "cultural norm" of my circumstance, it is not my tendency. I often go marching after my goals in the way that best suits me and my circumstance. And frequently, the consequences of my choices are not pleasant.

In this instance, I read books about hermit life and monastic life. I read much about the people who made these ways of life famous, and then I decided: I want to do that! I want to be like those people in the books! This way of life is for me! These practices are the way things are supposed to be for me! And I simply dropped everything I was invested in and started walking in a radically different direction. My sense from Jesus was that it might be too late for me to achieve my intention. But I decided to go for it anyway, not in defiance of Jesus but in hope. For all things are possible with God. And just maybe he would let me get to live like these people.

After reading many books that happened to be about Roman Catholic people, I decided to follow them - not yet realizing I needed to be Roman Catholic. And after investigating monasteries and seeking to visit one, I found out that most were Roman Catholic. And that I needed to be Catholic to join one. And after I became Roman Catholic and attended a Roman Catholic Parish, I found out that the type of monastery that held my interest required a two-year waiting period. I would also need to visit the monastery for various periods to become more familiar with Trappist's spiritual life. Saint Faustina's diary often discusses the difficulties of being in the monastery or convent. But no amount of reading can prepare you for encountering yourself in the monastery. And then there are the other people and monks around you! What could you do to help yourself prepare to accept them too!

And that was my little story in becoming Roman Catholic. Fr. Timothy listened intently to my story, and the conversation continued sincerely and cordially until it ended. Some days later, he departed for his next destination. And in my mind, I felt like I had just met the Pope or something like that. I felt like I had a session with someone important, even though he seemed pretty normal and approachable.

The Passing of Father Peter on The Feast of John The Baptist

By Br. Anthony-Maria

It was 12:48 a.m., and I needed to relieve myself badly! But I didn't feel like getting up from my bed to do so. Then, as usual, I remembered the magazine article that I read years ago, and that article is what I think of any morning under these conditions- never let your bladder stress this way, or you will ruin it far more quickly than you would like! So I got up from my bed and used the urinal.

Now, I was back in my bed, looking at the ceiling. And like two other mornings this week, I was not tired, nor was I sleepy. So I got up and dressed. This time it was because of a newspaper article I had read some months earlier. It indicated that you should never lay in bed if you are not tired or sleepy. Staying in bed under these conditions would ruin your sleeping habits. I did get up, and I started praying my morning Rosary. On the third attempt, I finally succeeded. At this time of the morning, brain fog meant difficulty keeping track of which part which mystery I was praying; it was a prolonged struggle.

By now, it was 1:35 a.m., and wearing my Habit, I decided to go through the church on my way to get some green tea from the serving area. I would turn on the church side entrance lights as I went. When I arrived at the Commons in the senior wing, I noticed the night nurse, Barbara, walking out of the infirmary. I waved to her, and she waved back. Soon I passed the small chapel and bowed to Jesus, and I could hear Fr. Peter gasping and gurgling. The light in his room was on, so I went in and found him sitting up. He was awake, but he did not seem to notice me in the room. So I spoke to him as I helped the nurse pull him up in the bed to adjust his bed pillows. We (Fr. Bartholomew and I) did the same yesterday to make him feel a little better. But because I never heard sounds of this nature coming from him, I was alarmed. He sounded like he was breathing and bubbling water in his lungs; I decided to wait to talk to the night nurse inside the nurse's office. It occurred to me that Father might be drowning in his fluids? But this was just a thought based on my active imagination and nothing more.

As I passed the infirmary to look in, I found her on the phone calling someone. It turned out that she was contacting the Hospice nurse. So I left the matter alone, thinking she already sees what I think I see. Something was seriously wrong with Fr. Peter. By the time I returned from getting clean towels from the towel closet, she was off the phone. She asked me if the front gate was still locked. I told her it probably was, but I would go and unlock it. The Hospice nurse needed to be able to drive onto the monastery grounds. Upon returning, I went down to Fr. Peter's room and asked the nurse if she needed any help with anything else, and she smiled and said no. As I said this, Fr. Peter began to expel fluids from his mouth, and the nurse was cleaning him up as he did. I asked her again (this time, I was even more alarmed). And she, quite calmly, said no, it was not necessary.

It was around 2:18 a.m., and I was back in my room. I set my alarm for a period of mediation. And a little before 3 a.m., I got up from my chair to light the candles in the church. From there, I went back to the senior wing to check on Fr. Peter. The Hospice nurse had arrived, and both nurses were working on Fr. Peter. I didn't go into the room as I didn't want to be in their way. So I went back to the church to finish my Rosary prayer. But as I sat there praying the second decade of the Glorious Mysteries, it occurred to me to stop praying the Rosary and to go to Fr. Peter's room in the senior wing and pray the Divine Mercy Chaplet for Fr. Peter. And so, I did. However, I saw the Abbot coming out on my way into the Senior Wing building, and he whispered that Fr. Peter was dying. I nodded to indicate my understanding. So instead of going into his room, I went into the small chapel across the hall so I would not disturb his care. I knelt and began praying.

I loosely concluded that his dying must be why I got up to return to the Senior Wing. It is now that I realize that I was participating in his transition. And I realize that our death is important us, but it is most important because God participates in it. Jesus says that he is "Mercy itself." Thus, he defines what is important not us. I prayed the Divine Mercy Chaplet three times before going to Vigils at 3:17 a.m.. By the time Vigils was over, I felt engulfed in peace. It seemed that I floated about from place to place. Everyone gathered at Fr. Peter's room with the Abbot. I stood outside his room during his Last Rites in something of a state of quiet joy. When I heard the gong indicating his death, I felt no reason to rush and see his body. So I strolled and prayed as I went. I felt intense gratitude and honor to participate in Fr. Peter's ritual as I walked.

Fr. Peter passed in such a personal way that I was overwhelmed with amazement. As the experience occurred, I wondered if it meant anything. But the sense of peace and the depth of solitude that surrounded me the remainder of the morning should have been proof enough that it meant something powerful! In any case, this is such a personal story that it may seem incredible to a few people other than myself. Still, I felt the need to share it.

"At the hour of their death, I (Jesus) defend every soul that will say this Chaplet as I do my own glory. When this Chaplet is said by the bedside of a dying person, God's anger is placated and His unfathomable mercy envelops the soul" (Faustina Diary, 811) [13]

The Diary of Saint Maria Faustina Kowalska Maria Faustina Kowalska, recognized in the Roman Catholic Church as Saint Faustina (born Helena Kowalska, August 25, 1905, in Głogowiec – October 5, 1938, in Kraków, Poland), was a Polish nun. Throughout her life, Faustina reported having visions of Jesus and conversations with him, which she wrote about in her diary, later published as the book The Diary of Saint Maria Faustina Kowalska: Divine Mercy in My Soul. Her Vatican biography quotes some conversations regarding the Divine Mercy devotion. [10]

Fr. Peter was a Roman Catholic Priest from East Asia. He migrated to the United States to enter Our Lady of Methuselah Abbey as a Trappist Monk back in the 1980s. He was 82 years old. He was buried July 1, 2014, at the Abbey in Monk City, SC, in the tradition of Trappist Monks.

She was a Trappist Monk in a monastery in Virginia. And we met at the Juniors Conference in Colorado. Every year all the Trappist monks in junior monk status travel to a central location in the U.S. to learn, share, and be "observed" by senior monks. She came from South Korea after direct communication with her local Bishop. As I remember her story, she left all she knew behind and became a Contemplative Nun. The year I met her was her last year (of three) as a Junior monk. She recently took her Permanent Vows.

July 11, 2014

Dear Sister Mary,
I wanted to drop you this little note. One point of the message was to say congratulations on your Solemn Vows! I am glad someone like you made vows. But I am also delighted you came to the Junior Conference. Fr. Mark just took his Vows, and the ceremony was quite beautiful.

While this is probably my last year seeing you any time soon, I am glad I did, which brings up the other reason I am sending this note. In hearing your story, I am strengthened. Especially in hearing the recommendation from your previous Bishop (while you were still in apostolic service). When I realized what you had to say, I felt a strengthening of my being. And even now, I think about the fact that you permanently left your homeland to be here and serve God as a contemplative nun. I wonder if I could have done the same? I hope you don't hesitate to tell that story to other people.

Anyway, that's all I wanted to say. I hope all is well with you. I am sure I met your Abbess while she was here for the Regional Meeting in June. Please tell her the dish-washing monk said hello!

May the Hand of God be with you Always,

Br. Anthony-Maria Odom
Voted Best Looking Religious - 2014 Junior Conference

I received a letter from a Junior Trappist Monk who was in a monastery in California. It took me some time to respond to him. In conversation with him in Colorado, we discovered we had many things in common concerning Religious life, even though he was much younger than I.

Our Lady of Methuselah Abbey
1234 Methuselah Abbey Road
Monk City, SC 29333

July 11, 2014

Dear Br. Joseph,

My most profound apology for taking so long to respond to your letter :((
As you know, I was voted 'Best Looking Religious' at the 2014 Junior Conference in Colorado. Now I am inundated with fan mail from around the world. It is challenging to keep up with it all! And I was equally surprised to see such a pleasant and friendly letter from you, the First runner up? So I was also at a loss as to how to respond to you.

In any case, I felt, as you did, that we had a unique rapport. I was impressed with your dedication to solitude amid all the socializing --- even though you seem to me to be a relativity social person. When your Abbot was here for the Regional Meeting (we spoke the same day your letter arrived). I told your Abbot that you had the misfortune of being near me while chanting, as I was lost during the instruction on proper chant. I mentioned that I had Br. L. on one side and Br. G. on the other.

By the way, we suffered through several bottles of your community's incredible wine during one day of the Abbot's conference here, and I must admit I am somewhat jealous that we don't produce such "magnificence" for a living. Not that I know that much about wine; I am just stating how I felt, and I was genuinely impressed.

Fr. Mark took Solemn Vows. He is now out of formation and part of the "formal community." It was a beautiful ceremony. And it made me think of my commitment to Monastic Life. Don't forget to pray for Sister Mary, whose vows are coming up in November. I am sure you will, but just in case it slips your memory chip in the busyness of the days. There is no financial bonus for these prayers, but think of it as another good deed for the day!

Anyway, in all seriousness, it was a pleasure and an inspiration to meet you and Br. G. You two guys give me hope for the future of the Order. Please let him know I asked about him and that I am not hurt that he didn't send me the traditional winner's double cheeseburger when I got home from our long trip. Oh Yes! Fr. Bartholomew sends his hello! He is knee-deep in Shiitake mushrooms even now, as I write. He recommends that there is no shame in being second runner-up for Best Looking Religious. Besides, there is always next year when the judges are not in my innocent favor? Between you and me, he does not stand a chance. I guess he is a dreamer?

I am looking forward to seeing you next year.

Sincerely,

Br. Anthony-Maria Odom, O.C.S.O.
Voted Best Looking-2014

Our Lady of Methuselah Abbey
1234 Methuselah Abbey Road
Monk City, SC 29333

September 28, 2014

Dear Mary,

I decided to send you a "keepsake" for your visit here. I know you said you would visit again. And I believe that. But I also know life gets busy out there and who knows what might come up. I wanted a picture of us together, but all the photos indicated **"he has not shaved in 300 years,"** so I decided to give you something you might not mind seeing! The problem is if I shaved in preparation for your visit, it would have caused all kinds of suspicions. So I did not want to cause a stir (smile).

The poem "the voice of my beloved" I wrote after you left. I wrote five poems after you left. Inspiration from somewhere, I guess? So I was hoping you wouldn't send me a bill until you get my little Christmas card. It will be a collection of all of them, including the two I wrote for you.

I am so sad to say that the pecan trees are not looking good. I guess my leaf theory is not panning out. Wishful thinking amid factual nonsense never worked for me either! Anyway, I hope all is well with you.

Warm Regards,

Br. Anthony-Maria

October 10, 2014

Dear Uncle John and Aunt Lorraine,

It sounds weird typing those words! Anyway, my mom told me that Jeffrey had passed away! It has been a long time since I have seen him; it was hard to hear and believe. And my mother also told me about his son visiting Philadelphia from school. So it seems some things just don't make any sense. And this is one that, to me, makes very little sense. I am genuinely sorry for your loss.

I immediately thought of Timmy [one of my older brothers who passed away in 2007], so, in a small way, I can relate to what you must be going through. It feels like a Big Empty Whole in my life. And with him being your son that much more "the big hole." I don't know if my mom mentioned to you that Brian Singleton passed away recently. He recently retired from 20 years in the Air Force. He was only 54 years old with two children. He lived in California and passed away due to a heart attack (or so I am told). We all grew up together, and Brian lived across the street from us on thirteenth street. I met his children once when they were about four or five. I remember them being very shy and quiet. [Kelly Hogart, who lived around the corner on Camac Street, also passed by heart attack and she was only 55 years old.]

I wanted you to know that when I heard about Jeffrey's death, we offered a prayer for him and your family at Mass here at Methuselah. That was some time ago, but I am just getting around to writing you to let you know.

Warmth and Love,

Br. Anthony-Maria Odom, O.C.S.O.
(Methuselah is a Trappist Monastery)

Keith Odom

October 12, 2014

Other Conversations with God by Br. Anthony-Maria

So I asked Jesus, why did you make us so small compared to the rest of the universe? It seems to me that we should be relatively larger? There was a silence. Then I answered my question in my mind: the physical universe is not all that relevant to me now, and I need not concern myself with it so much.

The "monastic honeymoon" is a panacea from the first day for some. On the other hand, I have found that seeking God in the monastery is like trying to move an immense boulder a mile down the road with my bare hands while tiny fire ants are crawling all over my feet and legs, biting me. I often feel my struggle is a wasted effort. Despite the frustrations, I feel over-rewarded for being here, and self-discovery alone is sufficient compensation. I often look at the matter in the following way: if you ask a mother giving birth if she would instead go without the pain, she would probably say yes. But most mothers are still happy to have given birth even with the pain.

I look at the giant mountain of a boulder that I need to move. And it towers over me going up so far. But I am like a child, I do not see any limitations, so I proceed to struggle with this enormous problem. I think to myself, "This is silly; why would I be able to move this giant rock?" I say to myself, "I cannot do this and see no reason to waste my time trying." And after some time of discernment (I tend to be a little simple-minded about life) and because I like to experiment, I decide to be obedient, and I come up with a plan to try. After all, I do have some faith. I think to myself that all things are supposed to be possible. And despite that, I see no way my little plan will work.

Then I put all my energy, mind, body, and efforts to move the boulder. And I get what I expect - Nothing! But because I have been reading the Holy Bible, it says I should give my all and have faith. And because I have been reading my religious books, and they indicate, I should talk to Jesus to get help. So I do; I pray and ask God for help. And I try again. And right as I am so exhausted that I'm about to drop to the ground, the million-ton rock moves half an inch, and the earth shakes, and the walls start to vibrate. I say to myself, Oh my goodness! It moved!

After doing my little "touch down" dance and feeling more confident, I try again, and the boulder moves a little more. But the third time I try it, not only does it not move the way I need it, it comes back at me several feet in the wrong direction! And I cannot help but wonder, "What is going on here? It worked before!" And as I fall to the ground in a childlike tantrum, I remember that I am supposed to trust God. My scripture says I'm supposed to have faith, so I get up off the ground and wipe the tears from my eyes, meditate for a few weeks, and I come back to this boulder and start trying to move it again.

Then after a few hundred more tries and struggles with this giant rock and after I have moved the boulder a few hundred feet in the proper direction, I naturally start to think that I have moved the boulder myself. After all, who would not get a little self-assured after experiencing a miracle like that?

And then there is spillover from God answering prayers. I start to ask God for more. After all, having prayers answered is like discovering the goose that lays gold eggs. And I begin to pray more and more: help this situation, aid this person, please do this, and help with that. And God answers. Sometimes I forgot I asked when the holy answer comes forth. Pretty soon, I think to myself, I'm on to something here! And every time another temptation passes my way, I run and pray.

At some point, I start talking to Jesus, just like I talk to my neighbors (I'm not always talking to myself, you know!) And I begin to treat Jesus in a very personal way. After all, anyone who would help me like this is extraordinary! Then I begin to understand what it means to have a real relationship with a God that few people can see and many don't believe as real. They wonder why is he "wasting his life in a monastery when he could be out here eating double cheese-burgers? Something must be very seriously wrong with him! But I want to protect this relationship, and I don't want to fail it in any way. So I ignore the comments and keep talking to God anyway!

`The kingdom of heaven is like this. Something worth a lot of money is buried in a field. A man found it and covered it again. He was so glad that he went and sold everything he had. Then he bought that field.' `The kingdom of heaven is like this. A trader was looking for fine stones called pearls. He found a pearl that was worth a lot of money. Then he went and sold everything he had and bought it.' `The kingdom of heaven is like this. A fish net was thrown into the sea. It caught all kinds of fish. When it was full, the men pulled it to the land. They sat down and picked out the good fish into baskets. But they threw the bad fish away. **Matthew 13:44-48.** (14)

October 17, 2014

The Enemy in the Garden by Br. Anthony-Maria Odom

I was certainly glad to have read that he lost his legs and subsequently had to crawl on his belly. Otherwise, running might not have been much help. And after seeing his viciousness, I would not want to have the heel that crushes its head! So there I was going for a walk after appreciating my invitation to the volunteer picnic on Sunday, October 5th (we had delicious fried chicken compliments of Dotty and Ursula). The monastic dinner took place only an hour before the picnic, so I was desperate to go for a long, pleasant stroll through the forest- I was feasting for a second time! But as I headed toward the forest via the rear area of the chicken houses, I heard a slithering sound in the grass.

Now you need to know that my hearing is horrible, so I don't know how I heard him slithering through the grass. But as I was passing the artificial pond behind chicken-house number 7, there he was - mean and evil! I was stunned by what I thought I was seeing. He lurched back in a very deliberate serpent-like fashion. Ready to strike! Maybe it was age, I just turned 49, or perhaps because monks are just not used to moving but so fast, my body was slow to respond to my need to run. And so there I was, frozen in time. I was in a sort of physical limbo where I stood staring forward toward my death or, indeed, serious injury. Then when my body eventually followed my instructions and moved with haste out of the way of this aggressive creature with his dazzlingly hostile stance, I didn't look back even once. I kept on moving swiftly toward the forest and safety.

Once in the quiet and serenity of the forest, I became a little puzzled by what had just occurred. This serpent was bathing in the sun! And after all the hype about his supernature, he was only three or 4 feet long. And for that matter, only four to five inches around with a sort of ashy black body. And I certainly never thought when he opened his mouth that it would look like a wad of cotton inside, but it did! What was even more puzzling is that I never once thought to stay around and have a conversation with it. You know what I mean! All that talk about wisdom-enhancing apples and being like God!

It took me about 10 minutes as I walked to calm down. Then it occurred to me; I have history on my side. I know about his kind. That must be why I ran? But even still, why would Eve be more concerned with eating a piece of fruit with this kind of threat looming in her midst? Could it be blind ambition? I just didn't get it! I suppose we all have our unique perceptions of the world around us. And some things I am simply not meant to understand. And thus, I was pretty content to finish my little walk through the quiet forest and head back to the monastery for the evening.

Columbia is different than any place I have ever been and I have been a few places. I got a final time to see Fr. Augustine since he was there as Chaplain. When I first came to Mepkin, he went over many of the subjects of the Roman Catholic Catechism with me. Another first was seeing a Chinese car dealership - I know that sounds odd. But I have never actually seen one - even while in Hong Kong. It was my first-time walking half way between the North and South Poles. The equator on the ocean while onboard a ship is not marked. The city we were in is laid out similar Philadelphia, PA – with 4 parks surrounding a city hall building. I noticed that the Sisters entertain different than the Brothers. They seem more attentive. And they interact more. During the free times, they entertain each other with skits, singing and even comedy. And their meals are GREAT! We Brothers usually watch a movie and have pizza.

November 11, 2014

Dear Mary,

Columbia - The Sisters, before Sunday Mass, lined up to process into the church.

You are getting your Christmas card early because I am mailing everything earlier this year. I am probably one of the few people here at the monastery that sends anything to people. The older monks just don't have any relatives or friends around, or they simply don't celebrate Christmas in the same way as us newcomers. There is a generational difference in our behaviors that does account for our different ways. Their monastic practices were developing under other circumstances. And the longer I am here, the less I will mail to people too! From what I hear, they were far more isolated in their monastic journey than we are now. They certainly had fewer monastic guests. The monastery had more and thicker forests. I must assume that what happened between you and me when you visited would probably never have happened 40 years ago. Me going alone with a female visitor to offer a tour of the monastery? And to think all we did was tour the facility and talk. Anyway, I included some information in this letter that I found personally interesting regarding monastic life.

I understand that community life in the monastery developed from hermit life of North Africa and community life from the monks of West Asia (Syria, etc.) I can be very social from afar for someone who interacts with people as little as I do. It is mainly my family that I correspond with through letters because I am trying to explain my religious practices (being a catholic monk). I don't want them to think I simply dumped them in the name of "God." Although in some ways, I must accept that that is what I have done. In Catholicism, we believe our "sacrifice" of living a "life of prayer" affects society, so I am spiritually helping my family. By the way, since you have a massive capacity for devouring books, I sent this extra material if you choose to read it. If not, there will be no test!

Well, I hope you are doing well. I looked up the population of Charlotte, and it is roughly 775,000. It has been far more populated since 2009 when I left. It is still considered the banking capital of the South. I hope you received the card I sent earlier in August or September. And the short notes before that? This card that I am sending you is slightly different than the one I sent to others. There is no picture in theirs. And I discovered some mistakes in yours after I printed the final copy. I really shouldn't keep printing copies to eliminate every error. So please do your best to overlook the mistakes. If, as a professor, you find the work simply unacceptable, donate the picture to a worthy cause. Speaking of donating, the jellies I sent are harmless and pleasing to eat. But if you are not comfortable with them, don't open them; donate them to a local shelter or give them to someone else unopened. It is the best way to preserve preserves!

Anyway, other than Fr. Luke turning 100 years old, there is nothing else going on here. Mushrooms, prayer, and more prayer! I will be going with three other monks and the Abbot to visit our sisters in Bogota, Columbia. They are called Trappistines. I look forward to that; I hear we get spoiled while there. I don't speak much Spanish, so I guess I'd better smile a lot? We will be down there for a week. So much for "never leaving the monastery?" Every time I contact you, I am coming or going somewhere!

Let me say that I appreciated your being here, and please feel welcome to come back and visit ME only! Not all those other monks (smile) - anytime whatsoever. God bless you and your family for a really "groovy" holiday season!

Warmest Regards,

Br. Anthony-Maria

The monastery store had a small but significant number of jars of preserves of various flavors that they took off the store shelves because the Sell-By date marked on the container passed. It was more than we could eat. After some research on the actual nature of the preserves, I realize that throwing them away would be a great waste. So I convinced the Abbot to allow me to send them to various people and organizations with explanations of why. Most people enjoyed the contents. Some of the people who received them just did not eat preserves, but most were quite satisfied with their little gift, including a group of contemplative sisters in Saint Louis, MO who graciously sent us a thank you note!

November 20, 2014

Dear Jesus, Mary, and Joseph,

Thank you! Thank you! Thank you! for the really great boxes of goodies that you send me. It makes a difference around here. And this last one, I am a little ashamed to say I am not sharing that much! I just could not see doing it. I gave some to Fr. Bartholomew and a little to the kitchen, but the rest the Abbot had no problem with me keeping it, and I will freeze most to eat a little at a time. It is very caring and thoughtful of you to support me this way. I thought to myself, I am one of the few people who get these gifts from their family. It is incredible to me, in general, how many people in life have poor relations with their family members. They don't talk or communicate whatsoever with their brothers and sisters, and even some hate their parents. Even if I did hate my folks, the family politics would dictate that I fake it to keep getting little surprises like what you send me (smile). Fr. Bartholomew has some cousins in New Jersey that send him stuff from time to time, and there is a community down here that supports him somewhat, so he is not entirely alone 10,000 miles from home.

All in all, I am feeling the love right about now. Fr. Matthias' family visits him annually from Virginia; luckily, that is not that far away. The older monks are not that involved with their family the way I am. When someone is 85 or 95 years old, they don't have many living relatives of their generation.

There is another new Postulant here from Columbia, who is still married and who has his wife's permission to spend the rest of his life here at the monastery. He is Br. Angel. He is fluent in Spanish and is in the process of improving his English. His children are all older, so I might have to share a little more with him as long as you send it. For the most part, the volunteers and benefactors here take to donating stuff they think you like, especially if they like you. I talked a lady named Gail into making all of us homemade pizza. It was delicious!

We are supposed to welcome a monk from Nigeria (if he can get in the country), which may take some time. There is not much else going on otherwise. I hope you like the jellies. Tell the people don't complain about the expiration date. In this case (preserves from 2014), a date is just a number and not much else. Appropriately handled, preserves don't go bad as regular food does; they are "preserved."

There is one case from 2010-2011 (I marked it). I contacted the monastery who made it, and they said if it has not been opened and is stored at even temperatures, it is okay! Just make sure the jar is still vacuum sealed and has no foul odor when you open it. It should smell like fruit.

Love you all,
Praying for you all,
Wishing you a Merciful Christmas Holiday!

Br. Anthony-Maria, Keith, Rodney Odom, etc.

P.S. Sorry, the trees have stopped producing pecans. Everyone loves the pecans.

I sent some Preserves to Deacon Todd in Charlotte for some of the Parish members at Our Lady of Consolation.

November 20, 2014

Dear Deacon Todd,

I hope all is well with you. There is not much going on here. Life at the monastery is as usual. My time to vow and sign for another year of Temporary Vows is coming up, and I expect to do so. Though just between you and I, I had a friend visit that made me think about what I am giving up to live a life as a monk. She is talking as if she is thinking about doing apostolic service. I think I'll be okay; we must all learn to deal with the choices we make, don't we?

Anyway, I decided to send these jellies to you, mostly because I wanted to leave it up to you whether people would like them. I'm not trying to create work for you! While monks wouldn't hesitate to eat something past the Sell-By date, others may not. If you feel people would not take too kindly to it, please donate it to a shelter.

I labeled one for Charleen, the pastor, and some of the West-African ladies who often came to Mass during the weekdays. Oh! And please don't forget the Joseph's. Maybe if you leave it in a specific place, they will see it and take it. I mailed Ms. Brown some separate because of her condition.

Sincerely,

Merry Christmas. Praying for you.

Br. Anthony-Maria

2015

The Curious Experience of Seeking God

In the quiet, sometimes chilling cold,
Other times steamy, muggy hot
Conditions of a retreat to nature,

I occasionally rest in special illumination.
Thoughts, words and even deeds.
Trigger insight as to some opaque corner of my heart.

And a new magical encounter presents itself.
Though a vague familiar mental presence,
He was never fully conscious till now.

Upon pondering, my thoughts resonate.
A discovery, that this "me" is so causal in effect.
Yet ingeniously operates in stealthy secret.

That this one has miscalculated,
Misunderstood and thus misbehaved.
For untold years of frustrating efforts.

And I, in some hidden way, am agreeing with this
Horrible, inscrutable, menacing operative,
Who comprises a weirder, darker path to life.

Continued,

And then there is the long, tedious chatter-filled
Journey of constant wrangling within.
Me trying to convince me to cooperate.

To change our covertly contracted agreement.
To see life in a slightly modified way.
I am praying clandestinely to Jesus about him.

Dear Lord, please have even more mercy,
Help "us" do better and live properly under this one
   roof,
And do well by your Holy temple.

Chapter Introduction

It is the most difficult decision I will ever make in my life. At least, that was the way I saw it at the time. Why was I here in this monastery? Why was I thinking of abandoning such a mighty effort on God's part that took place over so many years? How could I leave so much behind? Who was I pleasing by going? Did I please some selfish part of me? Or maybe I did not belong in the monastery in the first place? Was it God's will for me to stay? By going, was I disposing of an incredible opportunity to offer myself to God in such a tangible way? Being here was a great privilege, but, given the way I think, I was probably not coming back once I left. Because of how my mind works, this decision to go is more or less final.

My prayer was for someplace like this, and God answered my prayer. God helped me over all the hurdles and strengthened me for the challenges. Was I abandoning the path, and if I was leaving it, was there really anything wrong with doing so? Should I stay, or should I go? It was a choice I had been making for years. Yes! That is correct! My decision was going on for five years and seven months exactly. While arriving, I didn't focus on leaving. But once I came, I started weighing mentally the costs versus benefits of the decision to stay. And in all this deciding was the idea of "God's Will."

Still, I had to decide for myself. I would not lean on others to resolve this for me. I asked those involved to pray for me. Since some people think the monastery is an utter waste of time, I didn't dare ask them for insight. Others say it is so "close to God," and you should never leave anything like this. I made my decision. Maybe one day, I will know why I did what I did. As of now, I can only rationalize my answers. And even this, not to my satisfaction.

The journey to the monastery was just as beneficial as being here. The lifestyle here was beneficial to my relationship with Christ, and it was profitable in ways that I don't think I can express with words. Anything I focus on day and night persistently and intelligently benefits me this way. Still, when God is intimately involved, I don't have to worry too much about destroying myself for the wrong reasons.

The entire time I was here, my health was a background concern. My diabetes was an issue that was not going away, and truthfully it is not a monastery's job to deal with such matters. Medical people can give advice, but my condition may not improve if they are wrong or I don't take the advice. Was staying here just condemning myself to a slow and unnecessarily painful death? The truth is, diabetes aside, I was never in better health than in the monastery. My diet was healthy, as evident from how my clothes fit when I left. I wore the same dress leaving the monastery as when I arrived. And they hung off me several sizes too large.

Methuselah was a smaller monastery. And when someone leaves, it affects everyone dramatically. People do not always admit that effect, but it was clear to me. The longer I stayed, the more dependent the monastery would be on my presence. I believe that the sooner I left, the better off the monastery would be. As a monk, this practice of making decisions for the monastery is generally inappropriate. Who was I to decide what was best for the monastery? Though I had many conversations with the Abbot, the subject never came up. But previous instances indicated that the monastery would replace me with a new employee and spread my responsibilities amongst other monks. So how my leaving affected the monastery was not a significant factor in my decision to leave.

Leading up to my decision to leave were several short conversations that I had with senior monks from other monasteries. In one case, during a visit from Abbots and Abbesses, two Abbesses commented to me in front of my Abbot that I was doing too much. It was unclear whether they spoke "with the Abbot of Methuselah" or "in front of the Abbot of Methuselah." But in retrospect, when I left Methuselah, I realized that I was mentally exhausted and stressed beyond my comprehension. When speaking with people who live this life, sometimes they make superficial comments that are meaningless in consequence. Other times, they communicate deeper, and their words imply recommendations leading to something more profound. The advice they offered that day was undoubtedly one of those more profound communications meant to inform on a deeper level. I would have been better off heeding their comments and withdrawing from extra activities. But I did not. Perhaps Abbot Melchizedek, too, should have said something, but under the circumstances, he did not.

Another incident involved the visit of the superior monastery of Methuselah for evaluation of our monastery. During this visit, two Abbots were working together for evaluation. They interviewed all the monks. And in their interview with me, they asked questions, and I offered answers. Their response to one of my comments was sharp and pointed. I asked if I could restate something I said earlier, but they responded, "but you have already said it!" In my mind, there is already a mild nervousness associated with such interviews in the first place. And their behavior left me in a confused state. It was clear that I communicated information that was disturbing to them. And my intuitive response to their reaction was one of a decision to leave Methuselah. What was the disturbing information I communicated? I do not know. But this was another example of my poor social skills in action.

Sometimes, we make intuitive decisions while not being conscious of why we are making them. I have learned to trust that process, which was telling me that in no uncertain terms: leave and do not come back. In retrospect, and this is just a guess, there were probably conversations about me between the Abbot of Methuselah and these two Senior Monks. I was responding intuitively to this sudden and exposed knowledge of their conversation. After the meeting ended, these two senior monks did not seem offended by me in any way. On the contrary, they seemed pleasant and cordial toward me. But it was too late. My decision was made. Very little would or could have changed my decision. To this day, I am not consciously aware of any facts they may have known that contribute to my decision to leave.

Time was a serious concern in my decision to leave Methuselah, I was no longer 30-something, and if I waited too much longer to decide to go, life outside would probably be much more difficult. Monks live in a community. The monastic rule guides them to survive off work and donations. But no individual monk is planning these matters tactically or strategically. The senior people in charge design it. The individual monk's job is to pray and seek God. The idea of retirement or encountering a crippling disease is much less of an issue for the monk in Permanent Vows. Since I was in Temporary Vows and in my early fifties, I had no assurance of Permanent Vows. Also, financially, I had no personal assets. I made the mistake of giving all I had away far too early in my monastic life. I realized there was not much time left in my life to earn money for a reasonable retirement if I waited too late to leave. Faith is a factor in making this decision, but so is the reputation of the decision-makers around me. What was their reputation concerning these matters? It was not strong enough for my confidence. The Abbot always said that it was not him I needed to trust but God. Was I still dealing with those trust issues they talked about earlier? I do not know.

And most important was my understanding of God's Will. Did Jesus prefer me to be here, and if I did not stay, what would be the consequences of leaving? It is my opinion that it was God's Will for me to be in that monastery; however, it was no longer within my capacity to keep asking God for help to stay. I asked others to pray for that intention since I could not. And since it is the most important thing to do God's Will, this decision left me mentally stressed.

Were my relationships with the Abbot and fellow monks healthy? I think they were as healthy as one could expect for someone with my issues. I battled with some powerful issues. I was a somewhat anti-social, over-analytical, overly-complex, cynical person with many hidden and vain personal ambitions. That, together with my general sense of anxiety and diabetes, made me a daily handful! And I was far from immune to reacting to other people's issues. As one elderly monk once stated, you would think that some of these matters would not be such a problem after sixty years! But yet they continue. In other words, we are all struggling with something, whether six years or sixty years and the ones around us must learn to deal with each other person's struggles also.

Ultimately, I think deep, hidden, yet powerful cultural conflicts along with age are why I left the monastery. I certainly lacked specific social skills that would have allowed me to fit in the group a little better. There is a subtlety with the interaction of people when they think they are communicating, but, in fact, they are simply speaking two different versions of the same language – limited communications. It can be a rather sloppy, inaccurate form of information transmission between you and others. Inherit in that miscommunication is the resulting conflict, pain, and suffering, repeating itself daily.

My thinking processes were simply different than the others. My age of entry, 44 years old, brings me a person with a well-established value system. And it was clearly in conflict with the values and fundamental behaviors of the monastery. In six years, I made significant progress fitting into the culture. But I still had the choice of an immense and painful effort of mental change toward conformity versus the constant conflict that goes on with people that see life in somewhat different ways. First, I was not always confident that changing was a great idea. Secondly, genuine change for someone like me is excruciating. While I improved since entering, change was like a rigid, locking, metal device. It was why it would have been difficult for me not to enter the monastic life, hard to another monastery, and not very pleasant to leave one. To me, I had a decision that needed immediate attention. I was all out of "struggle" to keep going.

In an overarching sense, I was asking myself to counter my understanding of reality and how things should be in favor of a giant question mark for a future. And ultimately, I did not trust committing my future to this question.

My memory of the great gifts I received while at the monastery was not the ultimate deciding factor in leaving. Survival, intact, to keep going, and seeking God in the way I understood as the relevant one. I lived with a sense of self-importance. Not as my fantasies about life directed me - God forbid. But according to my perception of God's love for me. I seem to have a sort of scorch and burn mentality. Nothing stands in my way. If it is in the way, I need to move it out of the way. It is my simple truth. In my mind, if I could not finish seeking here, I would finish where it seemed I could. My hope was to move beyond it onward. And that presented another hassle, protecting myself as I left Methuselah to find another place on my own.

When it was time to leave, I tried to say goodbye in a non-harmful way. But it was a painful separation. I was in a horrible state of confusion, repressed only long enough to make it out the front gate. I attempted to stay in contact with some of the people I met during my time there. After all, most of the people were genuinely decent, well-intentioned folks. But I purposefully allowed those contacts to wither away also. Ultimately, I realized that many people I knew were simply another connection to a world I needed to leave behind. My relationship with these people and the monastery was the same. I realized there was no sense of independent, personal relationship with these individuals. I was, despite my efforts, thinking as an individual and not a member of a herd.

Failure, anger, bitterness, sadness, and a quiet sense of unfairness permeated my thinking. But the truth is the entire journey was beyond the scope of my ability. I did not do any of it on my own. I obtained where I was only with God's help. And now my fate was in the hands of Mercy still! If anything, I need to move beyond my thinking and opinion and go back to God - once again.

Now that the decision was made to leave, I had strong concerns about what I needed to do to continue to seek God efficaciously. I needed to continue to evolve according to my sense of righteousness. I knew reasonably well what I left behind when I came into the monastery and had no intention of returning to my previous way of life. Others around you think you will go back to fishing as the disciples did when Jesus died.

But I had decided and utterly refused to be distracted by worldly concerns that ultimately have nothing to do with seeking God. In my mind, there was nothing wrong with socially "crawling under a rock" to defend my relationship with God until I felt comfortable enough to walk the streets without being mentally destroyed by the aggressive nature of worldly demands. I observed busyness for the sake of busyness, demands to fill out applications and forms, more and ever-increasing bills to pay, social obligations for the sake of vain ritual, and more. These things meant sacrificing relationships and more. Over time conversations with God are drowned in life's "noise."

During the trip to Columbia for the 25th anniversary of the monastery there, Fr. Bartholomew captured over 700 photos, and I recorded many hours of video of the various events, speeches, and entertainment. We then put it together as a finished collection of five videos and video photo collages commemorating the anniversary. It was a historic event attended by guests, some coming from as far away as Spain. The Sister's Abbess was very impressed with our work. She appreciated what we created with them. Soon the sisters started calling me by a new nickname, "Hermano Techie."

March 27, 2015

Dear Mary,

I hope all is well. I am the culprit behind sending this card to celebrate the fifth day after your birthday. I believe that day is March 30? Yes, I wanted something unique. We all think about you here at Methuselah, although not as often as you might like. Let's face it, you didn't donate riches to Methuselah while you were here? Nor did you bring us a Giraffe or Elephant back from your global travels! What more should you expect from a bunch of busy monks anyway!

Photo: Mary Kathleen Rudy is a volunteer, musician, and frequent visitor to Methuselah. She played the harp during my Junior Vows ceremony. She is leaving to enter a monastery as a Postulant.

As for me, I am back from Columbia, where I fell in love with 50 sisters all at once. They are simply marvelous. They find a way to serve their guests left and right, up and down, and back and forth. They didn't miss anything. And I truly appreciated their chanting. I have it in Mp3 format, but I don't suppose you have a way of listening to it?

What's new at Methuselah? Fr. Bartholomew is going to California to attend another brother's Solemn Vows. Both Abbots agreed to this. As you know, Br. Ezekiel passed on back in January. His last words were, "That darn Mary-Martha, darn her!" and then he said, "rosebud." Do you have any idea what that might mean? I'm guessing you are as confused about it as we are!

We had a Postulant pass away. He was Br. Miguel of South America. He was only here for two weeks when it happened. I can't write about the details since his situation is still in progress. The better part is that because he never intended to return to Argentina, we buried him here. His family is still grieving, of course. He was a genuinely decent person (may he rest in Peace). And I sensed that he was purified in a very powerful way. But I could also tell he was disappointed at the grittiness and sometimes harshness of the monks. His first day at work everyone left him at the worksite alone to walk back by himself. (We all used bicycles.) I saw him and that disenchanted facial expression at a distance. But I did not go back to retrieve him. I suspected that this was occurring for a reason - always being tested!

I don't ever see your mother, though Br. Ezekiel, who used to be Br. Philip, who used to be Br. Ezekiel (he changed his name back and forth), sees her, and they talk about you all the time. He is doing okay. Don't worry about them; it is primarily positive issues! He struggles with the insanity of monastic life, as some do, but it is a little worse with him because, as a programmer, he thinks more or less rigidly, ultra-rationally. And the monks are far from that way! They are, in fact, very fluid or "gray" in their thinking. We had particular conversations on how to perceive the monastic setting without trying to "solve its problems and create a rational solution to it all."

Too bad you cannot go into details about your life there in Saint Louis. (She entered a monastery in Saint Louis.) I would not want to hear it anyway. I have already had dull enough pathetic talk bogging me down as it is. But still, it is too bad. They say only two things come from Saint Louis, steer and giant art displays. So which one are you? Last time I saw you were a pint-size little woman. So you can't be a huge art display!

Ed Magee passed away. Ed Magee went to Poland before he passed away. He obtained and gave me a picture of The Divine Mercy obtained while visiting Saint Faustina's Convent. He knew of my devotion to that saint and The Divine Mercy. Since then, I have been amazed that people pay attention to so much detail of your lifestyle.

He was already medically complicated when you played with him at my Junior Vows. His health pretty much went downhill from then. He suffered from illness and was in and out of the hospital. He is a loss around here. Age ques you as you get older! Everybody you know starts dying. I have had at least two high school classmates die since I came to Methuselah. A classmate, Charlene, told me through Facebook about them. One named Teresa (may she Rest In Peace) had Leukemia, and her death broke my heart. The last time I saw her was in a Taco Bell in Philadelphia. We just stared at each other. We had a crush on each other in high school. And it all came back in that one moment. We never went out on a date or anything like that, but we adored each other from afar.

Anyway, it took me a long time to recover from her death. The other young woman was someone I didn't socialize with at all, but because I saw her five days a week for 4 years in high school, it took me a while to get through her death, too (may she too Rest In Peace!) The more people I know go away, the more I realize how much I am attached to them and their situations. So much of life is a purely emotional experience hiding somewhere inside.

Rather suddenly: Farewell, I must go now. Tell me if you need anything? Can we send you stuff? Anything? Mushrooms!

AMO

I included some pictures in this letter to make it more interesting: We had Buddhist monks from India visiting (Tibetan monks).

Tibetan Monks visiting Methuselah Abbey while transiting South Carolina on a US visit.

The Monks are introduced to the Brothers of Methuselah Abbey.

Learning to photograph at night. A photo of the South Carolina moon.

We had a fantastic full moon one night and I manage to get a shot for you while practicing my photography!

This farewell letter I mailed to most of the people who had some critical part as I entered the monastery. I felt an obligation to let them know I was now leaving.

April 3, 2015

Dear Mary,

Just a short note to let you know that as of mid-April 2015, I will no longer be at Our Lady of Methuselah Abbey as an active member of the monastic community. As you know, the formation period is a period for discernment, and I have discerned (primarily at least) that a disciplined life as a hermit is what I need right now. It won't be effortless since I do not exist in a vacuum.

I have considered other possibilities, such as other monasteries and even a hermit's life "in community." Still, I feel I am best being a hermit on my own at almost 50 years old. I will be working in that direction according to my situation. My short (five years and eight months) stay at Methuselah has helped me in ways that I see as miraculous. And I don't wish to lose what I have gained in being here at the monastery. So pray that I stay focused on walking a straight and narrow road.

As for my future intentions, I will leave and take up as much of a hermit's life as possible on my own. With the help of my life here, I expect to continue working on my relationship with God in this way.

My new (temporary) address will be:

Rodney Odom
1234 Somewhere Street
City, State 12345
Email: anthonymaria3@gmail.com for the foreseeable future.

Thank you for your years of support for Methuselah Abbey. May God continue to bless you for your work.

Warm Regards,

Br. Anthony-Maria, O.C.S.O.

Jesus and his disciples went on their way. They came to a town. A woman named Martha took him into her home. She had a sister named Mary. Mary sat near the feet of Jesus and she listened to what he said. But Martha was very busy doing many things for Jesus. She came to Jesus and said, 'Lord, my sister has left me to do all the work. Do you not care? Tell her to come and help me.' The Lord answered her, 'Martha, Martha, you are worrying. You are troubled about many things. Only one thing is needed. What Mary has chosen is good. And it will not be taken away from her.' **Luke 10:38-42.** (14)

Welcome to Monastic Life! – My Last Day

Welcome to Monastic Life! – My Last Day

My Last Day

It was mid-morning when I left Methuselah Abbey for my last time. Angel, the store manager, was the last person I spoke to as I left. We had a big hug! I decided to stop for a snack and drink to accompany my drive on the way out of town. And I stopped to buy not so much because I needed to stop. I did it because I had the freedom to do so and felt the need to express that freedom.

I pulled into the BP Gas and Convenience store, and I gathered a single-serve soda and another for half price, along with a hot dog. I found myself mumbling out loud at the cash register that at least the last person I would talk to in Monk City would be a beautiful woman. She was an attractive young lady who blushed as she registered my order, and I quietly smiled.

I noticed that she had a photo attached to her shirt sleeve. And realizing that it was an odd spot to place a photograph, I asked her if the woman in the photo was recently killed. And she answered yes. She told me that the woman was her close friend.

Then I asked her if her death was the result of abuse. And I asked this question only because the young woman in the photo seemed about her age. And she answered yes. She told me that the young lady's boyfriend shot her to death. And as she spoke about her murder, I could feel my entire chest cringe. I could feel the pain in my heart. And my body bowed down, with my head nearing the counter.

I was genuinely sorry for her loss. But two things passed through my mind simultaneously: (1) I was flirting with this woman without even trying, and that was no way to start the plan I was pursuing, and (2) my entire body wrenched in pain hearing about the death of her friend. It turned out to be a prophetic event as to what I had to look forward to leaving the monastery and being exposed to the activities in society. And I reluctantly thought to myself, welcome back to "the world..."

For I will take you from among the nations and gather you out of all the countries, and will bring you into your own land. I will sprinkle clean water on you, and you will be clean. I will cleanse you from all your filthiness, and from all your idols. I will also give you a new heart, and I will put a new spirit within you. I will take away the stony heart out of your flesh, and I will give you a heart of flesh. I will put my Spirit within you, and cause you to walk in my statutes. You will keep my ordinances and do them. **Ezekiel 36: 24-27.** [2]

May 15, 2015

Dear Mary-Martha,

On April 11, 2015, I set out to Philadelphia to restart myself outside the monastery and develop a different prayer life. I fill this little letter with pictures of my route to Philadelphia. I will miss Methuselah and all her servants after almost six years there. But I freely admit that having 24 hour access to pizza makes it a little easier for me to leave.

Photo: Monk City, South Carolina, filling the gas tank of the blue 2008 Nissan Cube, I was driving to Statesboro, Georgia, to visit family and then Philadelphia.

I have had no trouble with the car they gave me thus far. I did have to read a manual to find the spare tire and jack. (I thought needing to search for something like a spare tire was a little odd.) While in Charlotte, North Carolina, my low tire pressure light lit the dash. But after using an air gauge and spending a dollar on air, I was back on the road.

My mind was overwhelmed by all the sensory sources of the open road; highway driving never seemed more overwhelming! A two-hour and 45-minute trek to Statesboro, Georgia, from Monk City, lasted essentially 4 hours because GPS kept "helping" me get there sooner, and in my fascination with this new way of driving, I accepted its recommendation. I also took my time and drove carefully.

I arrived safely in Statesboro at my Aunt Mae Francis' and Uncle Larry's home. There were already many people there as my cousin Lauren's daughter was going on her "Junior-Senior" prom. The families were gathering to take pictures. During the few days I was there, I had lunch with my Aunt Addie, and we visited the local park. It was very peaceful and quiet, probably because it

Photo: After we ate lunch, we went to the park. My Aunt Addie is feeding the fish and turtles.

Photo: Interesting street sign: Bell Arthur, North Carolina.

was the middle of the day. We fed the fish bread crumbs. I found it fascinating to watch these giant fish leap out of the water in competition for bread. I reached the little ones by tossing food away from the shoal. The park has eight baseball fields, 4 soccer fields, a water park, and an Olympic-sized indoor swimming pool. The city of Charlotte could not even fantasize about having a park like this one. Philadelphia might dream of such incredible use of public funds, but it would never amount to anything more than a dream. I should mention that the entire park was spotless!

After a few days in Statesboro, I went to Charlotte to visit my buddy Lin (we know each other from our time in U.S. Navy), his wife, Lisa, and their children. And I planned to say good-bye Sister Jeanne-Margaret at Belfast, NC, and possibly Deacon Todd. But none of that worked out. Sometimes it is just easier not to say goodbye?

Photo: Front wall, St. Patrick Roman Catholic Cathedral: Charlotte, North Carolina,

I did cook during my visit, and it turned out well. In 2009, I held Lindsey in my arms like a small jet plane while talking to her mother. That was in San Francisco. I was flying her around because then she was two years old and light as a feather. And now look at her! Then Lance was a very heavy 4-year-old. I could lift him, but I had to drop him quickly. After some time in Charlotte, I headed east to Greenville, North Carolina, to visit my Aunt Mary, one of my mother's sisters. I wanted to visit my cousin Deidre in the hospital for heart surgery. But it turned out she was in the hospital in Raleigh. And as I drove east, it occurred to me that I was taking the same path back to Philadelphia that I took coming to Methuselah. I was visiting each city but in precisely reverse order.

It is easy to know you are in Greenville when you start to see giant East Carolina University (ECU Pirates) buses. It always confused me how a university could have a more elaborate bus system to get its people around than the general public. But there they were arriving and frequent! The apartment complex where I lived has a new beach theme. Near that same apartment complex, the East Carolina Mall was partially demolished, and there were now twice as many stores.

The beautiful tobacco fields are still there. Although I think they are growing soybeans. The Bell Arthur Chapel is still standing. It has expanded into where my Great Uncle's house used to stand. My grandfather, who built houses, helped build the main church building. My family burned down my grandparent's house some time ago and built another in its place. And my Great Aunt's house across the road from my grandparent's house was overgrown with trees. Somebody was missing a tremendous real estate investment opportunity; Bell Arthur was rapidly developing.

Photo: The Bell Arthur Free Will Baptist Church. Monk Family history (mother's maiden name.)

Selfie: I stopped in Greenville, North Carolina, and saw Aunt Mary. My cousin Deidra, her daughter, was in the hospital in Raleigh for heart surgery.

My mother wanted me to stop in Maryland to visit my Aunt Hester and Uncle Vincent (May they Rest in Peace). But I instead opted to head straight to Philly. Heading north: traffic approaching Washington D.C. was heavy. I encountered at least two hours in bumper-to-bumper traffic. The driving speed changed radically. I drove 60 mph for a minute, and then suddenly, we slowed to five mph for 15 minutes. The tolls going through Maryland, Delaware, and Pennsylvania are horrendous. I paid two tolls for $8.00 and one for $4.00. If it is $20.00 to go through Maryland, I cannot imagine what the tolls to New York City

-are now! What happened to the days of tossing a few coins into a toll booth?

Anyway, goodbye, everyone. It seems I am constantly struggling to let go of something. The minute I get a little comfortable, it starts all over again!

(l to r) Mom, Dad, and Me. After finally arriving at the Bayard Street address in Philadelphia, PA.

Welcome to Monastic Life! – Authenticity And Humility

Authenticity and Humility

I have somehow fooled myself into thinking that my politeness is my nature. That using kind words genuinely represent who I am. This perspective is a misunderstanding of myself. The "polite me" is the socializing, outward-facing part of me. This is the "me" that faces the community I live in, wherever that is.

But there is also at least one other "me." I'll call it the inner me. And sometimes, the inner me varies based on place, time, mood, etc. Often the inner me is not the same as the outer me. But still, I seem to think it is okay to live many different personal behaviors outwardly and inwardly. I change based on my need to persist through social circumstances. If I am very dark inside but must smile, sometimes I adapt the outer me.

Because of Monastic Life, I am forced to live differently. I am struggling to live from within. And I must let that bidirectional communication process take place in its own time. I think about life this way: the entire "me," however that comes about, is required to focus on God. The often superficial outer-me is probably not acceptable to God. If I am not feeling well, I cannot lie to God and claim to be okay! Therefore, I should struggle to be the same thoroughly authentic person throughout all circumstances all the time! Authenticity and humility demand it.

I suspect one of the primary benefits of monastic life is that all the brothers have a strong sense of God's presence despite having distinctly different relationships with God. That sense is strong enough that they are willing to leave the world behind and struggle to focus on God alone.

Outside this setting, people want you to smile and be pleasant. "Don't be a downer!" "Lighten up, okay?" "I like him, he is always happy and smiling." "Don't be so serious all the time!" There is no regard for living from within and deepening that relationship with self in everyday life. And there is no use for allowing that process to play out naturally.

After leaving Methuselah, I communicated with the Abbot by writing letters. I did so primarily because of the obligation of my annual Simple Vows. Once my annual vow expired, so did my obligation to stay in touch. I usually contacted him once a month.

May 12, 2015

Dear Abbot Melchizedek,

I hope all is well with the brothers. I pray for Methuselah. I often pray for you and Fr. Thomas. How am I? Well, I am doing okay. If you read my little adventure story, you know I am taking things gradually and with caution. For the most part - it seems I am trying to adapt to the changes around me in an organized and purposeful way. My family is adjusting to my presence as well. I am trying to stay focused on what I intended to do when I left Methuselah. I go to my sister's house mornings to work. She has Wi-Fi. My parents don't know what Wi-Fi is, but they know my goals. I spend most evenings at my parents' home. I study at the Park (Kelly Drive) or the public library. Having Wi-Fi is convenient because I don't have to be in the library.

I have not visited other family members since I have been in Philadelphia. I have not socialized much with anyone. I occupy my time between studies and helping my parents with repairs around their home. I am proud of the safety bar I put on their shower walls. They truly appreciated it. The difficulty was finding wood behind the tile without drilling needless holes. A stud-finder is not as reliable as one might think. That's what makes it a challenge for an amateur like me. With the proper drill bit, the tile is easy to penetrate. Next, I will be cleaning the brick and repainting the window shudders on the 2nd-floor front bedroom windows. The guy they paid to do it didn't finish the job.

I am far more at peace with my decision to leave Methuselah. However, I am still dealing with the sense of failure from my original goals. The evidence is more apparent, indicating I had little or no choice but to leave. However, I find myself humbled by the struggle. God is the one who makes me worthy and not my effort to do his Will. I have started attending

Mass at a catholic church with three different congregations (St. Michael, St. Therese, and Holy Cross). They speak as if they are one congregation now. I attended Holy Cross in Philadelphia in 2012 for my parent's 50th anniversary. I have an appointment to talk with the Pastor of Saint Michael, who was an Anglican Priest. He has agreed to speak with me and do the best he can. He says he knows nothing about Trappists. He did spend a year at a Benedictine Monastery. They have a small congregation at the 9 a.m. Sunday Mass. It is spiritual direction I seek. I seek the Spirit.

Though I still have much work to do, learning all this new web technology is essentially grunt work. You must plow away at it daily until the information comes together as one piece. That's how I felt when I completed my first website. It was as though I had accomplished something miraculous. Sometimes I must take a deep breath in my studies and try not to panic! But the truth is the more you learn, the more you see there is so much more to learn.

The car is holding up well, though gas is far more expensive here than there. And because of my poor memory, I plan to get an extra key made. I do not wish to get locked out. I mention this because the Nissan dealer wants $200.00 to make and program the key. The keys have chips in them now! I found a place to do it for $85.00.

I try to do all this while trying to stay focused on Jesus. So most mornings, when I awake, I pray the Rosary. I spend about 20 minutes in meditation and try to read scripture, though often not much. Most evenings, I pray Divine Mercy Chaplet. I listen to audiobooks that I get free off the internet. I am currently listening to Revelations of Divine Love by Julianne of Norwich. Her English is a little different, but I understand some of it. I used iTunes to make CDs for my car.

Farewell for now.

Sincerely,

Rodney Odom

Welcome to Monastic Life! – Church Is Different Everywhere

Church is Different Everywhere

After leaving the monastery, one of the things I found is how people perceive the church's Sanctuary. In the monastery, the church's Sanctuary is also a sacred space. But it is kept quiet, and all social activity happens outside the Sanctuary. There is little or no talking inside the Sanctuary. The Altar in the Sanctuary is sacred, and when you pass it, you acknowledge it. Outside the monastery, a Sanctuary is a place for socializing, talking, greeting, and giving information. It is a place to be friendly and kind to each other. People evaluate each other for how well they fit into the parish culture. Sometimes the church business is passed to the parishioners in the Sanctuary. There is often fun-natured frivolity, including discussing a favorite sports team playing a game that day. I also noticed that in Philadelphia services, few people genuflect, and few bow in acknowledgment the birth of Jesus to the Mother of God during the Creed. In Charlotte, more people seem to acknowledge Mary and God, but it is still much different than in monastic practices.

Work is a part of monastic life. Monks do so to earn a living and as a way of serving God. It is a form of prayer. It is a part of the Monastic routine. Outside, people speak of dreading Monday because of work, but they say, "I have bills to pay!" In some cases, they have projects to accomplish. Frequently, they have some goal or routine to complete. As a result of the diversity of issues associated with work and life, their perspective after leaving the church may not align with the person's religious intentions.

What people do outside the church life is essential to earning a living. It often dictates what they do and why. But they may not see such issues as having to do with their relationship with God. Thus, they risk separation from focusing on God in their work or career. When I left the monastery, I knew it would not be easy to be in the world around me and stay focused on God as I wished.

But it is still another experience ending up mentally "deformed" because the person next to you has no interest in God; and behaves accordingly.

Or the person next to them thinks going to church on Easter and Christmas is sufficient for thinking about God. I left the monastery. And now I discover I am deforming: I am away from a personal and community prayer schedule so that I might sell raffle tickets and activities of that sort. Challenged, removed from a unique place of prayer to attend a birthday party. And also distracted: drawn from listening for God because "nobody else is doing that, and I should be like others!" I find I must struggle to be less religious/offensive and be more like the people around me.

If I have it in my heart and mind that God needs to mean everything and you have in yours that a double cheeseburger will suffice, your influence on me may not be trivial. Depending on my state of being, you may be ruinous for me. And if I already have a similar attraction toward double cheeseburgers, I find myself drawn back toward that previous, improper habit, leaving God further behind.

I am satisfied that what I learned and developed in the monastery is a mental fiber that seeks to defend my relationship with God with a realness I never had before. I have received a method for education and a sense of cooperation with tradition that keeps me from going too far away from God. And probably just as important, I have received the freedom to live according to specific values. I have learned to protect my relationship with God over and above the values offered by the world. But that state of defense is not sufficient. It is better to make continuous progress in my relationship with God - offense, and defense together.

Having left the monastery, it was an onslaught of noise every day. I felt my entire nervous system under attack. I spent years monastically sweeping up and "cleaning house," and now I was back outside, being mentally penetrated by every piercing distraction possible. It was like being thrown into a fierce ongoing battle; that only I noticed. And the war was not going to stop for me; I needed to find my bearings to survive it. My immediate response was to withdraw for protection, attend more Holy Mass, indulge in more prayer, and seek more meditation and the Eucharist. My response was to seek priestly advice. I see this as an example of putting on the "full armor of God" and seeking to rest in God's protection.

I was in contact with Len Goyke, the volunteer who lived in the Chicago area. He is one of the few people I kept in touch with outside the monastery. We often talked by phone about matters. He gave me a 35-year-old camper van that I could take to the forest on retreat. I flew to Chicago to pick it up and drive it back. It was so valuable that I could not describe the benefits of it all.

June 6, 2015

Dear Fr. Bartholomew and Br. Scott,

Please let the brothers know that after a short phone call with Len (the volunteer) last night, he told me he might not be able to visit Methuselah this year. He did ask about Br John.

His daughter in California is sick from lung cancer. It has spread. She is finishing up rounds of chemotherapy but is not expected to live very long. He will be with her. Also, his ex-wife had a heart attack. Apparently, during the attack, she went a long period without oxygen. She also has dementia. Another daughter recently had her tonsils removed. She has not yet recovered her speech. So please Pray for them!

I got an email response from Br. Angel. Thanks for letting me know about his wife.

Sincerely,

Rodney Odom

June 15, 2015

Dear Mary and Joseph,

Perhaps I should get straight to the point. Happy Birthday. I wanted to get this Birthday celebration card in because it will be my last to you. Since I have left Methuselah, I have realized the error of my ways. Birthdays are empty, pathetic celebrations, and I'll have nothing more to do with them! So I have taken my future into my own hands through the organization: **www.FormerGoodlookingMonksAgainstBirthdays.org**.

I learned about this enlightened group when I moved to Topeka, Kansas. I intended to start a new career making blockbuster movies. Topeka is the new "Hollywood!," or so the people say.

Would you please tell Joseph that if he needs a recommendation to join this great organization: **www.FormerGoodlookingMonksAgainstBirthdays.org**, I will gladly write him a personal recommendation (for a small fee). Anyhow if you feel, as I do, that those birthdays are a complete and utter waste of your time, then feel free to give this birthday poem to some less enlightened person.

There is not much going on here in Topeka, Kansas. Other than a sale on McDonald's 1/3-pound Sirloin burgers. But that sale expires soon, so don't concern yourself with that. Please give Mary-Martha a big kiss and hug for me if you see her. She is special to me! But, she can't join the organization because she is not unique enough! I miss you all.

Love and bliss to you! God Bless you and your family too!

Rodney Odom

PS I'll eat a 1/3-pound burger for you. Yes, I know; I am the same nice generous guy I used to be.

The year before I left Methuselah, the Abbot permitted me to interview some of the Monks getting along in age. As I saw it, the idea was that it would be nice to have a record of some of their lives, especially concerning their movement leading to Monastic Life. One of the people who freely accepted was Fr. Luke. I truly enjoyed him as a person. While he had a demeanor for "appropriate words," he was optimistic and authentic. To me, he struggled to be factual and accurate. Fr. Luke was in his late 90's and was a former Abbot. I videotaped our interview, edited the copy, and gave it to the Abbot. To me, Fr. Luke had an incredible memory. After we finished, he enthusiastically thanked me for doing the interview, just the opposite of the interview's purpose. I told him that I appreciated what I learned too! When each brother passes away, so does much of their story, wisdom, and knowledge. I attempted to preserve some of it.

June 17, 2015

Dear Abbot Melchizedek,

I waited to send this update to you (month two) until after your Funeral. Sorry to hear of the death of Fr. Luke. As you know, I was very fond of him. I found him to be a very positive influence at the Abbey. I have offered a prayer for him and the monastery at Mass. And for Fr. Jude (may he rest in Peace,) my pastor from Our Lady of Consolation in Charlotte, who recently passed away in Beacon, NY.

I had dinner with Br. Joe Payne in King of Prussia after he dropped his mother off in Malvern. We had a festive time at the Cheesecake Factory. The place was loud and busy. I suppose that is normal for a Friday evening? He sends greetings. He says he is always in touch with Ursula. He told me Ursula struggles with her vision. Would you please send greetings to all the brothers from him? Also, I have contacted Mary several times since she left her convent.

My family adjusts to my presence. One significant conflict I have with my parents is that they pretty much eat meat at every meal, and they want me to join in a little too often. Hopefully, not too much longer. I have been studying for long hours. I have found that the longer I am here, the more I grow in strength and focus. I was fragile when I left Methuselah. Please tell David my throat is still hurting, but I checked with the Veteran's Hospital and have another appointment in July. High doses of Vitamin C seem to help a little. The doctor thinks it is a virus and doesn't recommend drugs. He believes it will go away on its own. It could be stomach acid since it started about a week and a half before leaving the Abbey.

I am going to Mass at two different churches now compared to the last time I wrote. The pastor of St. Michaels has given me a key, and I can spend time in prayer at the Chapel at St. Therese. (It also used to be a Roman Catholic middle school.) My sister Barbara attended it for a short while. Now it's a charter school. He's the same priest who "used to be" an Anglican priest. Sorry, I can't pronounce his name yet! He pastors two different small flocks in this area. But they have no church yet. The people from Princeton, NJ, are too far in one direction, and the People on the Mainline are too far in another. They will come together and decide on a church building at some point. He spent time in a Benedictine Monastery before leaving. His Ph.D. is some subject generally related to the monastic lifestyle.

I am looking at the possibility of buying Dream Weaver 6.0 because it is trendy and an excellent platform for design. It would go a long way to integrating all this modern stuff and automating some of my programming possibilities. It looks like I have about eight weeks of study before I will feel more comfortable with my skills. And this is assuming no distractions or ridiculous new headwinds. So far, most barriers have been technical, and I get help online from unique websites set up for this purpose. Usually, the problem I encounter is poor communication. Technical people are often poor writers. Sometimes my ability to understand is the problem.

I have finished repainting my parent's window shudders and removing paint from the brick and have moved on to re-screening their back porch. This task is about 85% complete. I have nearly installed the new screen door my father decided to buy yesterday. My next project will be installing a ceiling fan and a new kitchen light fixture and checking the house for electrical safety hazards. I am doing simple work - no significant projects. I might also be helping my father clean the carpets.

Peace to you all,

Rodney Odom

Welcome to Monastic Life – It Was Already That Way

It was already that way!

I discovered in the monastery that I was not too fond of certain aspects of human behavior. I did not want any part of it. And because I found this in the monastery, I thought it was because of the monks. When I left and came home, I found my family behaved similarly. And not just my family but most people in society seemed to have the same characteristics; I did not realize any of this before going into the monastic setting.

When I first arrived at the monastery, I criticized the monks for not responding to anything. I asked someone, "Are we supposed to end up like bumps on a log?" At the time, it seemed to me that the brothers did not respond to anything. And I saw this as deadness. I was offended by it. I now realize that it was not deadness or a lack of response. It was Peace. There was no need for a response. The brothers I observed were in monastic life for decades. And unlike me, they were no longer lackeys to every idea, sensation, and inclination that popped into their heads. They sat satisfied with simply being present. There is no odder feeling than to sit in a room full of monks in absolute quiet. And then, one day, you finally get used to that peace you observe in others around you. In fact, one of the most challenging issues I dealt with was letting go of the need to respond to every idea that came to me. No matter how great an idea it may be. The Peace comes from not being a slave to it all and learning to rest quietly.

Other things I discovered about myself and others is that we are horribly dependent creatures. We have all kinds of secrets that we hide away from ourselves. We are unreliable and flaky. We are self-seeking, pleasure-seeking, and far more corrupt than we allow ourselves to accept. I am listing areas of criticism - do not be offended.

What I discovered about human nature that I did not want to see before entering is that human existence is messy and entangling, even in the most basic form. It certainly was not as immensely evolved as I thought. And it is easily destroyed. I eventually perceived human existence as one loosely connected being flowing down a river. The being can rearrange itself according to people's choices. But ultimately, we (the being) do not control where the river flows. We can only fool ourselves into thinking so.

July 14, 2015

Dear Abbot Melchizedek,

How am I? I am hanging in there. My health is pretty good. Diabetes and the heat have me dragging a bit. I am attending Mass 4 days a week. The routine I talked about in a prior letter is pretty much the same. I am old now, so I start to drag much faster after a hard work week than I used to when I was in my thirties. No boundless energy to charge forward into the abyss! I am much more cautious about my endeavors.

My family is surviving. My poor sister Kim is struggling with her ailments as best she can. Her husband James is doing much better, considering he was in a coma last year. His karate school seems to be doing okay. My parents are older than I so your guess is better than mine about how they may be. My dad would not know what to do with himself if he didn't work during the school year. He seems to fall much more than he used to, so his knees are sore, and he may need a hernia operation---before the new school year. Barbara (my younger sister) is in her unique world, but she is still lovely to me - most often!

The Church of St. Michael is soon to vote on accepting a new Parrish Building near Bridgeport, P.A., near King of Prussia. So I may be losing my quiet chapel in August or so. The Anglican version of Mass is fascinating. They have lots of chant and kneeling, but no touching and shaking hands. I enjoy the small size, though. All is well for my purposes. I have been thinking I might locate myself a nice little room somewhere. This move is better for me since my intended lifestyle is somewhat of a quiet clash with my family's. It is summer, and people don't wear as many clothes: "I have found that I have little or no control of my eyes or my mental response to what I see!" Seclusion is better for my circumstances. I do not know how else to put it!

Anyway, I continue to pray for the Church, Methuselah, my old family, and my new one down there. Sorry to hear about the murders/martyrs and plane crash (U.S. Air Force F-16 fighter jet). It makes you wonder if anywhere is reasonably safe anymore. Tell the Brothers I say – Hello!

Peace to you all,

Rodney   Odom

In 2020 with the spread of the Covid-19 virus throughout the United States, both state and federal governments encountered massive fraud due to the improper proliferation of people's personal information in our society. Even my sister had to reject approval for Unemployment Benefits someone else illegally applied for in her name.

August 13, 2015

Dear Abbot Melchizedek,

I hope all is well with Methuselah. All is well here. Thoughts of letting go are on my mind. I am looking at the future here in this general area. There seem to be plenty of jobs. But I have learned a bit from my past. It seems straightforward; I don't belong full-time in a corporate atmosphere. So I am very reluctant to go into that situation.

In the meantime, I have applied for a few temporary positions, but for every temp position, there are 40 other competing resumes! The online businesses I earlier spoke about seem to take a while to respond. After these companies collect your personal information, they tell you about the 20 thousand other people applying. They say, "they'll be in touch" [a polite, online rejection method– never heard from them.] Nice to know I am not alone in my situation! We all must be a little flexible.

My question is, what are these online businesses doing with all the personal information they collect from people applying for positions? I doubt they delete it! This information we submit to them is not the same as sending in a generic paper resume. The laws and regulations are not up to date to deal with the potential issues. And if "secure" government agencies can lose tons of personal information, companies will eventually lose some or all our personal information. I suspect we are headed for severe problems with people's identity as a society.

On another topic, Catherine, the Spiritual Guide that comes to Methuselah, knows many of the people at the Abbey where I will be for a retreat in September (we exchanged emails). It is a small world! I received an email from a lady going on retreat at Methuselah via Linkedin.com indicating that she would be there and would say a prayer for me. She is from Columbia, SC. I emailed her a message for Br. Vincent. "Tell Br. Vincent, I have had two double-burgers."

In the meantime, I am trying to stay focused on my studies. I am finally approaching a point where I feel some potential for the future in the coming months. I left Methuselah with the idea that it would take three to 4 months to accomplish what I had planned. I now see that there is far more to learn to function reasonably in this area. So I am looking at part-time work. I am determined to see this through, probably precluding working full-time.

Peace to you all,

Rodney Odom

Welcome to Monastic Life! – My Miraculous Medal Story

My Miraculous Medal Story

How many people are genuinely grateful for Mary? Most of my social group are Christian in understanding, if not in practice. They know about Mary. They know that Mary was Jesus' mom. So when I was at the main Library of Philadelphia, I would lose myself in the books on whatever subject was my focus. And at the time, I was trying to understand what I truly believed about Christianity. To my surprise, in the area of religion, there were two long rows of books for Mary. That fact struck me as really odd. To me, Mary was in the Christian Bible, but that was pretty much it. Even in the Gospel of John, Mary is referred to as the "Mother of Jesus." What could justify so many books? I decided to take a few books on Mary home to see what these writers would convey.

Photo: Miraculous Medal Shrine*, February 2021, Philadelphia, PA

Mary, the Mother of Jesus, appeared to people as various titles of the Blessed Virgin. She was said to be doing so all over the world. And at different times in the last hundreds. At first, I found it fascinating, but then I accepted it as fact. And when I returned to the library, I got more books on Mary. I especially liked the story of Our Lady of Guadalupe from the 1600s primarily because I could relate to Juan Diego. The man minded his own business, trying to get medicine to save his sick uncle, and Our Lady appeared to him, telling him not to worry about that. She had something else for him to do. And after all that, he still tried to avoid seeing the lady but could not. He finally gave in and cooperated with her direction. And now, as a result of God's Mercy, another piece of the eternal puzzle makes its definitive stamp on our human story!

When I read the books on the Miraculous Medal, I was so convinced of its nature that I wanted one for myself. But in retrospect, I was not Roman Catholic and knew nothing of Catholic practices. It never occurred to me that I probably should not make my medal. But because of the way I think, I did. I took 50 dollars down to the local mall and asked one of the local jewelry vendors to make me one.

The young lady working the jewelry booth seemed fascinated that customers were willing to spend so much money to have something inscribed on a bit of metal. And she seemed intrigued by my request: Could you please fit the words, "O Mary, conceived without sin, pray for us who have recourse to thee" on one of your large dog tags? She assured me she could fit the entire prayer on the tag. To me, she seemed fascinated that the prayer was to Mary. I freely admit I wondered about that myself for years. It seemed sacrilegious to my Christian background to pray to Mary, even if she was Jesus' mom.

In my mind, I now had a Miraculous Medal, and according to the instructions, I never took it off. Well, except when going through metal detectors as in the airports. I was not quite sure what the prayer on it meant. But I decided to have faith and hope in Mary's help and protection. All the while, I did not know that you don't make your medal or that the medal I made was not blessed. Nor did I know that that big building on Chelten Avenue, near where I lived and drove past so often, was a shrine to the actual Miraculous Medal and the apparition event!

I did not get an actual Miraculous Medal (pictured above) until I entered the monastery. During my stay, I talked with another monk who told me he found a medal as a child and kept it. He offered it to me! And while I was surprised he was willing to give it away, I did accept it with great gratitude. I cut my version from hanging around my neck and found a shoelace to tie on the real one. It was only at that moment that it occurred to me that I did not have an actual Miraculous Medal on my neck all those years.

*I have attended Masses and offered Mass cards from the Miraculous Medal Shrine on Chelten Ave. I no longer attend its Masses or have formal or informal ties to it in that way.

If you read the history of monastic life in western culture, it has always gone through various phases of germination, growth, upheaval, and disintegration. I am especially thinking of the French Revolution when I think of disintegration. I wonder where monasticism stands in our society as it continues to disintegrate. God is first, society is second, and not the other way around. But we exist together. If we were not relevant, Christ would not have bothered to come to us in the first place. My ability to understand my circumstances is limited. If I continue to seek God but see no path forward in this place being consumed by the community around it, what else can I do? There is a part of me that utterly refuses to merge with the society at hand!

April 14, 2016

Dear Deacon Todd,

I received your letter and read it. I have much to say on the various subjects, but I think things are best left alone because of the nature of this situation. I don't know if you wanted a response to your letter? I can see that you are aware of the severe nature of my decision. I, unfortunately, am aware to some extent of the seriousness of it also. I love God. I try to love God. I have nothing else. But (as you well know) I am not Jesus. And the older I get, the more I recognize my limitations. Methuselah is beyond anything I can deal with at this time in my life. And frankly, at 50 and because of how I think, I choose not to spend my time seeking Christ in this way. While monasteries have not lost their saltiness, one might interpret the situation as dire. Monks call it poverty. Forgive me for being blunt or insensitive, but this is my take on things. Also, don't tell the monks I said this because there would be no mercy (smile).

I have come to know that life is short, and I can only seek that path in which I see and know a sense of hope for "success." My hope is in God's Mercy when I choose this path. Formal monastic life for me has always been a means to an end. It has never been an end in itself. Beyond me trying to seek God, I have no power. It is not mine to talk about-- it is in God's hands.

So while I agree with what you have to say, I would be better off in a monastery than driving the streets of Philadelphia. But unfortunately, I cannot "see" that path with "eyes of hope." The issues are probably many: cultural, personal ability, true faith, and spiritual support. I am not different than other people in that way of thinking. So for me, the hermit's life is the best path available. And as you know, I am not totally without experience in struggling while blind with ignorance (i.e., my path to Roman Catholicism). Ignorance is my friend now because my sense of practicalness would cause me to back away quickly.

There are many reasons I left Methuselah, most of which I had no control over whatsoever. Yes, I made an actual choice to go, but only in the name of long-term survival. My thinking was/is that I must survive to seek God. I did not see that happening at Methuselah and have little hope of it elsewhere.

I have been in contact with a Fr. David up here, and he says (not his exact words - and I agree with him): if I have given my honest best effort, God can make up for my failures. This is mercy. I gave all that I had, and it was not enough. Having said all that, I honestly believe if I asked Jesus to help me stay, he would have gladly helped. I thank you, however, for caring so much.

You can be sure I will burden you with my status in the future (smile). For now, I need to spend time healing from my encounters. And for dealing with issues more in tune with my size. I think the invisible is invisible because it is its nature to be so. Let me learn what my nature is. Say a prayer for me as I pray for you also.

Always sincere,

Rodney K. Odom

Discovery and Understanding

All data and knowledge are local. The wisdom derived from such data and knowledge is local too! As I learn more, I expand my understanding of my local worldview. To develop the idea of locality a step further, any new "destination" for our local knowledge is, consequently, creating an expanded local destination or expanded local worldview. As individual human beings, we get a limited opportunity, a lifetime, to expand on our local knowledge beyond the local destination or local worldview. Thus, when we get a chance to do so, life dictates that we identify the seriousness and consequence of seeking an expansion in our worldview [in other words, we reap what we sow.] Eternity would probably remove such obstacles for a non-temporal "being." And it seems to me that God is not limited in any way at all.

If Jesus says no one comes to me except that the Father sends them, if Jesus says while I am in this world, I am the light of this world, if Jesus says those who follow me do not walk in darkness, and if Jesus says some people will never die, and those who die, still they will live forever, he is offering (in my opinion) and expanse on our local knowledge to a new, "non-local" destination. His words expand the human world view to a "dimension" beyond our current local destination. It is an expansion even beyond our current potential or maximum local development. The knowledge Christ gives is the knowledge you do not verify except through Grace from God. Verification is not through the study of our local world or local destination. In fact, and this is speculation on my part, but I suspect that without God's help, we would not know of God at all. The human-derived world view or local destination is only a local knowledge resource. It can never be a resource for the new non-local dimension that Christ offers.

There are experts in every significant evolution of the human worldview. And these experts proclaim the local truth of the local destination to help create an expanded local destination. From learning to control the use of fire to the notion of a spherical earth, from the splitting of atoms to quantum reality, we help each other accept more and different local knowledge. To me, what we call science is billions of people covering thousands of years attempting to understand reality as we experience it. And more and more we do "science" in a systematic way. Never, I repeat, never is "science" the same as God and nor should we worship it as God. But nowadays, it has become, in many ways, a false god like the little silver god statues of old. We put our hopes and dreams in it like it is a real God. Science is a process of discovery and understanding, reflecting how we exist as creatures and nothing more. We believe some experts because enough reliable people verify the expanded worldview. Eventually, we let go of older local knowledge and accept the extended version or new one. But it was with help from God that early Jewish people helped new Christians come to take the idea of one God. It helped us let go of the notion that objects like pieces of wood, gold, or even creatures can be God. While not always understood, God's workings came to be sufficiently comprehended. And through this new understanding of God, human existence is given form and direction amidst nothingness. Realizing the significance of this expansion beyond our local destination, we still hold dear the Jewish Holy Scripture as part of our understanding. We even study their scripture and meditate on that "Word of God."

From their local knowledge descriptions, we can deduce that they believed that the earth was flat. To them, God "built" the world on structures. Their writings indicate that the heavens are up in the sky and is the dwelling on the one God. Additionally, they thought that rain (so crucial to life) was from the heavens and came from that one God. Through his charity, God allowed rain by opening the skies to share it with his creatures. This general description, implying their worldview, sounds very reasonable to me (as I look back on history). My worldview includes much of theirs with additional local information. I expand on their local destination to a further developed local destination. And with the general acceptance of the "Jewish God," I extend my "new further developed local destination" to include a new, non-local destination.

Jesus came into our world and confirmed a "knowledge" of separate but somehow connected worlds. These were at least three realms in which the facts or workings about each were radically different. Humans would have no practical way to connect their locally accepted domain to these new ones - at least not safely. Nor would they know how they would function in this new destination. Jesus safely "connected" us as beings to a knowledge of this new realm by his words and actions. He commanded both the local world and its beings and non-local sources alike. His Word transformed our perspective or understanding. As a result, Christians now have a new, expanded local destination (to include a new non-local destination). It includes our worldview, which entails all the known universe as we understand it for our current time. But it also now has new non-local realms that we transition to as we die. This world that we transition to is where our current local knowledge seems virtually useless. In other words, we shall be as the angels, not needing marriage; life and death are no more.

Through his presence on earth and in cooperation with his Father's will, he added dimensions to the human experience that exceeded our local potential. And he did so without needing to expand the local knowledge or understanding of our physical world. He demonstrated these truths throughout our history by directing various peoples using faith. He thus confirmed that we could evolve past our local knowledge to a greater, more expanded understanding of our intended existence. In our studies of the "modern world," our new perception only leads to a new local destination: beyond the sky is outer space, not heaven's dwelling place. For us, the earth is a sphere-like object, and the sky is not just up but outward from the sphere. The modern worldview is essentially an infinite presence far beyond our complete awareness or understanding.

Interestingly, Jesus did not need local knowledge, of the stars, for instance, to help us reach beyond our local grasp and accept a new, non-local realm. If you cannot believe me, Jesus said at least consider my works. See what abundance I offer you at no cost.

My personal experience and education led me to believe that human experience is primarily physical and factual. In my circumstances, I wrongly concluded that the human being's ultimate goal was to discover the "ultimate facts" through studying the local destination. This way of thinking permeates me, frustratingly, to the depth of my being. Unfortunately, my struggle to understand my physical existence paralyzes me in accepting this new non-local destination offered by God. In other words, my discovery method limits my potential understanding of the eternity of my being.

Trying to understand what is more permanent and fixed in my local reality allowed me to decide where to build my life or best utilize ways to earn a living. My limited methods allowed me to live my story of life. But this way of thinking is like a house built on sand. It is inherently unstable because, as we learn, it is shifting, changing, and expanding to a new local destination. Indeed, and in the local sense only, this knowledge is the basis for wheels rolling and fires burning. It is the basis for wind and rain. It is the basis for the stars and planets revolving around each other. We call it the "laws of nature." And, for us, it changes with each new scientifically accepted breakthrough.

But the laws of nature are local to our physical perception. It leads to a life of guesses, conspiracies, fantasies, lies, and speculation with an occasional local fact included. In this process, we are far too often functioning against our created purpose. As a result of our human frailty, we spend a good deal of time fumbling about in authentic darkness. We seem to be a baffled people following the one who sounds correct at a particular moment in time. We create solutions based on what makes sense to us at a specific moment. And when something remains factual long enough, we accept it as a fundamental truth. When I glance up at the sky during the day, I speculate that the sky is there, around the earth. The sky is blue, perhaps with clouds floating by underneath it. When I glance at the sky at night, I speculate that the sky is gone; the stars emerge as infinite in number and go on forever. This situation is the human being processing local information for practical use. But when a new perspective is eventually proven too limited, it only serves as some local purpose or local point of clarity for further expansion and change.

So if Jesus says, I am the truth, I am the way, to me, he is saying don't spend too much time wondering about what life is about locally: save up for heaven and spend more of your time seeking Me, I am the only truth that is, I am the sole truth, not fact, that matters. The heaven you seek is within you, and when you desire it, then and only then will your local world or local destination be proper and complete.

I came that they might have life: once, I encountered an empty cabin while walking alone in the forest. It was below ground level. To enter the front door, I had to go down several steps. Then I observed a turtle with its head turned toward a corner of the lower enclosure that surrounded the cottage. It became clear to me that the turtle was stuck. Maybe it washed down the steps during a rainstorm. Maybe it did not realize it was trapped when climbing into the enclosure. Initially, I wondered if it was safe to try to pick it up and place it back on ground-level where it could get back to the water independently. When I did so, the turtle didn't respond much. It was weak. It obviously could not climb the steps. Its limited awareness could not know that climbing up the steps would get it from the enclosure to freedom. So I carried it. We went back to the water bank, and there I left it.

To me, we are very much like this turtle. We are a species learning to understand ourselves and our world safely, but we do so with a minimal capacity to know all the options. Besides, we do so with modest tools within a very constrained time (compared to billions of years or even eternity). We are people trying to trace the dots that we think make up our existence. Our limited, local understanding is one of our frailties. As a result, quickly, our journey of life collapses and is snuffed out. Thus, Jesus promises not to leave us to ourselves. He already knows the consequences of doing that. And if we do not choose to follow, by default, we choose death. The presence of God is like a moral or "life-gravity well". It draws those who "hear my voice". Those who do not remain in the darkness. And oh how great is that darkness and the trouble it causes.

We respond to our world or existence with much emotion, inspiration, intuition, and charity. But we also respond with indifference, fantasy, ignorance, fear, pride, and arrogance. And we probably do all of this rather clumsily. I am sure my little lists are not complete. But they make my point. Right now, we don't outnumber all species on earth, but we seem to dominate the planet in many ways. Our ability to discern what is proper and accurate will determine our collective and individual fate now and for eternity. "He came that they might have life" connects us to this source in ways we do not fully comprehend, but we need to follow in faith.

To me, it is only through God's mercy that we can overcome our limited, blind, feeble nature and stop guessing or speculating at what is. So Jesus says: that they may have life more abundantly. We should not pursue more life as we see it, for that will only lead to death. But life as was intended. If we seek God's mercy and involve God in our decisions, the journey will be a God-approved destination. Hence: where I am, there My servant will also be. As Christ says in our Christian scripture's last book, I Am the Alpha and the Omega. Jesus, the person who walked the earth and is the Christ is the start and end of all. The beginning and end of every idea, thought, word, development, condition, etc., and thus 'Is All' that matters for us both locally and non-locally.

I and others like me always struggle with this notion. When I improperly ask the "meaning" of life without reference to Christ, I acknowledge that the rules guiding my thinking are of a limited local nature. I am, in frustration, searching for something I simply cannot and will not find. Because I am a creative being, I can create an answer to my question in my local destination. I give it meaning with my imagination, but it genuinely has none. The meaning of life is defined and given non-locally by Christ. With God's continued help and support, we move beyond our local understanding to a new and non-local one. We evolve wisely and eternally, not in random, short-sighted, "physically limiting," or local ways. Through mercy, we have the benefit of eternal wisdom to guide us.

My Little Story of the 'Holy Rosary of The Blessed Virgin Mary'

The books from the Free Library of Philadelphia led me toward the Rosary of the Blessed Virgin Mary. The books on the lives of the Saints and how Mary was personally involved in their lives helped me understand the prayer's importance. But it was the meaningful and faithful use of the "Hail Mary" as a prayer over time that lay the trail of proof of Mary's involvement in my own life.

I do not know what distinguishes me from other people regarding our holy mother. I met people who looked to Mary for help and realized the authenticity of her presence through them. But, I have also met those who only know Mary as a name in the story of Jesus and saw their real relationship with Christ only! One day recently, as I stood in line, I prayed with my rosary beads in hand. And the person behind me was an older gentleman who said to me, "I have not seen rosary beads in a long time!" And I asked him if he was born Roman Catholic. And he said yes. He spoke with such pride. He spoke about going to catholic schools and attending Mass. I appreciated his comments and his pride.

But what baffled me was how he could have been a member of the Roman Catholic Church and not have seen rosary beads "in a long time." For me, Mary was synonymous with Roman Catholicism. Her name was the one I used as I thought more and more to talk to Jesus directly. It occurred to me; maybe this encounter was yet another situation where I joined a Roman Catholic church with a different cultural timeframe than my own. But, Mary has always been prevalent through most of the church's history! I just did not understand his comment whatsoever! Was I overanalyzing the situation? I just did not know.

The library books laid the groundwork for praying the Prayer of the Holy Rosary. Laying on my little mat for a bed in the living room of my near-empty one bedroom apartment in Greenville, N.C., I had a short conversation with one I could not see but could hear. I had a chance to think about this prayer in detail. I learned to pray the Rosary Prayer when I could listen to my inner voice and recognize the presence of heaven in my life. It was there alone that I could live without fear of my uniqueness and recognize the quiet influences of my mind and heart.

I had complaints about the prayer. And I needed to work through each one mentally. What kind of prayer repeats so many of the exact words? What purpose did the repetition serve? Why was the prayer so long? What type of prayer takes so long to pray that I did not feel I would complete it? How would I know if I was using it correctly? Would Mary listen to a non-Catholic person praying her prayer?

Though no one was present, I asked if I could help? I did not know who I was talking to; all I knew was it concerned me that I could help and was not doing so. And in the process of doing research online on Christianity, I came across what I call a mini version of the Rosary prayer. They involved sequences of prayers that often mentioned the "Hail Mary." And, in faith, I started praying these little mini rosary prayers.

And through a personal intercession, I realized that if I wanted to help, I needed to pray the complete Rosary of the Blessed Virgin Mary. It was an odd experience and challenging to describe. After a strange sort of electrostatic interaction, I felt free of any limitations I created in my mind about the prayer. She said, "You asked to help!" In thinking about this event, I realized my excuses were silly. Over time, when I did become Roman Catholic, I prayed the Rosary Prayer in groups before Sunday Mass at church. And when I went into the monastery, I mixed the Rosary Prayer with my increased knowledge of scripture and made fantastic discoveries about the story of Christ. This praying became my holiday version of Lectio Divina.

Nowadays, the Rosary is more than a prayer for me. It is an anchor to assure that I think about Jesus every day and remind myself of my commitment to Mary, his earthly mom. Whenever I recite this prayer, it is my protection from evil and my elevator to the top of life. I am as grateful as I can be for this prayer, and I am always doing my best to love Our Blessed Mother through its recitation.

To me, and me only, Monastic Life is about discovering that despite the herd psychology of everybody thinking the same, needing the same things, receiving the same information, and drawing the same conclusions about life and reality, we each have an individual relationship with God. And in seeking God this way, we discover more and more our unique creation. Not just superficial differences like the size of your aorta or the color of your eyes, but you walk slowly into your unique, eternal creation. There is no other resource than God for this progress. And focusing on God seems to be the only way to make this progress.

Monastic Life seems to be about slowly discovering your rebellious nature and coming to God 7 by 77 times for aid in correction. It is in the details of monotony, with help from Grace, that you will allow your mind and heart to expand into greater truth and awareness. It is with help from God that you allow yourself to receive like little children and accept a far greater reality than the world you live in is willing to accept. And once you accept this more complex reality, you do not turn to self-destruction in fear of its incredible nature. God fills you with himself to maintain your survival. Vast is this creation, far from the simple human goals of running the fastest or spelling the most words. My sense is that it is awesome beyond human understanding, and it takes God's "ambition" to survive its nature.

When I look at the street as I walk, my mind forms to see what is required. Yet there is so much more present as I walk down the street. My mind blocks out that that is not required. With Monastic life, I focus on God through all the activities, and I am reforming my mind to see more than the minimum requirements for everyday life. I am learning to see more details of myself, and more importantly, I am learning to see the "next" world to come and some of what that entails. And as my behaviors change, I, too, am perceived as different. The key is God. Whether you are being tracked as a terrorist (as in Jesus), pursued as a criminal, screened as a church member, or raised to sainthood, the key is always God. Stay focused on Christ through prayer or what some call "turning to Christ."

A scribe came and said to him, `Teacher, I will go anywhere you go.'
Jesus said, `Foxes have holes to live in. Birds have nests. But the Son
of Man has no place to lie down to rest.' Another man who was a

follower of Jesus, said to Jesus, `Lord, let me go first and bury my father.' But Jesus said to him, `Come with me. Let those who are dead bury their own dead people.' **Matthew 20 (19-22)** [14]

Letters From The Desert Home - Part II

Operational Readiness

It is second nature for me to look at a situation and try, in my mind, to make it more productive and efficient. One day after Mass, a non-monastic priest, who was on retreat at the monastery, once chastised me for speeding up the end of Mass. I explained to my superior the following: I was not speeding anything up; I was simply making the process more efficient. I figured, "why make three trips to clear the Credence table of implements when I can do it in two?" In monastic life with fewer and fewer people, it only made sense to reduce unnecessary labor. Why use two people to hand-carry a folding table when you can roll the table into place on a cart using one person.

Constant change and Monastic Life do not do well together! Still, in Monastic Life, we are often at war. If not with ourselves, then with other spiritual forces. And in war, one needs a plan to carry out the fight or win the race (so to speak). And unfortunately, that may require detailed planning and tedious implementation. And accomplishing it all takes expertise and experience. Monks do not often have the skill sets required for this. Nor do they realize they do not have those skills. Often, it does not even matter to them that they do not have the skills required. They simply go about their business in isolation as if they do! However, the monastic must learn to balance efficiency with tradition! Efficiency as determined by experts - not monks. And tradition, as determined by monks, not outsiders.

To eliminate the planning and operations part of organizations from interfering with Monasticism, I strongly recommend monasteries come together and form a sort of internal consulting organization. That organization would handle housing all aspects of business and social operations across all Religious and Monastic organizations. This "business unit" would offer information to improve the operation of monasteries without interfering with the lifestyle or practices. They would provide information and direction. They would consult, not determine, or mandate.

This internal consulting process would help implement up-to-date business practices. They could help monasteries keep updated with the latest facility security methods, accounting practices, financial investments, legal matters, building planning, human resource, and technology issues. The monastery group creating this business unit could start small and build a more detailed organization over time, at first taking up the most critical issues challenging Monasteries. This organization would actively offer practices across monastic walls to all monasteries involved.

I never knew until up close and personal in my own activities how important Public Relations was to Religious institutions. How people perceive those who claim to represent God in anyway have a special need to "present well." I noticed it especially in the Priesthood. I think a consulting organization like this could carry part of the burden of directing the public face of monasteries and convents. This would leave Abbesses and Abbots of monasteries to focus on forming monks and nuns.

Creating such an organization would be an enormous undertaking. And assuring that the people employed to run such an organization are appropriately chosen would be difficult. But given the cost efficiency and strengths gained by frequently sharing each other's efforts ideas and especially successes would undoubtedly make it worth the struggle.

By pooling resources and continually sharing information, the religious organizations would be far more potent achieving its goals and in interfacing with the world around it. They would not have to find solutions to objectives independently. This would make them temporally efficient, financially productive, and more secure in their true purpose. They would probably be far less dependent on direct, close-working. Their public relations methods could offer a more uniform front in dealing with the forces of change. Monasteries and Convents could be assured of the latest and most secure methods to deal with society and each other properly.

Glossary

Altar Server – a lay assistant to a member of the clergy during a Christian liturgy. An altar server attends to supporting tasks at the altar such as fetching and carrying, ringing the altar bell, helps bring up the gifts, brings up the book, among other things. If young, the server is commonly called an altar boy or altar girl. In some Christian denominations, altar servers are known as acolytes. [4]

Brothers, Br. - Members of a male religious community who have not taken Holy Orders or who do not aspire to Holy Orders but live a religious community life and devote themselves to various works of a religious nature. [16]

Cell - (1) A small unit of a monastery. (2) The room or separate dwelling of a monk; his living quarters. [16]

Commons – Area where monks or brothers eat meals.

Contemplative Nun – A woman who in a life long journey to God in prayer and worship, turning from all else that could make the journey less direct. Contemplative nuns and monks are concerned less with themselves and more with God and all those whom God loves. Prayer is essential for all Christians, but contemplatives are called to make their whole lives a prayer in solitude and silence and community. [19]

Chant - The official music of the liturgy, called Gregorian because of its final development by St. Gregory; and prescribed for those parts of the liturgy which are to be sung. [16]

Father, Fr. - A title universally given to all priests. (2) The title reverently applied to the first person of the Blessed Trinity, God the Father. [16]

Habit - The clothes or garments worn by members of a religious order as a mark of their profession in religion; the external garb of nuns or monks. [16]

Hail Mary – A prayer. "Hail Mary, full of Grace, the Lord is with the, Blessed are you among women, and Blessed is the fruit of your womb, Jesus."

Last Rites - also known as the Commendation of the Dying, are the last prayers and ministrations given to an individual of Christian faith, when possible, shortly before death. (4)

Lectio Divina - is a traditional monastic practice of scriptural reading, meditation and prayer intended to promote communion with God and to increase the knowledge of God's word. In the view of one commentator, it does not treat scripture as texts to be studied, but as the living word. (4)

Monastic Guest – A person visiting a monastery to live temporarily, but according to the rules, activities, and schedule of the monks.

NABRE - New American Bible (Revised Edition)

Schola – according to https://www.wordnik.com/: a musical school attached to a monastery or church. A group of musicians, particularly one which specializes in liturgical music.

Observer – A person visiting the monastery for the purpose of entering as a monk.

Trappists or O.C.S.O. - The Order of Cistercians of the Strict Observance (also known as "Trappists") is a Roman Catholic contemplative religious order, consisting of monasteries of monks and monasteries of nuns. We are part of the larger Cistercian family which traces its origin to 1234. As Cistercians we follow the Rule of St Benedict, and so are part of the Benedictine family as well. Our lives are dedicated to seeking union with God, through Jesus Christ, in a community of sisters or brothers. (18)

Pastoral Associate - Collaborates closely with the Pastor and with other members of the Parish Staff in the overall pastoral ministry of the parish. Collaborates in the overall process of parish administration including:

assessing needs, pastoral planning, decision-making, implementation, and budget management. (17)

Religious - The name frequently applied to a member of an order who has de- voted himself to God by the three vows of religion; a member of a religious institution. (16)

Senior Wing - Area or building where sick or very elderly monks are housed.

Permanent Vows - Solemn Vows. A deliberate, free promise made to God by which one obligates himself under pain of sin by the virtue of religion to the performance of some act more pleasing to God than its opposite. Public vows or Solemn vows invalidate any act against the vows. **(16)**

Trappistine - The female gender form of the word Trappist.

Vows - A deliberate, free promise made to God by which one obligates himself under pain of sin by the virtue of religion to the performance of some act more pleasing to God than its opposite. Public vows arc either solemn or simple. Solemn vows invalidate any act against the vows; simple vows merely forbid or render unlawful any act against the vows. (16)

References

(1) The Meaning of the Miraculous Medal | Marians of the ....
https://www.marian.org/news/The-Meaning-of-the-Miraculous-Medal-2942 (2022)

(2) World English Bible™ Public Domain,
https://www.biblegateway.com/

(3) Diagnostic Sleep Center of Midland | Midland Health.
https://www.midlandhealth.org/main/diagnostic-sleep-center-of-midland

(4) https://www.wikipedia.org/

(5) https://www.merriam-webster.com/(2010)

(6) Moinfort, de Louis Marie. Preparations for Total Consecration according to Saint Louis de Moinfort, Montfort Publications 2005.

(7) https://www.medjugorje.org (2021)

(8) *https://www.webmd.com/brain/sudden-confusion-causes (2021)*

(9) https://www.thefreedictionary.com/hermit *(2021)*

(10) The Divine Mercy Message and Devotion | Shrine of Divine Mercy. https://www.jpiidivinemercyshrine.org/divine-mercy-message-and-devotion *(2021)*

(11) https://south-carolina-plantations.com *(2021)*

(12) Keating, Father Thomas. "The Contemplative Journey (Vol 2)" Audio Cassette, Sounds True, Incorporated, 1999.

(13) Faustina, Maria. Divine Mercy in My Soul: Diary of Saint Maria Faustina Kowalska, Marian Press, 2009

(14) "Taken from THE JESUS BOOK - The Bible in Worldwide English. Copyright SOON Educational Publications, Derby DE65 6BN, UK. Used by permission."

(15) Gomer Pyle, U.S.M.C... Created by Aaron Ruben. Ashland Productions, Andy Griffith Enterprises, T & L Productions. 1964 – 1969.

(16) Traditional Catholic Dictionary Online http://laudatedominum.net/dictionary/index.php (2022)

(17) LA Catholics https://lacatholics.org/pastoral-associates/ (2022)

(18) Order of Cistercians of the Strict Observance https://ocso.org/ (2022)

(19)   Poor Clares of the Franciscan Monastery of Saint Clarehttps://poorclarepa.org/what-is-contemplative-life/

(20)   Odom, Rodney K., "*Writings from the Desert, A Compilation of Poems on the Way to First Vows as A Trappist Monk, pp. 56 - 57.*" Philadelphia, Pennsylvania: Self-Published, 2021.

My Assignment, My Task.

Christ is leaving now; he's going away.
But he suggested that I might stay.
And wait here at this little bus stop, and I should pray.

He said try, if you can, to feel the warmth of my Sun,
And try, if you will, the glimmering hope of my moon.
Do this that I ask of you.

For 33 years, I'll be here.
Comprehending, contemplation of this sacred space.
Until my friend Jesus comes back for me.

Crouched on this worn, rusted little bench,
Every moment of each day,
This oddly mystical duty, I must pray.

Hail Mary, full of Grace, the Lord is with you.
Blessed are you among us, even today.
And Blessed is the fruit of your womb, Jesus!

Back Cover

Photo: Close up photo of Mary's face. Mary is traveling with Joseph and the baby Jesus in this sculpture.

www.ingramcontent.com/pod-product-compliance
Lightning Source LLC
Chambersburg PA
CBHW070905100426
42737CB00047B/2612